Stewart Kyd

A treatise on the law of bills of exchange and promissory notes

Stewart Kyd

A treatise on the law of bills of exchange and promissory notes

ISBN/EAN: 9783337110673

Printed in Europe, USA, Canada, Australia, Japan

Cover: Foto ©Suzi / pixelio.de

More available books at **www.hansebooks.com**

A

TREATISE

ON THE

LAW

OF

BILLS OF EXCHANGE

AND

PROMISSORY NOTES.

BY

STEWART KYD, OF THE MIDDLE TEMPLE, ESQ.

BARRISTER AT LAW.

THE THIRD EDITION,

WITH CONSIDERABLE ADDITIONS.

London:

PRINTED FOR J. JOHNSON, ST. PAUL'S CHURCH-YARD, J. BUTTERWORTH, FLEET-STREET,

AND B. C. COLLINS, SALISBURY.

1795.

ADVERTISEMENT

TO THE

PRESENT EDITION.

WHEN the firſt edition of the following treatiſe was publiſhed, ſeveral points of importance remained doubtful; moſt, if not all, of theſe have been decided in caſes which have ſince occurred; the alterations rendered neceſſary by theſe deciſions have been made in the preſent edition, and the author is not aware that any thing material has been omitted which might be found uſeful in ſuch a work.

No. 4, Hare Court, Temple,
Trinity Term, 1795.

ADVERTISEMENT

TO THE

FIRST EDITION.

Two Treatises are already before the public on the subject of the following sheets : Without attempting to appreciate the respective merits of these performances, or to compare them particularly with his own, the author of the present publication feels it necessary to observe, that the plan of his work differs very materially from either of the others. He has endeavoured to produce a composition, which, without disgusting the professional reader, may be easily comprehended by men of business, and serve as an elementary treatise to the student. In executing this plan, he has given, under each division, an historical deduction of the opinions which have been held on the point immediately under discussion, and concluded with the law as settled by the latest decisions, where, in fact, it has been settled. Where the point remains still in doubt, he has stated the arguments on both sides of the question. How far he has succeeded in the execution, the public only can decide.

No. 4, Hare Court, Temple,
October, 1790.

TABLE OF CONTENTS.

CHAPTER I.

Of the Origin and Nature of Bills of Exchange and Promiſſory Notes.

PAGE.

ORIGIN of Foreign Bills of Exchange - - 1
Their object and uſe - - - - 2
Parties neceſſary thereto - - - 3
Definition of a Bill of Exchange - - 3, 4
Uſance - - - - 4
Mode of Computation on Bills - - 5—7
Old and New Style - - - 7
Days of Grace in different Countries - - 9
Forms of Bills of Exchange - - 10
Origin of Inland Bills - - - 11
Difference originally between them and Foreign Bills - 11
How far they are ſtill different - - 12
Examples of the different forms - - 13—17
Origin of Promiſſory Notes - - 18
When put on the ſame footing with Inland Bills of Exchange 19
Forms of Promiſſory Notes - - 20
Stamps to which Bills and Notes are ſubject - 21—27

CHAPTER II.

Who may make a Bill of Exchange or Promiſſory Note, and be Parties in the Negociation of them.

PAGE.

How far an Infant may be a party to a Bill or Note - 28, 29
How far a Married Woman - - 30, 31
How far Partners are bound by the acceptance of one - 31
How far a Corporation can be a party to a Bill or Note 32
Procuration, what - - - - 33

CHAPTER III.

Of the Reſemblance which Bills of Exchange and Promiſſory Notes bear to one another, and of their different kinds.

Bills and Notes in their original form bear no reſemblance
to one another - - - 34
When the reſemblance begins - - 34, 35
When the reſemblance is fixed, the law is the ſame as to both 35
Bills and Notes divided into two kinds, payable to bearer
and payable to order - - - 35
Difference of theſe two as to the mode of transfer or
negociation - - - 35, 36
Hiſtory of the opinions on the negociability of Bills pay-
able to bearer - - - 36—39
Negociability of Promiſſory Notes payable to bearer - 39
Bank

PAGE.

Bank Notes, Bankers Cafh Notes, and Drafts on Bankers 40
Within what time Bankers Cafh Notes and Drafts on
   Bankers muft be demanded -   -   41

———

CHAPTER IV.

*Of the Privileges of Bills of Exchange and Promiffory Notes,
and the Circumftances neceffary to make them good.*

Diftinction between Special and Simple Contracts - 47
In what refpects Special are more highly privileged than
   Simple Contracts -   -   -   47
Bills and Notes privileged as fpecialties -   -   48
Diftinction between things in poffeffion and things in
   action -   -   -   -   -   48, 49
What things are requifite to make a good Bill or Note 49—67
   Muft be for the payment of money only -   50
   Muft carry a *perfonal* and certain credit -   50
      Diftinction in this refpect between Bills and
      Notes -   -   50—55
   Muft be payable at all events -   -   55
Whether the words " value received" be effential -   61
——————————— " to order" or " to bearer" -   63—67

       CHAPTER

CHAPTER V.

Acceptance.

PAGE.

Acceptance, what - - - 68
Circumſtances concurring therein - 68
Manner in which it may be made - 68
    Written or verbal - 69—72
Time when it may be made - - 72
By whom made - - - 73
To whom made - - 73
When an agreement to accept amounts to an
    acceptance - - 74
General or abſolute - - 74
How it may differ from the tenor of the Bill 74, 75
Conditional - - 75, 76, 77, 78
    When it becomes abſolute - 78
    When diſcharged - - 79
What will amount to - - 80—86
By a ſervant - - 86, 87

CHAPTER VI.

Transfer of Bills aud Notes.

By delivery only - - - - 88
By indorſement - - - 88
Indorſement in full or in blank - - 89
    When it may be made - - 89
    May be made on a blank piece of paper 89, 90
                    How

PAGE.

How far a transfer by delivery only, without indorfement,
    is a fale of a Bill or Note   -   -   90—95
He to whom a blank indorfement is made may take the
    bill as indorfee or as agent to the indorfor - 95, 96
Indorfement needs not contain the words " to order" 97—100
    May be reftrictive   -   -   100—102
Transfer by delivery may be made by any perfon who
    has obtained poffeffion   -   103—106
——— by indorfement can be made only by him who
    has a right   -   -   106—108

CHAPTER VII.

Engagement of the feveral Parties.

Engagement of the drawer of a bill   -   109—111
——— of the indorfor   -   -   111—117
Refemblance in this refpect between the parties to a
    bill and the parties to a note   -   -   117
Engagement of the holder of a bill or note   -   117—126
What fhall be confidered as reafonable notice of the
    difhonour of a bill or note   -   -   126—129
When notice is not neceffary   -   -   129—136
Form of notice   -   -   -   136
Proteft on foreign bills   -   -   136—142
——— on Inland Bills   -   -   142—152
——— acceptance *fupra*   -   -   -   153
——— payment *fupra*   -   -   154—156
Engagement of the acceptor, &c.   -   156—165
Holder of a Bill or Note may recover of an indorfor
    without attempting to recover againft the drawer
    of the one or the payee indorfor of the other 166—173

Diftinction

PAGE.

Diftinction antiently made between a bill given in payment of a precedent debt, and for a debt contracted at the time the bill was given   171—174

———

CHAPTER VIII.

Of the Remedy on a Bill or Note.

By what action in ordinary cafes   -   -   175—177
What things it is neceffary to ftate   -   -   178—193
By what action the drawer or indorfor after payment
    by them refpectively   -   -   193, 194
What things it is neceffary to ftate   -   -   194
Indorfor cannot maintain an action on a reindorfement
    to him   -   -   -   194, 195
In what action an acceptor without effects may re-
    cover, &c.   -   -   -   196
——————————————————fupra proteft   196
Holder may fue all the preceding parties   -   198
But can recover but one fatisfaction   -   -   199
Plea to an action on a Bill or Note   -   -   200
Remedy in cafe of bankruptcy   -   -   201

CHAPTER IX.

Of the Proof necessary at the Trial, and of the Defence that may be set up there.

PAGE.

What is admitted in an action against the acceptor - 202
When the acceptor may dispute the hand-writing of the
   drawer - - - 204
What must be proved in an action against the acceptor 205, 208
When the plaintiff may be called upon to prove a
   good consideration, &c. - - - 206
What must be proved in an action by indorsee against
   the drawer - - - - 208
History of fictitious indorsements - 208—268
What must be proved in an action by indorsee against
   indorsor - - - 268, 269
————————————by drawer against acceptor 269
————————————by acceptor against drawer 269, 270
What proof required of signatures - 271, 272
What is required to be proved on judgment by default 273
A writ of inquiry not now necessary - - 276
Defence from want *or* illegality of consideration 276, 277
By whom and in what cases advantage may be taken
   of the illegality of the consideration - 280

LIST

OF THE

PRINCIPAL CASES

CITED IN THIS WORK.

PAGE.

ACHESON v. Fountain. 1 Str. 457.   -   97
Allen v. Dockwra. 1 Salk. 127   -   -   120
Ancher v. Bank of England. Doug. 615, (637)   -   101
Andrews v. Franklin. 1 Str. 24   -   -   57
Appleby v. Biddulph, cited 8 Mod. 363   -   -   56
Auriol v. Thomas. 2 Term. Rep. 52   -   141
Bacon v. Searles. 1 H. Bl. Rep. 88   -   -   160
Banbury v. Liſſet. 2 Str. 1211   -   53, 61, 63, 76
Bank of England v. Newman. 1 Ld. Raym. 442. 12 Mod.

241   -   -   -   -   90
Beardeſley v. Baldwin. 2 Str. 1151   -   -   56
Bellaſis v. Heſter. 1 Ld. Raym. 281   -   -   6
Bevis v. Lindſell. 2 Str. 1149   -   -   -   274
Bickerdike v. Bollman. 1 Term Rep. 405   -   130
Biggs v. Lawrence. 3 Term Rep. 454   -   277, 278
Billers v. Bowles. Barnes 233   -   -   274
Biſhop v. Chitty. 2 Str. 1195   -   -   75
Biſhop v. Hayward. 4 Term Rep. 470   -   -   190
Black v. Peele, cited Doug. 237, (249)   -   157
Bleſard v. Hirſt. 5 Bur. 2670   -   -   118, 119
Bowyer v. Bampton. 2 Str. 1155   -   -   281
Bromley v. Frazier. 1 Str. 441   -   -   167
Brown v. Davis. 3 Term Rep. 284   -   -   284
Brown v. Harraden. 4 Term Rep. 148   -   -   124
Brough

PAGE.

Brough v. Perkins. 2 Ld. Raym. 992 - 146
Buckley v. Campbell. 1 Salk. 13 - - 188
Buller v. Cripps. 6 Mod. 29 - - - 11
Burchell v. Slocock. 2 Ld. Raym. 1545 - 54, 185
Burrows v. Jemino. Str. 733 - - 160
Butler v. Maliſſey. Str. 76 - - 186
Carvick v. Vickery. Doug. 653, (630) - 106, 273
Chadwick v. Allen. 1 Str. 706 - - 61
Chamberlyn v. Delarive. 2 Wilſ. 353 - 63, 198
Cheſter v. Smith. 1 Term Rep. 654 - - 207
Chilton v. Wiffin, 3 Wilſ. 13 - - 201
Clark v. Mundal. 1 Salk. 124. 3 Salk. 68 - 172
Clark v. Pigot. 1 Salk. 125 - - 95
Claxton v. Smith. 3 Mod. 86. 2 Show. 441, 494 112
Clayton's Caſe. 2 Ventr. 308, 310 - - 6
Coleman v. Sayer. 2. Str. 829 - - 6, 120
Collins v. Emett. 1 H. Bl. Rep. 313 - 182, 208, 214
Connor v. Martin. 1 Str. 516 - - - 107
Cooke v. Colehan. 2 Str. 1217 - - 56
Cooper v. Leblanc. 2 Str. 1051 - - 271
Cox v. Coleman, cited B. R. H. 75 - - 69
Dale v. Lubbock. 1 Barnard. B. R. - - 272
Darrack v. Savage. 1 Show. 155 - - 120
Dehers v. Harriot. 1 Show. 163 - 95, 139
Dingwall v. Dunſter. Doug. 235, (247) - 158
Edie v. Eaſt India Company. 2 Bur. 1216 - 32, 98
Ellis v. Galindo. Doug. 238, (250) in the Notes - 159
Ellis v. Wall. Barnes, 234 - - 274
Ereſkine v. Murray. 2 Ld. Raym. 1542 - 188, 190
Eſſington v. Eaſt. 2 Ld. Raym. 810 - - 190
Evans v. Cramlington. Carth. 5. 2 Vent. 309 - 108
Evans v. Underwood. 1 Wilſ. 262, 263 - 57
Faikney v. Reynous. 4 Bur. 2069. 1 Bl. Rep. 638 278
Fenn v. Harriſon. 3 Term Rep. 757 - - 91
Fletcher v. Sandys. 2 Str. 1248 - - 44
Gibſon and Johnſon v. Hunter in Error. 2 H. Bl.
    187—209, 288—298 - - 261, 268

Golding

PAGE.

Golding v. Grace. 2 Bl. Rep. 749 - - 198
Goodall v. Dolley. 1 Term Rep. 712 - 118, 119
Gooftrey v. Mead. 2 Term Rep. 713 - - 137
Gofs v. Nelfon. 1 Bur. 227 - - 57
Grant v. Vaughan. 1 Bl. Rep. 485. 3 Bur. 1516 - 37, 103, 197
Green v. Hearne. 3 Term Rep. 301 - 275
Guichard v. Roberts. 1 Bl. Rep. 445 - 277
Hankey v. Wilfon. Sayer 223 - - 206
Hankey v. Trotman. 1 Bl. Rep. 1 - 41
Harris v. Benfon. 2 Str. 910 - - - 144
Hart v. King. 12 Mod. 309 - - - 271
Haydock v. Lynch. 2 Ld. Raym. 1563 - - 58
Hayward v. Bank of England. 1 Str. 550 - 43
Heylin v. Adamfon. 2 Bur. 676 - 34, 171
Hemmings v. Robinfon. Barnes, 436 - - 272
Hoar v. Dacofta. 2 Str. 290 - - 43
Holman v. Johnfon. Cowp. 341 - - 279
Howis v. Wiggins. 4 Term Rep. 714 - 202
Hull v. Pitfield. 1 Wilf. 46 - - 166
Jackfon v. Pigot. 1 Salk. 127. 1 Ld. Raym. 364.
          12 Mod. 211. Carth. 459 - - 72
Jenny v. Herle. 1 Str. 591. 2 Ld. Raym. 1361. 8 Mod. 265 51
Jenys v. Fowler. 2 Str. 946 - - 202
Jocelyne v. Laffere. Fort. 281. 10 Mod. 294, 316 - 51
Keflebower v. Timms. Bayley 47 - - 177
Kilgour v. Finlyfon. 1 H. Bl. Rep. 155 - 31
King v. Thorn. 1 Term Rep. 487 - - 107
Kingfton v. Long. Bayley's Appendix, No. 2 - 55
Lambert v. Pack. 1 Salk. 128 - - 90, 95
Lambert v. Oakes. 1 Ld. Raym. 443 - 169
Leftley v. Mills. 4 Term. Rep. 170 - 137, 149, 151
Lloyd v. Skutt. Doug. 63, in the Notes - 122
Louviere v. Laubray. 10 Mod. 36, 37 - 269
Lowe v. Waller. Doug. 736 - - - 282
Lucas v. Haynes. 1 Salk. 130. 2 Ld. Raym. 871 95, 96
Lumley v. Palmer. B. R. H. 74. 2 Str. 1000 - 70
Maber v. Maffias. 2 Bl. Rep. 1072 - 58

Macarty

PAGE.

Macarty v. Barrow. 2 Str. 949 cited 3 Wilf. 16, 17 - 110

Macdonald v. Bovington. 4 Term Rep. 825 - 200

Martin v. Chauntry. 2 Str. 1271 - - 50

M'Leod v. Snee. 2 Ld. Raym. 1481. 2 Str. 262 - 54

Mafon v. Hunt. Doug. 286, (299) - 74, 80, 162

May v. Cooper. Fort. 376 - - 122, 124

Miller v. Race. 1 Bur. 452 - 39, 103, 206

Minet v. Gibfon. 3 Term Rep. - - 183

Mitford v. Mayor. Doug. 55 - - 110

Mitford v. Walcot. 1 Salk. 129. 1 Ld. Raym. 574.

    12 Mod. 410 - - - 73

Moore v. Paine. B. R. H. 288 - - 65

More v. Manning. Comyns' Rep. 311 cited 2 Bur 1222 97

Morris v. Lyne. Bayley's Appendix, No. 7 - 276

Morris v. Lee. 1 Str. 629. 2 Ld. Raym. 1396. 8 Mod.

    364 - - - - 61

Neale v. Ovington. 2 Ld. Raym. 1544. 2 Str. 819 186

Nicholfon v. Sedgwick. 1 Salk. 125. 1 Ld. Raym. 180 36

Peacock v. Rhodes. Doug. 633 - - 104, 206

Pearfon v. Garrat. 4 Mod. 242 - - 56

Pierfon v. Dunlop. Doug. 571 - 54, 74, 78

Petre v. Hannay. 3 Term Rep. 418 - - 278

Pinkney v. Hall. 1 Salk. 126. 1 Ld. Raym. 175 - 273

Pillans v. Van Mierop. 3 Bur. 1663 - - 82, 277

Popham et al' v. Bathurft et al' cited 1 Bur. 459 - 40

Powell v. Mormier. 1 Atk. 717, (613) - 72, 74, 81

Price v. Neale. 3 Bur. 1354. 1 Bl. 390 - 202, 204

Rafhleigh v. Salmon. 1 H. Blackftone 252 - 276

Rawlinfon v. Stone. 3 Wilf. 1. 2 Str. 1260 - 107

Roberts v. Peake. 1 Bur. 323 - - 56

Rogers v. Stephens. 2 Term Rep. 714 - 131

Rufhton v. Afpinall. Doug. 679, (654) - 192

Ruffell v. Langftaffe. Doug. 514 - - 90, 277

Salomons v. Stavely. Doug. 684 - - 193

Smith v. Abbot. 2 Str. 1152 - - 75

Smith v. Boheme, cited 2 Ld. Raym. 1362, 1396 - 55

Smith v. Delafontaine. Bayley's Appendix, No. 5 75

PAGE.

Smith v. Niſſen. 1 Term Rep. 269 - - 196

Snowden v. Thomas. 2 Bl. Rep. 748. 3 Wilſ. 155 274, 275

Sparrow v. Carruthers. 2 Bl. Rep. 1197, cited 1 Term
Rep. 7 - - - - 31

Sproat v. Mathews. 1 Term Rep. 182 - 77, 161

Starkey v. Cheeſeman. 1 Ld. Raym. 538 - 196

Stone v. Freeland. 3 Term Rep. 176 - - - 209

Taſſel v. Lewis. 1 Ld. Raym. 743 - 120

Tatlock v. Harris. 3 Term Rep. 174 - 197, 210

Taylor v. Dobbins. 2 Ld. Raym. 1543 - 188

Tindal v. Brown. 1 Term Rep. 167 - 123, 128

Trueman v. Hirſt. 1 Term Rep. 40 - - 21

Vere v. Lewis. 3 Term Rep. 183 - - 213

Walmſley v. Child, cited 1 Bur. 459 - - 39

Walker v. Atwood. 11 Mod. 190 - - 75

Walpole v. Pulteney, cited Doug. 237, (249) - 157

Ward v. Honeywood. Doug. 61, (63) in the Notes 122

Wegerſlofe v. Keene. 1 Str. 214, (224) - 74, 190

Whitcomb v. Whiting. Doug. 652 - 272

White v. Ledwick. Bayley's Appendix, No. 3 - 62

Wilkinſon v. Lutwidge. 1 Str. 648 - 69, 76

Windham v. Withers. 1 Str. 515 - - 199

Wright v. Reed. 3 Term Rep. 554 - - - 41

A

TREATISE

ON

THE LAW

OF

𝕭ills of 𝕰xchange, and 𝕻romissory 𝕹otes.

CHAPTER I.

Of the Origin and Nature of BILLS OF EXCHANGE *and* PROMISSORY NOTES.

IN the infancy of mankind, nature pointed out
the fimple mode of exchanging one commodity for
another, by a comparative eftimation of their ref-
fpective values, dictated by the immediate wants of
the parties to the exchange. But when the occu-
pation of a merchant became a diftinct profeffion,
profpects of a more diftant gain introduced a more
exact appretiation of the value of the feveral articles;
and a common ftandard, under the denomination
of money, to which every thing elfe fhould be referred as its meafure, appears to have been adopted
at a very early period in the hiftory of mankind.—— Genefis.
It is probable, from the low ftate of navigation and

B   commerce

commerce in the ancient world, that the only im-
provement, till long after the fubverfion of the
Roman empire, was the reduction of the rude
pieces of antiquity to a more commodious form,
under the fanction of the ftate. It was referved for
an oppreffed people, confidered as the outcafts of
mankind, in an unenlightened age, urged by the
neceffity of their fituation, to introduce into Europe
at leaft, if not to give birth to, a method, by which
the merchants, of regions the moft remote from
each other, could convey the means of procuring
the value of their commodities, without the incon-
veniency of tranfporting gold or filver.—About
the middle, or towards the end of the thirteenth
century, the Jews, driven by the exactions of the
Prince, from England and France, took refuge in
Lombardy, and from thence gave to merchant
ftrangers and travellers, fecret letters on thofe to
whom they had entrufted their effects in the former
countries; who honourably difcharged the truft
repofed in them, by complying with the orders contained in the letters.—In the courfe of time thefe
letters received a fixed form, and had conferred on
them the name of BILLS OF EXCHANGE.

IT is by means of thefe bills of exchange, that
money is now ufually remitted from one country
to another: The parties to them are generally four,
two at the place where the bill is drawn, and two at
the place of payment; as where A, a merchant at
Amfterdam, owes money to B, a merchant in London, inftead of fending the money in fpecie to B,
he

Montef-
quieu, l.21,
c. 16.

he applies to C, another merchant at Amfterdam, to whom D, a fourth perfon, refiding in London, is indebted to an equal amount; A pays to C the money in queftion, and receives from him a bill directed to D to pay the amount to B, or to any one appointed by him, who fends it to his corref-pondent B, with an order that the money be paid to him by D.

But it frequently happens, that only three per-fons are concerned, as where A, refiding at Am-fterdam, and wifhing to remit money to B at Lon-don, for goods bought of him, and having C, a debtor alfo at London, addreffes his bill to the latter, defiring him to pay the fum mentioned to B, or to his order, to whom he then fends it by letter.

Or if I be at Exeter, and intending to go to Lon-don, and wanting money, I may take it up of a friend at Exeter, and give him bills drawn on myfelf, pay-able to whomfoever he fhall appoint in London.

Beawes, 450.

There may alfo be only two parties concerned in the formation of a bill, as where the perfon mak-ing it defires another to pay to himfelf or to his order.

1 Salk.130. 6 Mod. 29. Per Holt.

A Bill of Exchange therefore may be defined, to be an open letter of requeft, addreffed by one perfon to a fecond, defiring him to pay a fum of money to a third, or to any other to whom that third perfon fhall order it to be paid: or it may be payable to bearer.

Bill of Ex-change, what.

The perfon who makes the bill is called the

drawer;

drawer; he to whom it is addreffed the *drawee*; and if he undertake to pay the amount, he is then called the *acceptor*. The perfon to whom it is ordered to be paid is called the *payee*, and if he appoint another to receive the money, that other is called the *indorfee*, as the payee is with refpect to him the indorfer; and any one who happens for the time to be in poffeffion of the bill, is called the *holder* of it.

THE time at which the payment is limited to be made is various, according to the circumftances of the parties, and the diftance of their refpective refidences. Sometimes the money is payable at *fight*, fometimes at fo many days *after* fight; at other

Ufance. times, at a certain diftance from the *date*.—*Ufance* is the time of one, two, or three months after the date of the bill, according to the cuftom of the places between which the exchanges run. Double or treble ufance, is double or treble the ufual time, and half ufance is half the time.

USANCE between London and any part of France, is thirty days after date.

BETWEEN London and the following places,—Hamburgh, Amfterdam, Rotterdam, Middleburg, Antwerp, Brabant, Zealand, and Flanders,—is one calendar month after the date of the bill.

BETWEEN London and Spain and Portugal, two calendar months.

BETWEEN London and Genoa, Leghorn, Milan, Venice, and Rome, three calendar months.

THE ufance of Amfterdam, on Italy, Spain, and Portugal, is two months.

ON

On France, Flanders, Brabant, and on any place in Holland or Zealand, is one month.

On Frankfort, Nuremberg, Vienna, and other places in Germany, on Hamburg and Breflau, fourteen days after fight, two ufance twenty-eight days, and half ufance feven.

Half ufance, when the ufance is one month, fhall contain fifteen days, notwithftanding the inequality in the length of the months.

Where the time, after the expiration of which a bill is made payable, is limited by months, it muft be computed by calendar, not lunar months: Thus, on a bill dated the firft of January, and payable at one month after date, the month expires on the firft of February.

On this account it is faid in fome books, that where the bill is dated the laft day of a month, fome difficulty may arife from the manner in which that laft day is expreffed, on account of the inequality in the length of the months: Thus in cafes of bills payable one month after date, if the date be fimply the laft day, and the number of the day be not expreffed, it is faid the month expires the laft day of the fucceeding month; as if it bear date the *laft* day of February, the time does not expire till the 31ft of March; but if the *number* of the day be expreffed, the month expires on the day correfponding in number to the date: as if the date be the 28th of February, the time expires on the 28th of March. —On the fame principle it would feem, where the

date

date is the 31ſt of March, the time will not expire till the firſt of May, but where it is the *laſt* day of March, it expires the 30th of April.

But this difficulty can hardly ever occur in practice, as it is apprehended the inſtances of bills dated the *laſt* day of a month are very rare; and where one month is longer than the ſucceeding one, it is a rule not to go, in the computation, into a third: Thus, on a bill dated the 28th, 29th, 30th, or 31ſt of January, and payable one month after date, the time expires on the 28th of February in common years, and in the three latter caſes, in leap year, on the 29th.

The general rule of law is, that when computation is to be made from an act done, the day in *which* the act is done muſt be included; becauſe the law, unleſs to prevent miſchief or inconvenience, admitting no fraction of a day, the act relates to the firſt moment of the day, and is conſidered as done then. But when the computation is to be *from* the day itſelf, the natural conſtruction of the words imports that the day muſt be excluded:

Clayton's Caſe, 2 Ventr. 308. 310.

Thus where a leaſe is made to commence *from* the day of the date, the day is excluded, and it begins the next day, but if it be to commence from the *making*, the day is included.—With reſpect to bills

Bellaſis v. Heſter. Ld. Raym. 281. Coleman. v. Saver. Str. 829.

of exchange, however, the caſe is different: The cuſtom of merchants, which makes part of the law of the land, being, that where a bill is payable at ſo many days after ſight, or from the date, the day of

presentment

prefentment or of the date is excluded. Thus, where a bill, payable ten days after fight, is prefented on the firft day of a month, the ten days expire on the eleventh; where it is dated the firft, and payable twenty days after date, thefe expire on the twenty-firft. Where there is no date, and the payment is directed to be made fo many days *after* date, the date is taken to be the day on which it iffued.

THE vernal equinox, as the year was rectified by Julius Cæfar, happened to fall, in the year 325, on the 21ft of March : But from caufes which it is foreign to the purpofe of this treatife to explain, in 1582, the equinox having changed from the 21ft to the 11th of March, Pope Gregory XIII. ordered ten days to be taken out of the calendar, and the 11th day of March to be reckoned as the 21ft. This edict was generally obeyed by the nations who acknowledged his authority, but moft of the Proteftant countries continued the former method of reckoning their time, and from hence arofe the different modes of computation, which now obtain in Europe under the denominations of Old and New Style. Since the days of Gregory, the equinox has receded one day, fo that there are eleven days of difference between Old and New Style; or, in other words, the firft day of any month, according to the *old* ftyle, is the twelfth according to the *new*.

OLD Style now prevails in Mufcovy, Denmark, Holftein, Hamburg, Utrecht, Gueldres, Eaft Frief-land,

land, Geneva, and in all the Proteſtant principalities in Germany, and the Cantons of Switzerland.

NEW Style, in all the dominions ſubjeĉt to the
Crown of Great Britain, in Amſterdam, Rotterdam,
Leyden, Haerlem, Middleburg, Ghent, Bruſſels,
Brabant, and in all the Netherlands except Utrecht
and Gueldres; and in France, Spain, Portugal,
Italy, Hungary, Poland, and in all the Popiſh
principalities of Germany, and the Cantons of
Switzerland.

WHERE a bill, payable at a certain time from
the date, is drawn at a place uſing one ſtyle, and
remitted to a place uſing the other, the time is to
be computed according to the ſtyle of the place at
which it is drawn.—Thus, on a bill payable the 1ſt
of March, old ſtyle, and payable here one month
after date, the month is to be reckoned from the
12th of March, becauſe that day, according to the
new ſtyle, correſponds to the firſt according to the
old *.

SOMETIMES the drawer of a bill makes the date
both according to the old and new ſtyle, writing the
one above and the other below, a ſmall line drawn
between them, thus:

$$\frac{18}{29} : \qquad \text{March } \frac{28}{8} \quad \text{April}$$

* Beawes, in his Lex Mercatoria, page 484, ſeĉt. 251, ſays,
that a bill payable on a certain day, is due on the day mentioned,
according to the ſtyle of the place *on* which it is drawn, which
ſeems contrary to the reaſon and nature of the thing.

WHERE

WHERE a bill is payable at a time after fight, there can be no difficulty; the time muſt evidently be computed according to the ſtyle of the place where it is payable.

A CUSTOM has obtained among merchants, that a perſon to whom a bill is addreſſed, ſhall be allow-ed a little time for payment, beyond the term mentioned in the bill, called days of grace. But the number of theſe days varies, according to the cuſtom of different places. Days of Grace.

GREAT BRITAIN, Ireland, Bergamo, and Vienna, three days.

FRANKFORT, out of the time of the fair, four days.

LEIPSICK, Naumburg, and Augſburg, five days.

VENICE, Amſterdam, Rotterdam, Middleburg, Antwerp, Cologn, Breſlau, Nuremberg, and Portugal, ſix days.

DANTZICK, Koningſberg, and France, ten days.

HAMBURG and Stockholm, twelve days.

NAPLES eight, Spain fourteen, Rome fifteen, and Genoa thirty days.

LEGHORN, Milan, and ſome other places in Italy, no fixed number.

SUNDAYS and holy-days are included in the reſpite days at London, Naples, Amſterdam, Rotterdam, Antwerp, Middleburg, Dantzick, Koningſberg, and France; but not at Venice, Cologn, Breſlau, and Nuremberg. At Hamburg, the day on which the bill falls due makes one of the days of grace, but it is not ſo elſewhere.

IN

In England, if the laſt of the three days happens to be Sunday, the bill is to be paid on Saturday.

But bills payable at ſight, are to be paid without any days of grace.

Form of
Bills of Ex-
change,
Bcawes,
484.

The ſtyle admits of ſeveral variations, according as one or more bills are granted for the ſame ſum; or according to the *time* of payment, or the *place* of payment, (though the latter be ſeldom mentioned) as, at his own houſe,—at the houſe of A. B. &c. or according to the ſpecie in which payment is to be made, as in Engliſh money, French money, &c. or according to the different kinds of value received for them; for though bills in Britain bear only *value received* in general, yet bills drawn in other countries uſually particularize whether the value was given in money, goods, or bills, or according to the number of perſons concerned in the bill; for bills may be drawn by and upon, and payable to, not only ſingle perſons, but alſo perſons in company or co-partnerſhip; or according as the perſon on whom it is drawn is to expect further direction or not from the drawer, and ſo run thus, *as per advice from your humble ſervant;* or thus, *as per advice from A. B.* or *without further advice.*

Bills of Exchange are diſtinguiſhed by the appellations of *foreign* and *inland* bills; the firſt being thoſe which paſs from one country to another, and the latter ſuch as paſs beeween parties reſiding in the ſame country. The univerſal conſent of merchants had eſtabliſhed a ſyſtem of cuſtoms relative

to

to *foreign* bills, which was adopted as part of the law in every commercial ftate.

THOUGH the objeft of Bills of Exchange was at firft to be the medium of remittance between *different countries*, yet in Italy, Germany, and France, where the trading cities, though included within the limits of an extended government, were in effeft under the diftinft jurifdiftion of fovereigns independent of one another, the merchants of different cities of the fame country very foon adopted them in their mutual tranfaftions, and they were in every refpeft confidered in the fame light in the one cafe as in the other. But in this country, which was united under one firm government, where, in the infancy of commerce, the tranfaftions of one trading town with another were of but little importance ; and where, from the better regulated police and eafier communication between the different parts of the kingdom, gold and filver could be conveyed with greater fafety; it appears that this mode of negociation was introduced at a very late period, for Lord Chief Juftice Holt is reported to have faid, that he remembered *when* aftions on inland bills of exchange firft began, fo that inland bills themfelves cannot be fuppofed to have been very frequent before the reign of Charles II. And when they *were* introduced, they were not regarded with the fame favour as *foreign* bills, differing in fome circumftances, of which notice will be taken in a fubfequent part of this treatife. At length, however, the legiflature, fenfible of the advantage arifing

Mich.
2 Anne.
6 Mod. 29.

9 & 10 W.
III. c. 17.
3 & 4 An.
c. 9.

arifing to trade from this mode of payment, by two different ftatutes, fet them on nearly the fame footing with foreign ones; fo that what was the law and cuftom of merchants with refpect to the one, is now, in moft refpects, the eftablifhed law of the country with refpect to the other.

There is, however, one circumftance in which they differ with refpect to practice: Inland bills are generally fingle, there being only one of the fame tenor and date, whereas foreign bills are ufually in fets, confifting of three bills of the fame tenor and date, a method adopted by way of precaution to guard againft the rifk of mifcarriage.

Lex Mercatoria,
451.

The following precautions are recommended by Beawes, in the drawing of a Bill of Exchange. 1ft, That it have its date rightly and clearly expreffed. 2dly, That it have the name of the place where it is made. 3dly, That the fum be expreffed fo diftinctly, both in words and figures, that no exceptions can be taken againft it. 4thly, That the payment be ordered and commanded. 5thly, That the time of payment be not dubioufly expreffed, nor fooner nor later than has been agreed on. 6thly, The perfon remitting the bill muft particularly obferve, that the name of the perfon to whom payment is to be made, be properly fpelled; or if it be made to his order, that thofe words be clearly written. 7thly and 8thly, He muft obferve whether his own name be there, and the value *of him* be expreffed. 9thly, He muft obferve that the bill be fubfcribed by the drawer. 10thly, The drawer
muft

muft principally look to the direction of the bill, that it be true, and directed to the right perfon. 11thly, They muft both obferve, that the place where the payment is to be made (and the coin or fpecie in which the bill is to be paid) be fully expreffed in the fuperfcription or body of the bill; and if the drawer draw upon one not living at the place where the bill is intended to be paid, then the remitter muft obferve, that as well the place where the perfon lives that is to pay, as the place where payment is to be made, be expreffed.

The following are EXAMPLES of the different kinds of BILLS.

No. I.

London, Jan. 18th, 1782.

Exchange for £. 50 Sterl.

AT fight (* of this my only Bill of Exchange) pay to Mr. John Rogers, or order, Fifty Pounds fterling, value received of him, and place the fame to account, as per advice (or without further advice) from

SAMUEL SKINNER.

To Mr. James Jenkins,
  Merchant, in Briftol.

* This is not always inferted.

No.

No.' II.   (1.)

London, the 18*th of January,* 1782.
> *Exchange for* 10,000 *Liv. Tournoises.*

At fifteen days after date (or at one, two, &c. usances) pay this my first Bill of Exchange, (second and third of the same tenor and date not paid) to Meffrs. John Rogers and Co. or order, Ten Thousand Livres Tournoises, value received of them, and place the same to account, as per advice from

THOMAS BENCRAFT.

To Mr. Henry Kendrick,
Banker, in Paris.

––––––––

No. II.   (2.)

London, Jan. 18*th,* 1782.
> *Exchange for* 10,000 *Liv. Tournoises.*

At fifteen days after date (or at one, two, &c. usances) pay this my second Bill of Exchange, (the first and third of the same tenor and date not paid) to Meffrs. John Rogers and Co. or order, Ten Thousand Livres Tournoises, value received of them, and place the same to account, as per advice from

THOMAS BENCRAFT.

To Mr. Henry Kendrick,
Banker, in Paris.

No.

No. II. (3.)

London, Jan. 18, 1782.

Exchange for 10,000 *Liv. Tournoiſes.*

AT fifteen days after date (or at one, two, &c.
uſances) pay this my third Bill of Exchange, (the
firſt and ſecond of the ſame tenor and date not
paid) to Meſſrs. John Rogers and Co. or order,
Ten Thouſand Livres Tournoiſes, value received
of them, and place the ſame to account, as per
advice from

THOMAS BENCRAFT.

To Mr. Henry Kendrick,
  Banker, in Paris.

No. III.

London, January 18*th,* 1782.

Exchange for D. 1000.

AT uſance pay this my firſt of Exchange to Mr.
Ignatio Teſtori, (or to the *procuration of* Mr. Ignatio
Teſtori) One Thouſand Ducats Banco, value received of Mr. Gregory Laman, and place it to account, as per advice from

NICHOLAS REUBENS.

To Mr. James Robottom,
  Merchant, in Venice.

No.

No. IV.

London, Jan. 18*th*, 1782.

> *Exchange for* 1600 *perooo R's.*

AT thirty days fight, (or ufance, &c.) pay this my firft of Exchange, (fecond and third as above) to Samuel Fairfax, Efquire, or order, One Thoufand Six Hundred Mil-Reas, value received of ditto, and place it to account, as per advice from

JEREMIAH TOMLINSON.

To Meffrs. Brown and Black,
 Merchants, at Lifbon.   –

———

No. V.

London, Jan. 18*th*, 1782.

> *Exchange for* £. 273. 15*s. fterl. at* 35 *Sc.* 7 *G.*
> *per* £. *fterl.*

AT two ufo's and a half, pay this my firft of Exchange, (fecond, &c.) to Mr. Jofeph Jacobs, or order, Two Hundred and Seventy-three Pounds Fifteen Shillings fterl. at thirty-five fhillings and feven groots per pound fterling, value received of Mr. James Merryman, and place it to account, as per advice from

JOHN JOHNSON,

To Mr. David Hill,
 Merchant, at Amfterdam.

No.

No. VI.

No. 4. *London, 22 September,* 1789.

     For £. 200 sterl. at 35 Sh. Flemish.

 Two months after date of this my first of Exchange, (second, &c.) pay to D. E. or order, at his own house, Two Hundred Pounds sterl. at thirty-five shillings Flemish per pound sterling, value received of him, and pass the same to account, as per advice from

        Yours, &c.

          A. B.

To Mr. Peter Par,
 Merchant, at Amsterdam.

No. VII.

* *No.* 10. *London, Sept.* 22, 1765.   £. 200.

 Pay to me, A. B. grocer, in London, or order, on the first day of November next, the sum of Two Hundred Pounds in goods of

       Your humble servant,

         A. B.

To G. H. Vintner,
 in Westminster.

     Accepts G. H.

          As

---

 * It is usual when the drawer draws a bill or draft on a banker, or on a person on whom he usually draws, to number the bill in this manner.

       C

Origin of Promissory Notes.   As commerce advanced in its progress, the multiplicity of its concerns required, in many inftances, a lefs complicated mode of payment than by Bills of Exchange. A trader, whofe fituation and circumftances rendered credit from the merchant or manufacturer who fupplied him with goods, abfolutely neceffary, might have fo limited a connection with the commercial world at large, that he could not eafily furnifh his creditor with a Bill of Exchange on another man; but his own refponfibility might be fuch, that his fimple promife of payment, reduced to writing for the purpofe of evidence, might be accepted with equal confidence as a bill on another trader: Hence, it may reafonably be conjectured, Promiffory Notes were at firft introduced; and the period of their introduction appears to have been about 30 years before the reign of Queen Anne.

6 Mod. 30. 2 Anne.

A Promiffory Note may be defined to be an engagement in writing to pay a certain fum of money mentioned in it, to a perfon named, or to his order, or to the bearer at large; and at firft thefe notes were confidered only as written evidence of a debt; for it was held that a Promiffory Note was not affignable or indorfible over, within the cuftom of merchants, to any other perfon, by him to whom it was made payable; and that if, in *fact*, fuch a note had been indorfed or affigned over, the perfon to whom it was fo indorfed or affigned, could not maintain an action, within the cuftom, againft the perfon who firft drew and fubfcribed the note; and

Vid. 1 Salk. 129. 2 Lord Raym. 757, 759, and preamble to 3 & 4 Ann. c. 9.

that

that within the same custom even the person to whom it was made payable could not maintain such action. But at length they were recognized by the legiflature, and put on the same footing with *inland* Bills of Exchange, by a statute which enacts, " That from the first of May, 1705, all " notes in writing made and signed by any person " or persons, body politic or corporate, or by the " servant or agent of any corporation, banker, " goldfmith, merchant, or trader, usually intrusted " by him, her or them, to sign such Promissory " Notes by him, her or them, whereby such person " or persons, body politic or corporate, his, her or " their fervant or agent as aforesaid, doth or shall " promise to pay, to any other person or persons, " body politic and corporate, his, her or their " order, or to bearer, any sum of money mentioned " in such note, shall be taken and construed to be, " by virtue thereof, due and payable to any such " person or persons, body politic and corporate, " to whom the same is made payable; and also " every such note shall be assignable or indorsible " over in the same manner as Inland Bills of Ex- " change; and that the person, &c. to whom such " sum is by such note made payable, may maintain " an action for the same, in the same manner as " they might do on an Inland Bill of Exchange, " made or drawn according to the custom of mer- " chants, against the person or persons, body poli- " tic and corporate, who or whose agent signed the " same; and that any person, &c. to whom such

3 & 4 Ann. c. 9. made perpetual by 7 Ann. c. 25. f. 3.

" note

" note is indorfed or affigned, or the money therein
" mentioned, ordered to be paid by indorfement
" thereon, may maintain an action for fuch fum of
" money, either againft the perfon, &c. who or
" whofe agent figned fuch note, or againft any of
" the perfons who indorfed the fame, in like man-
" ner as in cafes of Inland Bills of Exchange."

PROMISSORY NOTES are in thefe forms.

£. 10.

London, December 15, 1789.

I promife to pay G. F. or bearer, on demand,
Ten Pounds, for value received.

S. R.

———

£. 30. 12. 6.

London, January 1, 1790.

Two months after date, we or either of us promife to pay to Mr. C. B. and Co. or order, Thirty
Pounds Twelve Shillings and Sixpence, value received.

D. E.
G. K.

Vid. 23
Geo. 3. c.
49.

TILL the twenty-third of George III. thefe notes
and bills were written on a plain piece of paper
unftamped: By a ftatute made in that year, certain
duties were impofed on every piece of vellum,
parchment or paper, on which Bills and Notes,
falling under certain defcriptions, fhould be written,
engroffed,

engroffed, or printed. By a fubfequent Act thefe 31 G. 3. c. 25, f. 1. duties are taken off, and others impofed in their ftead.

By this latter ftatute, the duties on Inland Bills and Notes vary according to the different claffes into which they are diftributed, by the provifions of the fame ftatute.

One diftinction is marked between thofe in which the fum expreffed does *not* exceed £. 200, and thofe in which it *exceeds* that fum.

Of thofe in which the fum does *not* exceed £. 200 there are two general divifions; thofe payable on *demand*, and thofe payable *otherwife* than on demand.

Of thofe payable on *demand* a diftinction is made between Bills of Exchange, Drafts or Orders, for the payment of money on *demand*, and *Promiffory* Notes, or *other* Notes for the payment of money to the *bearer* on *demand*.

The latter kind may be re-iffued without being Vid. f. 7, 8, 9. fubject to the duty a fecond time; and the holder has the fame remedy for the recovery of the fum expreffed in them, after their being re-iffued, as he would have had at firft. But of thefe there are two claffes—thofe which may be re-iffued from time to time, after payment at the place *where they were firft iffued;* and thofe which may be re-iffued from time to time, after payment *at the fame place*, or *any other place*, than where they were firft iffued. The firft may be for fums not exceeding £. 200, the fecond for fums not exceeding £. 30.

Duties

Vi l. f. 2.   Duties on Bills of Exchange, Drafts or Orders, for the
payment of Money on demand.

			s.	d.
For any sum amounting to 40s. not exceeding 5 Guineas			0	3
————— exceeding 5 Guineas,——£. 30	-		0	6
————— exceeding £. 30 —————	50	-	0	9
————— exceeding 50 —————	100	-	1	0
————— exceeding 100 —————	200	-	1	6
For any sum from - 200 upwards	-	-	2	0

Duties on Bills of Exchange, Drafts or Orders, payable
otherwise than on demand, and Promissory Notes, or *other*
Notes, payable otherwise than to the *bearer* on *demand*.

			s.	d.
For any sum amounting to 40s. not exceeding £. 30	-		0	6
————— exceeding £. 30 —————	50	-	0	9
————— exceeding 50 —————	100	-	1	0
————— exceeding 100 —————	200	-	1	6
For any sum from - 200 upwards	-	-	2	0

Duties on Promissory or *other* Notes payable to the *bearer on
demand*, and re-issuable from time to time, after payment
at the place where they were first issued.

			s.	d.
For sums amounting to 40s. not exceeding 5 Guineas			0	3
————— exceeding - 5 Guineas——£. 30	-		0	6
————— exceeding £. 30 —————	50	-	0	9
————— exceeding 50 —————	100	-	1	0
————— exceeding 100 —————	200	-	1	6

Duties on Promiſſory Notes, or *other* Notes, for the payment of money to the *bearer on demand*, re-iſſuable from
time to time after any payment at the *ſame* place, or any
other place than where they were firſt iſſued.

With reſpect to Foreign Bills, drawn here in ſets, according
to the cuſtom of merchants, every Bill of each ſet is ſubject to a Stamp Duty as under :

	s.	*d.*
For ſums not exceeding £. 100 - -	0	6
For ſums exceeding - 100 not exceeding £. 200	0	9
——————————— 200 - -	1	0

THE duties are payable by the drawers or makers ſ. 2.
of the bills or notes reſpectively; and the ſheet or ſ. 19.
piece of vellum or parchment, or the ſheet or
piece of paper, on which the bills or notes are ingroſſed, written, or printed, muſt be ſtamped *before* theſe are drawn ; and the Commiſſioners and
their officers are prohibited from ſtamping any
vellum, &c. at any time *after* any Bill of Exchange,
Promiſſory Note, or other Note, Draft, or Order,
ſhall be ingroſſed, written, or printed thereon.

AND it is enacted, that no Bill of Exchange,
Promiſſory Note, or other Note, Draft, or Order,
liable to the duties, ſhall be pleaded or given in
evidence in any court, or admitted in any court
to be good, uſeful, or available in law or equity,
unleſs the vellum, &c. on which it ſhall be en-
groſſed, printed, written, or made, ſhall be ſtamped
with a lawful ſtamp to denote the rate or duty, or
ſome higher rate or duty in the Act contained.

IT

f. 6.

IT is likewife enacted, that if any Bill, &c. for the payment of any fum amounting to 40s. or upwards, be engroffed, &c. on vellum, &c. which fhall not be ftamped, &c. or which fhall be ftamped with a ftamp of a lower denomination or value than by the Act directed, there fhall be due, anfwered and paid to his Majefty, &c. the full rate or duty chargeable thereon, which fhall be payable by and charged upon all and every perfon or perfons, feverally and refpectively, who fhall draw or make, and utter and negociate, or caufe to be drawn or made, and uttered and negociated, any fuch Bill, &c. on fuch vellum, &c. not ftamped, or ftamped with fuch lower duty, his, her and their refpective executors, adminiftrators, and affigns.

f. 10.

AND any perfon who fhall write or fign, or caufe to be written or figned ; or who fhall accept or pay, or caufe to be accepted or paid, any of thefe inftruments, without the *proper* ftamp, fhall, for every offence, forfeit the fum of £. 20.

f. 7.

A PENALTY of £. 20 is alfo impofed on any perfon who fhall re-iffue any of the re-iffuable Promiffory Notes, otherwife than is permitted by the Act.

f. 24.

THESE penalties may be fued for in any of the courts at Weftminfter, for offences committed in England; and in the Court of Exchequer, in Scotland, for offences committed there, by action of debt, bill, plaint or information, in which no effoin, privilege, wager of law, nor more than one imparlance fhall be allowed.

AND

AND any Juſtice of Peace, reſiding near the place ſ. 25. where the offence is committed, is authoriſed and required, on any information exhibited, or complaint made, to ſummon the party accuſed, and the witneſſes on either ſide; and, on due proof made, to give judgment for the penalty, and to iſſue his warrant for levying it on the goods of the offender; and unleſs they be redeemed within ſix days, to cauſe a ſale to be made of the goods taken under the warrant, rendering to the party the overplus, if any; and if goods cannot be found ſufficient to anſwer the penalty, to commit the offender to priſon, there to remain for the ſpace of three months, unleſs ſuch pecuniary penalty ſhall be ſooner paid and ſatisfied; but the juſtice may mitigate the penalty as he ſhall think fit, (reaſonable coſts and charges of the officers and informers, as well in making the diſcovery as in proſecuting the ſame, being always allowed, over and above ſuch mitigation) ſo as ſuch mitigation do not reduce the penalty to leſs than a moiety over and above the ſaid coſts and charges—provided that any one who ſhall feel himſelf aggrieved by the judgment of ſuch juſtice, may, on giving ſecurity to the amount of ſuch penalty, together with ſuch coſts as ſhall be awarded in caſe ſuch judgment ſhall be affirmed, appeal to the next general quarter ſeſſions for the county, riding, or place, which ſhall happen after 14 days next after ſuch conviction ſhall have been made, and of which appeal reaſonable notice ſhall be given, who are

impowered

impowered to fummon and examine witneffes upon
oath, and finally to hear and determine the fame;
and if the judgment be affirmed, the court may
award the offender to pay fuch cofts, occafioned by
fuch appeal, as to them fhall feem meet.

f. 27.

AND if any one, being fummoned to give evidence before fuch juftice or juftices, fhall refufé to
appear, without a reafonable excufe to be allowed
by fuch juftice or juftices; or, appearing, fhall refufe to give evidence, every fuch perfon fhall forfeit the fum of 40s. to be levied in the fame manner as directed with refpect to the other penalties.

f. 24, 25.

THE time limited for a common informer to
fue in is three months, either in the fuperior courts
or before juftices of peace; and if a common informer fue within that time, the penalties are divided in moieties between the informer and the
King.

f. 28.

IF no informer fue within that time, then the
penalties are only recoverable in the name of his
Majefty's Attorney General in England, or Advo-
cate in Scotland, by information in the refpective
courts; and the whole of the penalties go to the
King.

f. 29.

AND if any perfon fhall counterfeit, or procure
to be counterfeited, any ftamp directed to be ufed
by this Act; or fhall counterfeit or refemble the
impreffion of fuch ftamp on any vellum, &c. or
fhall utter, vend, fell, or expofe to fale, any vellum,
&c. liable to the duties, with fuch counterfeit mark
or impreffion, knowing the fame to be counterfeited;

feited; or fhall privately or fraudulently ufe any ftamp or mark directed by this Act to be ufed, with intent to defraud his Majefty, &c. he fhall be adjudged a felon, and fhall fuffer death as in cafes of felony, without benefit of clergy.

DRAFTS or Orders for the payment of money to f. 4. the bearer on demand, bearing date on or before the day on which the fame are iffued, and at the place from which the fame are drawn and iffued, and drawn on any banker or bankers, or perfon or perfons acting as a banker or bankers, and refiding and tranfacting the bufinefs of a banker within ten miles of the place where fuch Draft or Order fhall be actually drawn and iffued, are exempted from the duty.

AND all Promiffory and other Notes and Bills f. 5. iffued by the Bank of England are exempted from any ftamp duty, on confideration of the Governors and Company paying into the receipt of his Majefty's Exchequer the annual fum of £. 12,000, by half yearly payments.

IT is alfo provided, that nothing in the prefent f. 11. Act fhall be conftrued to give legality to any Bill of Exchange or Promiffory Note which was not legal before.

CHAP.

CHAP. II.

Who may make a BILL OF EXCHANGE *or* PROMISSORY
NOTE, *and be parties in the Negociation of them.*

Vid. Stat.
5 R.II.c.2.
Lutw. 891,
1585.

BILLS of Exchange having been first introduced
for the convenience of commerce, it was formerly
thought that no person could draw one, or be concerned in the negociation of it, who was not an

Carth. 82.
2 Vent.292.
Comb.152.
1 Show.
125. 2 Sho.
501. Lutw.
1585. 12
Mod. 36,
380. Salk.
126.

actual merchant: but the multiplied concerns of
society rendering it necessary for others, not at all
engaged in trade, to adopt the same mode of remittance, it has been since decided that any person
capable of binding himself by a contract, may
draw or accept a Bill of Exchange, or be in any
way engaged in the negociation of it, and shall be
considered as a merchant for that purpose; and
that it is not necessary in a declaration on a Bill,
to aver, that the defendant is a merchant.

3 & 4 Ann.
c. 9.

ON the same principle, since the statute of
Queen Anne, any man, though not a merchant,
may be party to a Promissory Note.

AN infant, or one under the age of twenty-one,
cannot be engaged in trade, and therefore, it being
impossible that the fiction or supposition of being
a merchant should extend to him, it has been de-

Carth. 160.

termined that he cannot be sued on a Bill of Exchange,

change, drawn in the ordinary courfe of bufinefs; and though it does not appear to have ever been exprefsly decided that he cannot be fued on a Promiffory Note, yet as the fame principle extends to the one as to the other, it is evident he cannot.

BUT as an infant *may* contract for neceffaries, or for his education fuitable to his rank in life, it may admit of fome doubt whether a Bill of Exchange or Promiffory Note given by him for either of thefe confiderations, and expreffed fo to be in the body of them, would not bind him; for though it be certain that even for *thefe* he cannot bind himfelf by a bond or other writing with a penalty, yet it has been frequently determined, that a fingle bond, that is, one *without* a penalty, given by an infant for neceffaries, will bind him; and unlefs the circumftance of the making a Bill of Exchange or Promiffory Note, being a mercantile tranfaction, and of the total incapacity of an infant to be a merchant, be a fufficient reafon for confidering *any* Bill or Note in which an infant is concerned as invalid againft him, there feems no reafon why either, really given and expreffed to be given by him for neceffaries, may not be confidered as equally binding with a fingle bond: for if it be faid that the jury muft inquire whether the articles mentioned as neceffaries be really fo or not, and into the reafonablenefs of the price, and therefore may give a lefs fum than that mentioned in the Bill or Note, it may be anfwered, that thefe objections hold equally againft a fingle bond.

Co. Lit.
172. a.

Vid. March
145. 1 Ro.
Abr. 729.
Pl. 8. &
1 Lev. 86.

Vid. 1
Term Rep.
40. Trueman v.
Hurft.

AN

An infant however may certainly fue on a Bill or Note, for that is for his benefit.

A MARRIED woman, in general, can bind herfelf by no contract; nor can fhe, without a fpecial authority, bind her hufband, except it be for fuch neceffaries as are fuitable to his rank: it is therefore clear that a Bill of Exchange or Promiffory Note to which fhe is a party is of no force.

But there are cafes in which a married woman is confidered as having an exiftence independent of her hufband, and then fhe may contract and be bound by her contract as if fhe were fingle; and in fuch cafes fhe may, amongft other contracts, certainly be bound by a Bill of Exchange or Promiffory Note.

Thefe cafes are,

1ft. WHERE by particular cuftom in fome places fhe is permitted to trade on her feparate account; but in this cafe, if fhe be fued in a *fuperior* court, her hufband muft be joined for conformity, and he may plead the cuftom in bar.

2dly. WHERE a woman lives apart from her hufband under articles of feparation, has a feparate maintenance, and acts and receives credit as a fingle woman.

But this does not extend to the cafe of a woman eloping from her hufband, and living apart from him.

3dly. WHERE the hufband is under a civil difability of being in the kingdom; as where he is banifhed, or has abjured the realm; or has been tranfported,

3 Burr. 1776,1784.
2 Bl. Rep. 1081.

1 Term Rep. 9.

2 Bl. Rep. 1079.

Co. Lit. 132. b. 133 a. Sparrow v. Carruthers,

transported, though but for a term of years; or where the husband is an alien enemy, residing out of the kingdom.

cited 2 Bl, Rep. 1197, & 1 Term Rep. 7. 1 Ld Raym, 147. Salk. 116.

NEITHER can a married woman, except in the foregoing cases, be the payee or indorsee of a Bill or Note, for she cannot sue, as she can possess no property in a capacity distinct from her husband.

WHERE there are two joint traders, and a Bill is drawn on both of them, the acceptance of one binds the other, if it concern the joint trade, because they trade for a common benefit, and therefore where one of them gives credit, it is the act of them both: but it is otherwise if it concern the acceptor only, in a distinct interest and respect.—And if a factor of an incorporated company draw a Bill on such company, and any member accept it, the acceptance shall not bind the company, nor any other member of it, because it is a private act of the party, and not a public act of the company.

1 Salk. 126, Gilb. L. E. 117, 118. 1 Ld Raym, 175.

ON the same principle, if ten merchants, each in his individual capacity, employ one factor, and he draw a Bill on all of them, and one accept it, this shall only bind him and not the rest, because they are separate in interest, the one from the other.

IF on a dissolution of partnership between three partners a power be given to one of them to receive all debts due to the late partnership, and to pay all debts owen by it, this will not enable him afterwards to draw a Bill on one of the *debtors* of the partnership, and, on its being accepted, to indorse

1 H. Bl. Rep. C. B. 155. Kilgour v, Finlyson & others,

it

it in the *name* of the partnerſhip ; and conſequently the indorſee cannot maintain an action on the Bill againſt the three as partners.

WHETHER a corporation, which has not a ſpecial power expreſsly given for the purpoſe, can be concerned in drawing or accepting a Bill of Exchange or Promiſſory Note, or in the negociation of either, or can be made the payee, is a queſtion which ſeems never to have had the conſideration of a court; perhaps, becauſe nobody has ever entertained a doubt on this head ; and it ſeems to have been taken for granted by the legiſlature, and it is conſiſtent with the general principles of law, that, by the intervention of an agent or ſervant, lawfully authorized, a corporation, on which no reſtraint is impoſed in its original conſtitution, might in this reſpect act as a natural perſon.   There is, however, a proviſo in the Act, which puts Promiſſory Notes on the ſame footing with Bills of Exchange, that no body politic or corporate ſhall have power, by virtue of it, to iſſue or give out Notes, by themſelves or their ſervants, other than ſuch as they might have iſſued if this Act had not been made.

THE Bank of England has a ſpecial power conferred on it for this purpoſe.

IT is aſſerted by *Marius* and others, that the wife, ſervant, or friend of a merchant, cannot bind him by their acceptance, without a power of attorney in form ; but it is a common practice for ſome one of a merchant's clerks, in the abſence of his maſter, to accept Bills in his name; and there is no doubt but,

Marginal notes: Vid. Edie v. Eaſt IndiaCompany. 2 Bur. 1216. 3 & 4 Ann. c. 9. ſ. 3. — 5 W. & M. c. 20. ſ. 28. — Mar. 26.

but, at this day, though there fhould be no inftrument made to either of the before-mentioned perfons, yet if either of them have formerly, in the Beawes
principal's abfence, ufually accepted his Bills, and 462.
he did not difapprove on his return, this will be
as binding on him as if there had been a legal and
formal inftrument.

SOMETIMES exchange is made in the name and Id. Ibid.
for the account of a third perfon, by virtue of full
power and authority given by him, and this is
commonly termed *procuration;* and fuch bills may
be drawn, fubfcribed, indorfed, accepted, and negociated, not in the name or for the account of the
manager or tranfactor of any or all thefe branches
of remittances, but in the name and for the account
of the perfon who authorifed him.

BUT a difcreet man will not rafhly hazard his Id. Ibid.
fubftance by fuch a fubftitution; but if obliged by
the neceffity of his affairs, will act with the utmoft
circumfpection in the choice of his agent; and
when he has appointed him, he muft advife thofe
correfpondents on whom fuch agent may occafion-
ally want to draw, of his having given fuch a power,
and defire them to honor the firm of his fubftitute,
whenever ufed for his account.

AND he who by fuch a procuration either ne-
gociates, draws, indorfes, fubfcribes or accepts
Bills of Exchange, by fubfcribing his own name
and quality, that is, as attorney of his employer,
as effectually binds his principal, as if he himfelf
affirmed, whilft the procurator is not in the leaft

bound:

bound : but if any one, under *pretence* of having a
full power from a perſon of credit, tranſact buſineſs
on his own account, he is bound, and not the perſon whoſe name he has uſed.

Id. Ibid.

THE poſſeſſor of a bill muſt admit the acceptance
of a procurator, provided his letter of attorney be
general, or expreſsly declaring that all bills accepted
by him are on account of the principal, or limited
only to thoſe bills which the poſſeſſor has; but if
the procuration be not clear and expreſs in theſe
particulars, then the holder is not bound to admit
the acceptance.

Id. 462.
3.

CHAP. III.

Of the Reſemblance which BILLS OF EXCHANGE *and*
PROMISSORY NOTES *bear to one another; and of
their different Kinds.*

Per Lord
Mansfield,
in Heylin
v. Adam-
ſon. 2 Bur.
676.

A PROMISSORY NOTE, in its original form of a
promiſe from one man to pay a ſum of money to
another, bears no reſemblance to a Bill of Exchange.
When it is indorſed, the reſemblance begins, for
then it is an order by the indorſer to the maker of
the note, who, by his promiſe, is his debtor, to pay

the

the money to the indorfee.   This is the exact definition of a BILL OF EXCHANGE.

THE indorfer of the note corresponds to the
drawer of the bill; the maker to the drawee or acceptor; and the indorfee to the payee, or party to
whom the bill is made payable.

WHEN this point of refemblance is once fixed,
the law is fully fettled to be exactly the fame in
Bills of Exchange and Promiffory Notes: and as
fome confufion has arifen in the books from an
inattention to the real analogy between them, it
may be proper to obferve, that whenever the law
is reported to have been fettled with refpect to the
acceptor of a bill, it is to be confidered as applicable to the drawer, or, as he may, with more propriety, be called, the maker of a note; when with
refpect to the drawer of a bill, then to the firft
indorfer of the note: the fubfequent indorfers
and indorfees bear an exact refemblance to one
another.

BOTH bills and notes are in two different forms,
being fometimes made payable to fuch a man or
his order, or to the order of fuch a man; fometimes to fuch a man or bearer, or fimply to the
bearer.

THE firft kind have always been held to be negociable, that is, transferable from one man to another:
but where they were made payable to the *order* of
fuch a man, exception has been taken to an action
brought by that man himfelf, on the ground that
he had only an authority to indorfe; but that

10 Mo 1.
286. 2
Show. 3.
Comb. 401.

D 2   exception

exception was not allowed, there being no difference, according to the cuſtom of merchants,
between " payable to the order of ſuch a one," and
" payable to ſuch a one or order."

Mar. 14.
2 Show.
23. Mich.
34. Car. 2.
B. R.
BILLS payable to bearer were originally thought
to be equally negociable with thoſe payable to
order. In the time of Charles II. one Hinton
brought an action as bearer of a bill of this kind,
againſt the drawer; no objection was made to his
right to bring the action, only Lord Pemberton
ſaid, he muſt entitle himſelf to it on a valuable
conſideration, for that if he happened to be the
bearer by caſualty or knavery, he ſhould not have
the benefit of it.

3 Lev. 299.
1 Salk. 125.
1 Lord
Raym. 180.
Nicholſon
v. Sedg-
wick.
BUT in King William's time, a diſtinction was
taken between a bill payable to J. S. or *bearer*, and
J. S. or *order*: the former, it was ſaid, was not
aſſignable by the contract, ſo as to enable the indorſee to bring an action againſt the drawer or
drawee, in caſe payment were refuſed, becauſe no
ſuch authority was given to the party by the firſt contract, the effect being only to diſcharge the drawee
if he paid it to the bearer, though the latter ſhould
come by the bill by finding, theft, or otherwiſe.

IT was alſo ſaid, that dangers might ariſe, if, on
a caſual loſs, the finder ſhould become intitled as
bearer, to maintain his action for it.

YET it was held, that as between the indorſer and
indorſee, the bill was good, and the inforſer liable
to an action for the money, for that the indorſement was in the nature of a new bill.

AND

AND even as between the bearer and the drawer, or drawee, if the plaintiff alleged a fpecial cuftom in London, or any other place, for the bearer to have this action, and the defendant demurred, without traverfing the cuftom by which he confeffed it, though in truth no fuch cuftom did exift, the plaintiff recovered; becaufe, faid the court, though we are to take notice of the law of merchants, as part of the law of England, yet we cannot take notice of the cuftom of particular places, and the cuftom alleged in the declaration being *fufficient* to maintain the action, and that being confeffed, the defendant admitted judgment againft himfelf. 1 Sak. 126. 3 Salk. 68. 12 Mod. 36.

IN equity too, it was held even then, " that a bill payable to A. or bearer, was like fo much money paid to whomfoever it was given; that whatever accounts or conditions might be between the party who gave the bill, and A. to whom it was given, yet it fhould never affect the bearer, but he fhould have his whole money." So that the whole intereft was transferred to the bearer.

AND Holt held, that if a bank note were loft, payable to A. or bearer, and a ftranger, who found it, transferred it to C. for good confideration, trover would not lie againft C. becaufe, by the courfe of trade, there is a property in the bearer. 1 Salk.126. 1 Lord Raym.738.

AND in a fubfequent cafe, which was fully inveftigated by the court, thofe cafes in which the diftinction was taken between bills payable to bearer and to order, were held to have been decided on erroneous principles. Grant v. Vaughan. 1 Bl. Rep. 485. 3 Bur. 1516.

FOR,

For, firſt, as to their not being intended by the contract to be aſſigned: the contrary of this is true; for when made payable to A. B. or bearer, it is clearly intended that they ſhould be transferred in the moſt eaſy manner, even without indorſement.

As to the dangers ariſing from a caſual loſs, the bearer muſt ſhew it came to him fairly, on a good conſideration, and then there is no more danger here than in loſing an indorſed Bill of Exchange, made payable to A. B. or order.

And as to any neceſſity that might be ſuggeſted of bringing the action in the name of the perſon to whom the bill was originally made payable, it may in many caſes be impoſſible, becauſe there may be no perſon originally named as the payee; many bills are payable to bearer only, without the inſertion of any perſon's name: in the very caſe before the court, which was an action againſt the drawer by the bearer, who had innocently received it for a valuable conſideration, from a perſon who either found it, or became poſſeſſed of it by ſome other accident:—the bill ran thus, " Pay to *Ship Fortune* or bearer:" however, if there were a perſon named, the reaſon will not hold, for that perſon may become bankrupt; may be indebted to the drawer, ſo as to give the drawer a right to *ſet off* ſuch debt againſt the demand of the money due on the bill; —may not be found;—may refuſe to lend his name, or may releaſe;—ſo that if the courts of law ſhould not allow the bearer to bring the action in his own name, there might be no relief at all. Be-
ſides,

fides, this would be giving a third perfon (the drawee) an option whether he would pay it to the bearer or not, an option which might be abufed to unjuft or corrupt purpofes.

WITH refpect to Promiffory Notes payable to *bearer*, the ftatute of Queen Anne exprefsly makes them transferable in the fame fentence in which it confers that privilege on notes payable to order: and as the profeffed intention of the ftatute was to put Promiffory Notes on the fame footing with inland Bills of Exchange, the legiflature muft evidently be taken to have fuppofed that bills payable to bearer had that privilege before

THERE has fince been no doubt but that actions may be brought by bearers of fuch Promiffory Notes againft the drawers or makers. In one cafe a Bank Note ftolen out of the mail, yet being negociated and coming to the bearer fairly on a good confideration, was held recoverable. In another, the defendant gave a Shop Note to A. or bearer. A. loft it, and demanded the money at the houfe of the defendant. He was ready to pay it, provided A. would give bond, with two refponfible fureties, (as is the cuftom in fuch cafes) to indemnify him againft the bearer, if the note fhould ever be demanded. A. not being able or willing to give that fecurity, the defendant ftill refufed, on which A. brought a bill in Chancery to compel the payment, but it was difmiffed by Lord Hardwicke.

Margin notes:
3 & 4 Ann. c. 9. f. 5.

Miller v. Race, 1 Bur. 452.

Walmfley v. Child.

11 Dec. 1749. 1 Bur. 459.

D 4   So

So that it is now decided law, that both Bills of Exchange and Promiffory Notes payable to bearer, are equally transferable as thofe payable to order, and the transfer in both cafes equally confers the right of action on the *bonâ fide* holder.

THE *mode* of transfer however is different; bills and notes payable to bearer are transferred by mere delivery, the others by indorfement.

THE bills and notes hitherto defcribed are confidered merely as a fecurity for money. But there is a fpecies of each which is confidered not barely as a fecurity, but as money itfelf. Thefe are bank notes, bankers' cafh notes, and drafts on bankers, payable on demand.

Per Lord
Mansfield.
1 Bur. 457.

BANK notes are not fecurities, nor documents for debts, nor are they efteemed as fuch: but they are treated as money or cafh in the ordinary courfe and tranfactions of bufinefs by the common confent of mankind, which gives them the credit and currency of money to every effectual purpofe. They are as much confidered as money, as guineas themfelves, or any other current coin ufed in common payments.

Popham et
al' v. Bath-
urft et al'
in Chan-
cery, 5th
Nov. 1748.

THEY pafs by a will which bequeaths all the teftator's money or cafh. On Lord Ailefbury's will, 900l. in bank notes was confidered as money: on payment of them, whenever a receipt is required, it is given as for fo much money, not as for fecurities or notes.

So on bankruptcies, they cannot be followed as identical and diftinguifhable from money.

IF

IF they be loft indeed and found, an action will lie againft the finder by the true owner, as it will alfo for money before it has paffed in currency. But after they have come into the hands of a third perfon, in a fair courfe of dealing, they can no more be recovered of him than money under the fame circumftances.

ON the annuity act too, which requires the real confideration of the annuity to be fet forth in the memorial, though the whole confideration be defcribed as *money*, and it appear that it was part money, part bank notes, that will be fufficient, bank notes being confidered as money.

17 G. III. c. 26. Wright v. Reed, 3 TermRep. 554.

IT has never indeed been determined that a *tender* in bank notes is *at all events* a good tender; but if they have been offered, and no objection made on that account, the Court of King's Bench have confidered it to be a good tender, becaufe thefe notes pafs in the world as cafh : though the Lord Chancellor once fuggefted a doubt whether they were money.

Per Buller Juftice, 3 Term Rep. 554.

BANKERS cafh notes, and drafts on bankers, are fo far confidered as money among merchants, that they receive them in payment as ready cafh; and if the party receiving them do not, within a reafonable time, demand the money, he muft bear the lofs in cafe of the banker's failure : but what fhall be conftrued to be a reafonable time has been fubject to much doubt; it was formerly confidered as a queftion of fact depending on the circumftances of the particular cafe, to be determined by a jury, the nature

Hankey v. Trotman. Mich. 20 Geo. II. 1 Bl. Rep. 1.

nature of the thing not admitting of any precife invariable rule; but it is now eftablifhed to be a queftion of law to be decided by the court, though the precife time is as undetermined as before.

Vide page infra.

IF, however, within fuch reafonable time, the money be demanded, and payment refufed, he who gave the note muft make it good.

1 Ld. Ray. 744.

A MAN received in payment a goldfmith's note, (goldfmiths being then what bankers are now) at two in the afternoon, and next morning at nine prefented it at the goldfmith's, who had a quarter. of an hour before ftopt payment. It was held that no credit had been given to the goldfmith, and that therefore the party who gave the note muft bear the lofs.

1 Str. 415.

IN another cafe it appeared that the defendant had paid the plaintiffs, who were the Sword-blade company, two goldfmiths' notes at three in the afternoon; the plaintiffs' fervant the next morning left the notes with the goldfmiths, in order that they might have the money ready for him as he came back a clearing; it being, as they proved, cuftomary for the Bank and the Sword-blade company to fend out their notes in the morning by their fervant, who then left them, and called for the money as he returned in the evening; and the goldfmiths on receiving the notes always cancelled them, and got the money told out againft the time when it was ufually called for.—The notes in this cafe were brought early in the morning, and received and cancelled: and between four and five in the

2 Str. 416.

the afternoon, the fervant who left them called again
for the money, when the goldfmiths had juft ftopped
payment: upon which the fervant takes new notes
of the fame tenor and date with the cancelled ones
which he left in the morning. And becaufe the
plaintiffs 'd done nothing but what was ufual,
in leaving the notes, inftead of taking the money on
the firft call in the morning, the Chief Juftice* di- * Pratt,
rected the jury to find for the plaintiffs, which they
did.

But in a fubfequent cafe this practice was difap- Hayward v.
proved of. The plaintiff, who kept cafh with the Bank of
Bank, had on *Saturday* left a note for 5ol. on Cox Engl.nd.
and Cleeve: on Monday they gave it to the runner, 1 Str. 550.
who left it at the fhop in the morning, and when he
called in the evening, he found the bankers had
ftopped payment, on which he took a new note of
the fame tenor and date. King, C. J. who tried
the caufe, directed the jury, that it would be dangerous to fuffer perfons to deal with notes in this
manner, and faid that the Court of Common Pleas
was of that opinion in a like cafe.

In Hoar and Dacofta, it appeared that Wood- 2 Str. 910,
ward's note was paid to the plaintiff at twelve on
the Friday, who put it into the bank at one; and
the next morning at ten, the runner of the bank
carried it to the fhop with other notes to the
value of 2600l. and left them (as ufual) to call again
for the money: he called at eleven, and they faid
their fervant was gone to the Bank: he called again
at two, and they faid they were going to fhut up,
and

and refufed to pay; but paid fmall notes for two
hours, and then ftopped; and the next morning
notice was given to the defendant, who had paid
the note to the plaintiff.—It was infifted on the
part of the defendant, that he fhould not fuffer by
the plaintiff's paying it into the Bank, who fent it
with other notes; whereas, if the note had been
tendered by itfelf, it would have been paid. On
the other hand it was contended, that if *no* demand
had been made, there would have been no laches,
as the goldfmith ftopped payment within a day
after the receipt. The Chief Juftice faid there
was no ftanding rule, but left it to the jury, who
gave a verdict in favour of the plaintiff.

Fletcher v.
Sandys.
2 Str. 1248.

In another cafe a Banker's Note was paid to the
plaintiff after dinner, who fent it the next morning
at nine, when the banker had ftopped payment:
and it was ruled that there was no laches in the
plaintiff fo as to fix the lofs on him; and that in
all thefe cafes there muft be a reafonable time allowed, confiftent with the nature of circulating
paper credit.

2 Str. 1175.

But in the cafe of the Eaft India Company
againft Chitty, it appeared that at half an hour
after eleven in the morning of the 18th of January,
the defendant being indebted to the plaintiffs, paid
to the cafhier a note of Cafwell and Mount, goldfmiths, in Lombard-ftreet; they continued to pay
all notes till the next day at two; and immediately
after they had ftopped payement, the company's
fervant came with the note. On the examination of
merchants

merchants it was held, that the company had made it their own, by not sending it out the afternoon of the 18th, or at surtheft the next morning, and there was a verdict for the defendant.

In a late case the plaintiff took the defendant's draft on his bankers, Brown and Collinson; the next morning they stopped payment, and the defendant refused to give cash for his draft, alleging that if the plaintiff had presented it for payment as soon as he might nave done after he received it, the bankers would have paid it. Lord Mansfield said, the whole rested on custom; and the question to be determined was, whether the plaintiff was obliged to go to the bankers on the day on which he received the draft, for if he had, it appeared he would have been paid. It was unreasonable to suppose, that a tradesman should be compelled to run about the town with half a dozen drafts from Charing-cross to Lombard-street, and other places, on the same day. The Jury were to consider that *twenty-four* hours was the usual time allowed, and the plaintiff kept it no longer from being paid, for the next day the town was alarmed by the bankers stopping payment. The jury however found for the defendant; and the Court of King's Bench is said to have rejected an application for a new trial *.

Beawes 482.

Sittings at Guildhall after Easter Term, 1782.

* But this appears to be a mistake in Beawes, who reports the case without a name; for all the circumstances correspond with those of Metcalfe and Hall, cited in a subsequent part of this treatise, in which a new trial was granted.

On

Beawes
482.

ON the whole, the beft rule in thefe cafes feems to be, that drafts on bankers, payable on demand, ought to be carried for payment on the very day on which they are received, if from the diftance and fituation of the parties that may conveniently be done; and when it is confidered that great part of the payments for the purchafe of fhares in the public funds is made by the purchafers in drafts on their bankers at the inftant of making the tranffer of the ftock, it is certainly advifeable to take the drafts for payment without delay.

C H A P. IV.

Of the Privileges of BILLS OF EXCHANGE *and* PROMISSORY NOTES, *and the Circumftances neceffary to make them good.*

BILLS and Notes having been introduced for the convenience of trade and commerce, are indulged with feveral privileges peculiar to themfelves.

WITH reference to the modes by which the performance of contracts is fecured, by the mere act of the parties, without the operation of law, or the intervention of any legal authority, they are ufually
confidered

confidered as divided into two kinds, fpecial and fimple; the firft being thofe which are formally afcertained by deed or inftrument under feal, the inftrument itfelf being denominated a fpecialty; the latter, fuch as are not afcertained by deed or inftrument under feal, but are either mere verbal agreements, in which cafe the proof of them depends on oral teftimony alone, or are reduced into writing without feal, for the purpofe of a more eafy proof, in which refpect only, they are better.than a mere verbal promife.

ONE circumftance, in which a contract by fpecialty is more highly privileged than a fimple contract, is, that the law allows, in its favour, a diftinct fpecies of action, of which the fpecialty or inftrument itfelf is the foundation, and in which no extrinfic facts are neceffary to be ftated, nor any confideration fhewn but what appears on the face of the deed; and where, from the nature of the deed, as in the cafe of a bond, the law does not require the infertion of any confideration, none is neceffary to be fet forth in the declaration; the law giving that credit to the folemnity of the inftrument, which prefumes a good confideration, and impofing the neceffity on the oppofite party of fhewing that it was improperly obtained.

Vid. 3 Bur. 1639. 1669. 1671.

BUT in actions founded on fimple contracts, not only the circumftances of the cafe muft be particularly ftated, but a fufficient confideration muft be fhewn, on which the obligation to perform the contract arifes; and though the terms of the contract

be

be reduced to writing, no reference can be made to that writing as the ſpecial ground of the action; it can only be uſed in evidence, as the proof of the contract ſtated in the declaration.

BUT Bills of Exchange and Promiſſory Notes, though, according to the general principles of the law, they are to be conſidered only as evidence of a ſimple contract, are yet in this reſpect regarded as ſpecialties, and are indeed on the ſame footing with bonds; for unleſs the contrary be ſhewn by the defendant, they are alway preſumed to have been made on a good conſideration; nor is it incumbent on the plaintiff, either to ſhew a conſideration in his declaration, or to prove it at the trial. However, though foreign bills were always entitled to this privilege, it was not without a conſiderable ſtruggle that it was extended to inland bills : and notes are indebted for it to the ſtatute of Queen Anne.

THE principal heads of diſtinction, under which perſonal property may be conſidered, are thoſe of things in poſſeſſion and things in action:—things in poſſeſſion are thoſe objects of property, to which a man not only has a right, but which he actually enjoys;—things in action are thoſe over which he has not actual dominion, but which he has only a right to recover by a ſuit at law: things in poſſeſſion might in general always be aſſigned or tranſferred from one perſon to another; but the jealouſy of the common law, carefully guarding againſt that litigious diſpoſition, which, it was thought; might be

1 Bl. Rep. 445. Peckham v. Wood. B. R. E. 18. G. III.

Vid. 2 Ld. Raym. 758. 1 Bl. Rep. 487.

2 Bl. Com. 389.

Co. Lit. 214. 2 Bl. Com. 442.

be encouraged, by permitting one man to purchase from another his right of prosecuting a suit, prohibited the transfer of things in action ; and even now, when the improved state of commerce requires, and the law permits an actual assignment of such property, so much respect is paid to the ancient principle, that the form of assigning it is in the nature of a declaration of trust, and an agreement to permit the assignee to make use of the name of the assignor, in order to recover the possession : and therefore, when in common acceptation a debt or bond is said to be assigned-over, it must still be sued for in the original creditor's name ; the person to whom it is transferred being rather an attorney than an assignee.

Vid. 1 Term Rep. 26, 619.

But Bills of Exchange, though only securities, and consequently things in action, are so highly favoured in the law, that not only they are assignable or negociable without any fiction, but every person to whom they are transferred may maintain an action, in his own name, against any one who has before him, in the course of their negociation, rendered himself responsible for their payment. The same privilege is conferred on Promissory Notes by the statute of Queen Anne.

But to be intitled to these privileges, the instrument or writing, which constitutes a good Bill of Exchange, according to the law, usage, and custom of merchants, or a good Note according to the statute, must have some essential qualities, without which it can neither be the one nor the other.

Per L.C.J. De Grey, 3 Wilf. 213.

E   One

Martin v.
Chauntry,
2 Str. 1271.
ONE of thefe qualities is, that it fhould be for the
payment of money only, and not for the payment
of money and the doing of fome other act: thus a
note to deliver up horfes and a wharf, and to pay
money at a particular day, cannot be reckoned a
note within the ftatute: for thefe inftruments being
originally adopted for the convenience of remittance, and at this day confidered only as fecurities
for the future payment of money, muft undertake
only for that: and it muft be money in fpecie, not
Bull. Nifi
Prius, 273.
Ed. 1785.
in good Eaft India bonds, or any thing elfe, which
can itfelf be only confidered as a fecurity.

3 Wilf. 213.
ANOTHER requifite quality is, that the inftrument muft carry with it a *perfonal* and certain credit, given to the drawer or maker, not confined to
credit on any particular fund.

BUT in the application of this principle, there
feems to be a material diftinction between Bills of
Exchange and Promiffory Notes. As to the former, where the fund is fuppofed to be in the hands
of the drawee, the objection holds in its full force,
not only becaufe it may be uncertain whether the
fund will be productive, but becaufe the credit is
not given to the perfon of the drawer; but where
the fund, on account of which the money is payable, is either in the hands of the drawer, or where
he is accountable for it, the objection will not hold,
becaufe the credit is perfonal to him, and the fund
is only the confideration for his giving the bill.

WITH refpect to a Promiffory Note, though, in
the analogy between the two fpecies of inftrument,

3   when

when their form is inconteftibly good, the acceptor
of the bill refembles the drawer of the note, yet
with refpect to this objection to their validity,
there is a difference; for if the drawer of the note
promife to pay out of a particular fund then within his power, the note will be good under the
ftatute: the payment does not depend on the circumftance of the fund's proving unproductive or
not, but there is an obligation on his perfonal credit, the bare making of the note being an acknowledgment that he has money in his hands.

THIS diftinction is apparent in the following
cafes:—Evans drew a bill on Jofcelyne, requiring
him to pay to Laffere 7l. per month, out of his
growing fubfiftence, and to place it to his account;
Jofcelyne accepted it according to the tenor of the
bill, but afterwards refufed payment; on which
Laffere brought an action in the Common Pleas,
and obtained judgment: Jofcelyne brought a writ
of error in the King's Bench, on which the judgment was reverfed, becaufe it was not a bill within
the cuftom of merchants; it concerned neither
trade nor commerce, and being payable out of the
growing fubfiftence of the drawer, if he died, or
his fubfiftence were taken away, it was not to be
paid; it might never be paid, and yet his credit be
unimpeached.

JENNY and others made an inftrument in thefe
words, " Pray pay to ———— Herle 1945l. on demand, out of the money in your hands, belonging
to the proprietors of the Devonfhire mines, being

Jofcelyne
v. Laffere.
Fort. 281.
10 Mod.
294, 316.

Jenny v.
Herle, 1
Str. 591. 2
Ld. Raym.
1361. 8
Mod. 265.

part

part of the confideration money for the manor of Weft Buckley," and directed it to one Prat, who refufed to accept it, on which Herle brought his action in the Common Pleas, as on a Bill of Exchange, againft Jenny and the others, and had judgment; on which they brought a writ of error in the King's Bench, where the judgment was reverfed, becaufe this was not a Bill of Exchange, but a bare appointment to pay money out of a particular fund, and did not anfwer the neceffity of trade, and if the party might be charged on fuch an inftrument as this, then every man who gave his fteward an order to pay money, might be charged as the drawer of a Bill of Exchange.

Dawkes & ux. v. Delorane, 3 Wilf. 207. 2 Bl. Rep. 782.

THE Earl of Delorane made an inftrument in thefe words :

" SEVEN weeks after date pleafe pay to Mifs Read, thirty-two pounds and feventeen fhillings out of W. Steward's money, as foon as you fhall receive it, for

" Your humble fervant

" DELORANE."

" *To* TIM. BRECKNOCK, Efq.
        St. Mary-le-bone."
        Accepted Timothy Brecknock.

BRECKNOCK refufed to pay, on which an action was brought againft the drawer as on a Bill of Exchange, but judgment was given againft the plaintiff for this among other reafons, that it was payable out of a particular fund ; and it being objected

at

at the bar, that this bill was accepted by Brecknock
generally, and in an unlimited manner; it was anfwered by the court, that if the bill had been drawn
accordingly in a general and unlimited way, both
the bill and the acceptance would have been good,
but the acceptance here muft mean that Brecknock
accepts it to pay out of Steward's money, not out
of the drawer's.

On the fame principle which governed thefe
cafes, an order from the owner of a fhip to the
freighter, to pay money *on account of freight*, has
been held to be no Bill of Exchange: Gibfon, the
owner, gave an order on Gilly and Company, the
freighters of a fhip, in thefe words:

"*Meffrs. Gilly and Co.*

"Pray pay to Mr. Richard Banbury, one month
after date, 200l. *on account of freight* of the Veale
Galley, Edward Champion, and this fhall be your
fufficient difcharge for the fame.

"J. Gibson."

This was accepted conditionally for Liffet and
Gilly, and not being paid, an action was brought
againft the acceptors, and among other objections
to the bill, the Chief Juftice faid, that it was payable out of a particular fund; but, with deference
to fo great an authority, it is conceived, that if
that had been the only objection to the inftrument,
it would have been a good bill, for its being payable
on account of freight, feems to be no more than a direction to the drawees to what account between them
and the drawer they are to place the payment.

E 3   However,

Banbury v.
Liffet, 2
Str. 1211.

Lee.

Pierſon v.
Dunlop,
Doug. 571.
HOWEVER, ſuch a bill from the freighters of a ſhip to the perſon to whom the freight is due, if good in other reſpects, would certainly not be bad becauſe it was made payable *on account of freight*, becauſe indiſputably there is a *perſonal* credit given to the drawer, the words *on account of freight* only expreſſing the conſideration for which the bill was given.

AND there may be caſes where the inſtrument may appear at firſt ſight to be payable out of a particular fund, and in reality be otherwiſe, of which M'Leod v.
Snee, 2 Ld.
Raym.
1481. 2 Str.
762. Barnard, 12.
K. B. deſcription the following caſe is one :—A. B. drew a Bill of Exchange, dated 25th of May, by which he requeſted M'Leod " one month after date, to pay to Snee, or order, 9l. 10s. as his quarterly half-pay, to become due from the 24th of June to the 29th of September next by advance." M'Leod accepted it, and on his refuſal to pay, was ſued in the Common Pleas, where judgment being given againſt him, he brought a writ of error in the King's Bench, and objected to the judgment that this caſe reſembled the former caſes, being payable out of a particular fund; but the court held that this bill was drawn on the particular credit of the drawer, not on that of the half-pay, for it was to be paid as ſoon as the quarter began, and whether that ſhould ever become due or not ; and the mention of the quarterly half-pay was only a direction how the drawee was to reimburſe himſelf.

OF the diſtinction taken between Bills and Notes Burchell v.
Slocock, 2
Ld. Raym.
1545. in this reſpect, the following is an illuſtration :—" I promiſe to pay to William Burchell, the ſum of

101l.

10il. 12s. three months after date, for value received out of the premifes in Rofemary-lane, late in the poffeffion of Thomas Rower Sherwin:" was held a good note under the ftatute.

ANOTHER effential quality to make a good bill or note is, that it muft be abfolutely payable at all events, and not depend on any particular circumftance which may or may not happen in the common courfe of things.—Of the application of this principle the following are examples: *3 Wilf. 213. 1 Bur. 325.*

THOMAS ROGERS made a Bill of Exchange, by which he requefted Roger Lynch to pay to Henry Haydock, or order, the fum of 14l. 13s. out of a fifth payment, when it fhould become due; this was held not to be a good Bill of Exchange, on account of the uncertainty whether any fifth payment might ever become due, as well as on account of its being payable out of a particular fund. *Haydock v. Lynch, 2 Ld. Raym. 1563.*

So, an order to pay money, " provided the terms mentioned in certain letters written by the drawer were complied with," is not a good bill, though the acceptance admit a compliance with thofe terms, for it was no bill until after fuch compliance, and if it was not a bill when drawn, it could never afterwards become one. *Kingfton v. Long, B. R. M. 25 G. III. Bayley, Appendix, No. 2.*

ITs uncertainty in this refpect was one reafon of the determination in the cafe of Dawkes againft Delorane, it being an order to pay out of Steward's money, when received, which might never happen. *Ante, page 52.*

So, a note " to pay a certain fum of money, or to render the body of J. S. to prifon by fuch a day," *Smith v. Boheme, cited 2 Ld. Raym. 1362, 1396.*

E 4

day," is not a note on which an action will lie by the ftatute, after failure of rendering the body to prifon, becaufe it was not neceffarily and originally for payment of money, but only became fo by matter *ex poft fa&to.*

Appleby v.
Biddulph,
cit. 8 Mod.
363. 4 Vin.
240. pl. 16.
So, neither is a note " promifing to pay money, if another do not pay it within a limited time ;" for this is only an eventual promife.

Beardefley
v. Baldwin,
2 Str. 1151.
Pearfon v.
Garret, 4
Mod. 242.
So, a note " to pay money fo many days after the defendant fhould marry," is not good under the ftatute; for it depends on a contingency which may never happen.

Roberts v.
Peake, 1
Bur. 323.
So, a note " promifing to pay to A. B. a fum of money, value received, on the death of a particular perfon, *provided* he leave me a fufficient fum to pay the fame, *or if* I fhall be otherwife able to pay it," is not good within the ftatute, becaufe it is not abfolutely payable at all events, but depends on two contingencies, neither of which may ever happen.

In the cafe of notes, however, it is not neceffary that the time of payment fhould be abfolutely fixed; it is fufficient if, from the nature of the thing, the time muft certainly arrive on which their payment is to depend.

Cooke v.
Colehan,
2 Str. 1217.
Thus a note "to pay to A. or order, fix weeks after the death of the defendant's father, for value received," was held to be negociable within the ftatute, for there was no contingency by which it might never become payable, but it was only uncertain as to the time, which, it was faid, was the cafe of all bills payable after fight. There appears

however

however some little difference, for it is in the power of the holder of a bill payable after fight to reduce the time to a certainty.

So, a note "payable to an infant, when he the infant fhould come of age," and fpecifying the time when that was to be, viz. "on the 12th of June, 1750," was held to be negociable within the ftatute, for it would have been clearly good, if it had been made payable on the 12th of June, 1750, which is a day certain, without mentioning that the plaintiff was then to come of age, and it is not the lefs certain from the addition of that circumftance. *Per Lord Mansfield. Gofs v. Nelfon, 1 Bur. 227.*

THE words of engagement make the debt; and it is no direction to *another* perfon: the former part of the note is a promife to pay the money, and the reft is only fixing the particular time when it is to be paid. It is fufficient if it be certainly, and at all events, payable at that time, whether he live till then, or die in the interim.

AND a moral certainty is fufficient: it is not neceffary that the time fhould be phyfically certain.

THUS, "a promife to pay within two months after fuch a fhip fhall be paid off," will make a good note: for the paying off of the fhip is a thing of a public nature, and morally certain. *Andrews v. Franklin, 1 Str. 24.*

So, "I promife to pay to George Pratt, or order, 8l. on the receipt of his the faid George Pratt's wages, due from his Majefty's fhip the *Suffolk*, it being in full for his wages, and prize money, and fhort allowance money for the faid fhip," was held a good note on the authority of the laft cafe; and there *Evans v. Underwood 1 Wilf. 262, 263.*

there being an averment that the wages were received, the plaintiff recovered.

But this seems to be carrying the indulgence to these notes abundantly far.

It is obfervable that of all thefe cafes, where the time for the payment of the money is not abfolutely fixed, there is not one arifing on a Bill of Exchange: fuch a latitude feems incompatible with the nature and original intention of that inftrument; and its allowance in favour of Promiffory Notes arifes entirely from a liberal conftruction of the ftatute on which the negociability of thefe notes is founded.

It muft alfo be obferved, that in moft of the cafes where the feveral inftruments have been denied the privilege of Bills and Notes, it is not, for that reafon, to be concluded that they are of no force: when the fund from which they are to be paid, can be proved to have been productive, or the contingency on which they depend has happened, they may be ufed as evidence of a contract, according to the circumftances of the cafe, or according to the relation in which the parties ftand to one another.

Maber v. Maffias, 2 Bl. Rep. 1072. WILLIAM WATTS, a merchant, who traded to Gibraltar, employed Mofes Maffias as his factor there, who ufed to confign Watts's goods to certain agents in Barbary for fale. Maffias ufed to keep an account with the agents, and another with Watts, but Watts had no communication with the agents. On the 21ft of May, 1772, Watts drew a bill in the following terms, for the balance of an account

that

that day ſtated between him and Maber and Ken-
tiſh, merchants, with whom he had dealings:

"SIR, pleaſe to pay to Meſſrs. Maber and Ken-
tiſh, or order, 195l. 14s. 1od. out of the produce
of goods you have of mine, now lying at Gibraltar,
Barbary, and Leghorn, as ſoon as the ſame ſhall
come into your hands, after diſcharging the preſent
acceptances.

WILLIAM WATTS."

"To Mr. Moſes Maſſias,
   No. 63, Preſcot-Street."

Which bill Maſſias accepted in the following words
underwritten "I agree to conform to this order,

"MOSES MASSIAS."

BEFORE this bill was paid, Watts became a
bankrupt, and Maſſias refuſing payment, an action
was brought againſt him for "money had and received to the uſe of the plaintiff." On the trial it
appeared that Maſſias had large quantities of goods
of Watts in his hands; in 1773 to the amount of
1657l. and more in 1772. That he had paid large
ſums for Watts, but whether for engagements prior
to 1772 or not, did not appear.

THE defendant gave evidence of ſeveral prior engagements, but theſe did not cover the whole account; and alſo that there was, at the time of acceptance, and ſtill remained, a balance due to Maſſias himſelf of 870l. There was a verdict for the
plaintiff; and an application being made by the
defendant for a new trial, the court obſerved that
the

the queftion was, whether the defendant had in his hands 195l. for the ufe of the plaintiff. He was proved to have had goods to the amount of 1657l. and that his acceptances, in the common and technical fenfe of the words, as applied to Bills of Exchange, together with certain other indorfements by which he had engaged himfelf to pay money for Watts, left a balance in his hands more than fufficient to pay the plaintiffs; if the balance of 870l. due to Maffias himfelf, be excluded. For this balance, then unliquidated, it never could have been meant to provide, nor was it meant that the bill or its acceptance fhould be fubject to it, for then there would have been fraud in the drawer, and alfo in the acceptor; both knew, or muft be fuppofed to have known, at leaft Maffias knew how the balance then ftood. If he meant to have referved his own balance, he fhould have made a fpecial acceptance; but having accepted it generally in the terms of the draft, fubject only to prior acceptances, he fhall not fhelter himfelf by this concealed balance due to himfelf in the courfe of a running account.

10 Mod. 287. 2 Ld. Raym. 1397. 1 Str. 629 1 Wilf. 263. 3 Wilf. 213.

No precife form of words is neceffary to make a Bill of Exchange, or a Note, under the ftatute; any order which cannot be complied with, or promife which cannot be performed, without the payment of money, will make a good bill or note. Thus an order to deliver money, or a promife that fuch a one fhall receive it, is equivalent to an order or promife to pay.

A QUESTION

A QUESTION arifing on a note in thefe words; Morris v. Lee, 1 Str. "I promife to *account* with T. S. or his order, for 629. 2 Ld. Raym. 50." it was objected that this importing only a 1396. 8 Mod. 364. promife to be accountable for the money, the maker was not obliged to pay it to the perfon to whom it was firft given, or to the indorfee, but that he might account for it another way, by having laid it out in goods, or otherwife applied it. But the court held that a promife to account was the fame as a promife to pay, more efpecially as it was to be accountable to A. or order, which implies an intention that it fhould be negociated; and it would be a ftrange conftruction to fuppofe that the meaning could be fatisfied in any other way than the payment of money when there might be any number of indorfees.

NEITHER will the addition of extraneous cir- Chadwick v. Allen, 1 cumftances vitiate a note. Thus, "I do acknow- Str. 706. ledge that Sir Andrew Chadwick has delivered me all the bonds and notes for which 400l. were paid him on account of Colonel Synge, and that Sir Andrew delivered me Major Graham's receipt and bill on me for 10l. which 10l. and 15l. 5s. balance due to Sir Andrew, I am ftill indebted for, and do promife to pay;" is good.

THE words "value received," being in general inferted in bills and notes, there feems to have been fome doubt, whether they were effential: in one cafe, where the want of thefe words was ob- Banbury v. Liffet, 2 jected, a verdict was given on that account againft Str. 1212. the inftrument, but that cafe feems to be a very

doubtful

Dawkes, v.
Delorane,
3 Will. 207.

doubtful authority: in a fubfequent cafe the fame objection was made, but as the inftrument was clearly defective on another ground, the court gave no opinion as to this point.

Fort. 282.
Barnard,
K. B. 88.
8 Mod. 267.
1 Show. 5.
497. 2 Ld. Raym. 1556, 1481. Lutw. 889. 1 Mod. ent. 310.

On feveral occafions it appears to have been faid incidentally by the court, and at the bar, that thefe words are unneceffary.

White v.
Ledwick,
B. R. H. 25
G. III.
Bayley,
Appendix,
N. 3.

And the point is now fully fettled, that they are not neceffary; for as thefe inftruments are always prefumed to have been made on a valuable con-fideration, words which import no more cannot be effential.

Beawes,
490.

But in France not only "value received" muft be inferted in Bills of Exchange, but alfo the nature of that value, in confequence of an ordinance of the King, in March 1673, whether it was in mo-ney, merchandize, or othe effects, to prevent feve-ral abufes which had crept into this branch of commerce, by the bare infertion only of " value received;" for it was common to give a note in payment of a Bill of Exchange, each having thefe words: and this practice was found to be of great prejudice to trade, by occafioning many failures, which it was the object of this ordinance to pre-vent; and in confequence of it, there are four forts of Bills of Exchange in that country, the firft ex-preffing fimply *value received;* the fecond, *value received in merchandize;* the third, *value in himfelf;* and the fourth, *value underftood.* The firft and fecond need no explanation, being alike in their negociation,

negociation, and their diftinction only anfwering fome ends that may occur between the drawer and deliverer in cafe of failure or fraud. The third fort is when a merchant draws a Bill of Exchange on one who owes him money, which he fends to his friend or factor, to procure acceptance and payment, and as the acceptor is his debtor, an inconvenience might arife to him, fhould he infert "value received," fimply, as his friend or factor might pretend it belonged to him, it appearing by the Bill that the drawer had received the value.—The fourth is when a perfon, taking a Bill of Exchange from one on whofe credit he cannot rely, gives the drawer his acknowledgment of receiving the Bill, the value of which he obliges himfelf to fatisfy, on having advice that the Bill is paid; but if the Bill return difhonoured, it is again exchanged for the Note, the drawer defraying the charges.

WHETHER it be effential to the conftitution of a Bill of Exchange, that it fhould contain words which render it negociable, as "to order" or "to bearer," feems not, hitherto, to have received a direct judicial decifion. There are two cafes in which the want of fuch words was taken as an exception, but as there were other objections on which the Bill was in both cafes held to be bad, it was not thought neceffary to decide on that point.

Banbury v. Liffet, 2 Str. 1212. Dawkes v. Delorane, 3 Wilf. 212.

In another cafe the fame exception was taken and overruled, but under fuch circumftances as that the point was not generally determined. The defendant had given the plaintiff a draught on one

Chamberlyn v. Delarive, 2 Wilf. 353.

Heddy,

Heddy, for the payment of a fum of money for work done by the plaintiff for the defendant: the plaintiff had neglected to demand payment for a confiderable time after the draught was due; and in the mean time Heddy became infolvent. The plaintiff brought his action for work and labour, and the defendant at the trial proved his having given this draught to the plaintiff in payment. But that not being payable to the plaintiff or order, the Jury confidered it as not being a Bill of Exchange, and gave a verdict for the plaintiff. On an application for a new trial, the court thought it unneceffary to decide on the general queftion, whether words importing negociability were effential to the conftitution of a Bill of Exchange, becaufe they were of opinion that by accepting the draught, and keeping it fo long after it became payable, the plaintiff had given credit to Heddy, and difcharged the defendant.

If, in a doubtful point, however, we might be allowed to reafon on general principles, it would feem, that it being the original intention and the actual ufe of Bills of Exchange that they fhould be negociable, fuch draughts as want thefe operative words are not entitled to be declared on as fpecialties, however they may be fufficient as evidence to maintain an action of another kind.

The words in the preamble to the ftatute, which gives the fame remedy on Promiffory Notes as there was before on inland Bills of Exchange, include only notes payable to order; thofe of the

3 & 4 Ann. c. 9. f. 1.

enacting

enacting claufe only fuch as are payable to order or bearer, and therefore in ftrict interpretation would feem not to confer that privilege on notes wanting fuch words, even if the want of them were no objection to inland Bills of Exchange.

YET it has been ruled that fuch words are not neceffary in notes, and that the perfon to whom they are made payable may maintain an action on them, within the ftatute, againft the maker. And there are feveral cafes in the books of reports where fuch words were omitted, and no exception taken on that account. The reafon of this indulgence to notes may be, that they have lefs reference to trade and diftant commerce, being properly no more than engagements between party and party; and the ftatute being remedial, the benefit of it has been extended beyond the literal words.

Per Ld. Hardwicke. Moore v. Paine. B. R. H. 288.

IT having been found by experience, that trade and commerce fuffered materially from the circulation of Bills, Notes, and Draughts for very fmall fums, which paffed as cafh, and many of them being made payable under certain terms and reftrictions with which the poorer fort of manufacturers, artificers, labourers and others could not comply, without fubjecting themfelves to great extortion and abufe, the legiflature has thought proper to lay certain reftraints on Bills or Notes under a limited fum.

Vid. Preamble to St. 15 G. III. c. 51.

ALL Notes and Bills for the payment of any fum under twenty fhillings, which had been iffued

15 G. III. c. 51. f. 8.

F   before

before the 24th of June, 1775, were made payable on demand.

S. 1.   Notes and Bills for lefs than twenty fhillings, iffued *after* the 24th of June, 1775, are declared

S. 2.   void. And any perfon publifhing or uttering fuch Bills or Notes, or in any manner engaged in the negociation of them, is liable to a penalty of not more than twenty pounds, nor lefs than five, to be recovered and applied in the manner pointed out

S. 13.   by the act, which was to continue for five years.

17 G. III.   The good effects of this act being found, fur-
c. 30.   ther provifions for the fame purpofe were made by another two years after.

S. 1.   All Promiffory or other Notes, Bills of Exchange, or Draughts, or undertakings in writing, being negociable or transferable, for the payment of twenty fhillings, or for any fum of money above that fum and lefs than five pounds, or on which twenty fhillings, or above that fum and lefs than five pounds, fhall remain undifcharged, iffued after the firft of January, 1778, fhall fpecify the names and places of abode of the perfons refpectively to whom or to whofe order they fhall be made payable; fhall bear date before or at the time of drawing or iffuing them, and not on any fubfequent day; fhall be made payable within the fpace of twenty-one days next after the day of the date; and fhall not be transferable or negociable after the time limited for the payment: and every indorfement fhall be made before the expiration of that
                                                                time,

time, and bear date at or before the time of making it, and ſhall ſpecify the name and place of abode of the perſon or perſons to whom or to whoſe order the money is to be paid: and the ſigning of every ſuch note, &c. and alſo every indorſement, ſhall be atteſted by one ſubſcribing witneſs at the leaſt; and all notes &c. of the above deſcription not having theſe requiſites ſhall be utterly void.

THE ſame penalties, recoverable in the ſame S. 2. way as in the former act, are impoſed on every one uttering, publiſhing, or negociating ſuch notes, &c. without the requiſites preſcribed.

AND all negociable notes, &c. iſſued before the S. 3. 1ſt of January, for any ſum between the ſum of twenty ſhillings and five pounds, or on which twenty ſhillings, or leſs than five pounds, remained undiſcharged, are made payable on demand.

AND this act and the former act are continued S. 4. not only for the reſidue of the five years of the former, but alſo for other five years.

AND by a ſubſequent ſtatute, both the former 27 G. III. are made perpetual. c. 16.

CHAP.

CHAP. V.

ACCEPTANCE.

AN acceptance is an engagement to pay a Bill of Exchange according to the tenor of the acceptance.

THE making of a Promiffory Note is equivalent to an acceptance of a Bill of Exchange, for it is an engagement to pay the money for which the note is given, and therefore nothing under this head is applicable to Promiffory Notes.

THE circumftances which generally concur in the acceptance of a bill, are that the party to whom it is addreffed, binds himfelf to the payment, *after* the bill has iffued, *before* it has become due, and according to its tenor, by either fubfcribing his name, or writing the word "accepts," or "accepted," or "accepted, A. B." But as a man may be bound as acceptor, without any of thefe circumftances, it may be convenient to confider this fubject under the following points of view.

FIRST, with refpect to the manner in which an acceptance may be made; fecondly, the time of making it; thirdly, the parties by whom and to whom it is made; fourthly, its different kinds; and, fifthly, what fhall amount to an acceptance.

I. AN

I. An acceptance may be either written or verbal; if the former, it may either be on the bill itself, or in some collateral writing.

Mol. 295. 300 Mar. 17. 1 Str. 648. 3 Bur. 1674.

In *foreign* bills it has always been understood that a collateral or parol acceptance was sufficient.

In an action against the acceptor of a foreign Bill of Exchange, it appeared that the acceptance was by a letter, in which the defendant said, I will pay it, if you will first let me send to my correspondent in Ireland. This was held as well as if the acceptance had been on the bill itself.

Wilkinson v. Lutwidge, 1 Str. 648.

In another case it appeared that a foreign bill was drawn on the defendant, and on non-acceptance returned to the drawer; afterwards, the defendant said to the plaintiff, if the bill come back I will pay it; and on the return of the bill this was held to bind him as acceptor.

Cox v. Coleman, Mich. 6 G. II. cited B. R. H. 75.

But on account of an ambiguity in the two statutes which extend the remedy for damages and costs to inland Bills of Exchange, considerable doubts had arisen with respect to the validity of a verbal or collateral acceptance of them.

9 and 10 W. III. c. 17. 3 & 4 Ann. c. 9.

The statute of William, which gives that remedy for non-payment after acceptance, requires that acceptance to be by subscribing the Bill by the party accepting.

S. 1.

The other statute provides, in express words, that no acceptance of any inland Bill of Exchange shall be sufficient to charge any person whatever, unless it be underwritten, or indorsed in writing on the bill.

S. 5.

* Two

* Two chief juſtices had at different periods
after the making of theſe ſtatutes, ruled that an acceptance by parol was ſufficient to bind the acceptor.

† Another had afterwards held that ſuch acceptance was not ſufficient.

But this point is now finally ſettled by a ſolemn
determination in the King's Bench in the time of
Lord Hardwicke.

An action was brought againſt the defendant as
acceptor of an inland Bill of Exchange, and at the
trial the acceptance appeared to have been by parol,
on which the point was reſerved for the opinion
of the court, and in delivering that opinion, Lord
Hardwicke obſerved that the caſes of foreign bills
were not applicable to the queſtion then before
them, as it wholly depended on the conſtruction of
the Acts of Parliament: the caſes on inland bills
that had ariſen ſince that act were indeed in point;
but it was by no means ſettled in the court of
Common Pleas, that this acceptance was not good;
for that he had been informed by one of the judges
of that court, that in a caſe which had lately come
before them, of an action againſt the acceptor of a
Bill of Exchange, exception had been taken at the
firſt

(margin: Lumley v. Palmer, M. 8 G. II. 2 B. R. H. 74. 2 Str. 1000.)

(margin: Orm. v. Holliday, Hil. 3 G. II.)

---

* Parker C. J. in Holdſworthy v. Thicary, P. 11 Ann. B.
R. and in Smith v. Plunket, Mich. 11 Ann. B. R. and Raymond
C. J. in Scott v. Anderſon, at Ni. Pri. M. 1 G. II.

† Eyre C. J. in Reay v. Meggot, at Ni. Pri. in London,
Hil. 7 G. II. C. B.

firſt trial, that the acceptance was not in writing, and therefore not binding. On an application for a new trial, the court being informed that the opinion of Lord Raymond was in favour of the acceptance, all inclined to the ſame opinion. No final judgment was indeed given, becauſe the defendant thought fit to acquieſce in the inclination of the court.

WITH reſpect to the Acts of Parliament, it muſt be allowed, that they are both, and eſpecially the laſt, very obſcurely penned: they were made to give a remedy againſt the drawer for damages, intereſt, and coſts, in caſe of non-acceptance or non-payment by the drawee, for no ſuch remedy exiſted at common law.

THE firſt gave that remedy, in caſe of non-payment after acceptance, but requires that the acceptance ſhould be in writing under the bill, but no proviſion was made for the caſe of non-acceptance; the ſtatute of Ann was made to extend the remedy to that caſe: and the proviſions of the two acts had evidently a reference to that remedy only: the fifth ſection of the laſt act indeed has expreſs words, that no acceptance ſhall charge any perſon whatſoever, unleſs under-written or indorſed; and if theſe words ſtood ſingly, it would be difficult to maintain that any remedy lay againſt the acceptor, by reaſon of a parol acceptance: but the generality of theſe words is reſtrained by the words that immediately follow; that if ſuch bill be not accepted by ſuch under-writing or indorſement, no drawer

F 4   ſhall

shall be liable to pay costs, damages, or interest on that account; so that the first general words are to be understood to relate to charging the drawer with interest and costs. Nothing is more common than for an act of parliament to have general words at first, which are afterwards restrained by more particular ones. And it has been said that this proviso was inserted by the committee, when there might not be so much time for drawing it up clearly, as if it had been done at the first drawing of the act.

THE proviso at the end of the act is also very material to the present question, " that nothing in the act contained shall be construed to discharge any remedy which might before have been had against the drawer, acceptor, or indorser of any such bill; and such acceptance being clearly valid at common law, it cannot be construed to be rendered void by this statute.

Powell v. Monnier, 1 Atk. 717. (613.)

AND if a verbal acceptance be binding, there can be no doubt but an acceptance by letter will be so too.

3 Bur. 1663. Doug. 284. 1 Atk. 715. (611.)

II. THE acceptance is usually made between the time of issuing the bill and the time of payment; but it may also be made before the bill is issued, or after it has become due: when it is made before the bill is issued, it is rather an agreement to accept, than an actual acceptance, but such agreement is equally binding as an acceptance itself.

Jackson v. Pigot, 1 Salk. 127. 1 Lord Raym. 364. 12 Mod.

WHEN the acceptance is made after the time of payment is elapsed, it is considered as a general

promise

promife to pay the money: and if it be to pay according to the tenor of the bill, this fhall not inva-
lidate the acceptance, though, the time being paft,
it be impoffible to pay according to the tenor, but
thefe words fhall be rejected as furplufage.

211. Cath.
459. Mit-
ford v.
Walcot, 1
Salk. 129.
1 Lord
Raym.574.
12 Mod.
410.

III. ACCEPTANCE is ufually made by the drawee,
or perfon on whom the bill is drawn, and when
made before the iffuing of the bill, is hardly ever
made by any other perfon; but after the iffuing of
the bill, it frequently happens, either that the
drawee cannot be found, or refufes to accept, or
that his credit is fufpected, or he cannot, by reafon of
fome difability, render himfelf refponfible: in any
of thefe cafes, an acceptance by another perfon, in
order either to prevent the return of the bill, to
promote the negociation of it, or to fave the repu-
tation and prevent the profecution of the drawer, or
of fome of the other parties, is not uncommon:
fuch an acceptance is-called an acceptance for the
honour of the perfon on whofe account it is made,
the effect of which will be more particularly explained in a fubfequent page.

Mal. 265.
Mar. 22.
Beawes,
456, 458.

THAT engagement which conftitutes an acceptance is ufually made to the holder of the bill, or
to fome perfon who has it in contemplation to receive it, and then the acceptor muft anfwer to him,
and to every one who either has had the bill before,
or fhall afterwards have it by indorfement: but it
is frequently made to the drawer himfelf; and then
it may be binding on the party making the engagement.

ment or not, according to the circumſtances of the caſe.

Beawes,
454. Pier-
ſon v. Dun-
lop, Cowp.
572,574. 1
Atk. 715.
(611.)
Powell v.
Monnier.

THE mere anſwer of a merchant to the drawer that he will " duly honour his bill," is not of itſelf an acceptance, unleſs accompanied with circum-ſtances which may induce a third perſon to take the bill by indorſement: but if there be any ſuch circumſtances, it may amount to an acceptance, though the anſwer be contained in a letter to the drawer.

Maſon v.
Hunt,
Doug. 286.
(99.)

AND an agreement to accept may be expreſſed in ſuch terms as to put a third perſon in a better con-dition than the drawer. If one man, to give credit to another, make an abſolute promiſe to accept his bill, the drawer, or any other perſon, may ſhew ſuch promiſe on the exchange, to procure credit, and a a third perſon advancing his money on it, has no-thing to do with the equitable circumſtances which may ſubſiſt between the drawer and acceptor.

IV. AN acceptance is generally according to the tenor of the bill, and then it is called a general and abſolute acceptance.

BUT it may differ from the tenor in ſome mate-rial circumſtances, and yet, as far as it goes, be bind-ing on the acceptor.

Mar.17,22.
Wegerſlofe
v. Keene,
1 Str. 214.
Mar. 21.

IT may be for a leſs ſum than that mentioned in the bill: or it may be at an enlarged period, which is uſually the caſe when a merchant on whom a bill is drawn has no effects of the drawer in his hands, and does not ſuppoſe he ſhall have any at the time of payment mentioned in the bill.

So,

So, the drawee may accept a bill which has no time mentioned for the payment, and which is held payable at fight, to pay at a diftant period; and fuch acceptance will bind him.

Walker v. Atwood, 11 Mod. 190.

A BILL was payable the firft of January, the drawee accepted to pay the firft of March; the holder ftruck out the firft of March, and inferted the firft of January; and when it was payable according to that date, prefented it for payment, which the acceptor refufed; on which the holder reftored the acceptance to its original form; and the court held that it continued binding.

Price v. Shute, P. 33. Car. II. Beawes, 481.

So, the acceptance may direct the payment to be made at a place different from that mentioned in the bill, as at the houfe of a banker; in which cafe if the holder neglect to demand payment within a reafonable time, and the banker afterwards fail, he muft ftand to the lofs.

Bifhop v. Chitty, 2 Str. 1195.

BUT if the banker continue folvent, the holder is not bound to prove a demand on the banker in an action againft the acceptor.

Smith v. Delafon-taine, B. R. T. 25 G. III, Bayley App. No. 5.

So alfo the acceptance may differ from the tenor of the bill in its mode of payment, as to pay half in money, half in bills.

Smith v. Sear, E. 14. G. II. Buller's N. P. 270.

AN acceptance may alfo be conditional, as " to pay when certain goods configned to the acceptor, and for which the bill is drawn, fhall be fold;" for it would affect trade if factors were not allowed to ufe this caution when bills are drawn on them, before they have an opportunity to difpofe of the goods.

Smith v. Abbot, 2, Str. 1152.

So,

Julian v.
Shobrooke,
2 Wilf. 9.
So, an acceptance " on account of the ship Thetis when in cash for the said veffel's cargo" is sufficient to bind the acceptor.

Banbury v.
Liffet, 2.
Str. 1212.
On the fame principle, an acceptance " to pay as remitted from the place where the perfon on whofe account the acceptance is made refides," feems binding after the remittance made.

1 Term
Rep. 182.
But what fhall be confidered as an abfolute or conditional acceptance is a queftion of law to be determined by the court, and is not to be left to the jury.

Wilkinfon
v. Lut-
widge, 1
Str. 648.
A Bill was drawn in New England for a fum of money advanced there, for the repairs of a ship, of which Lutwidge, the drawee, refiding at White-haven, was the freighter. Wilkinfon, the holder of the bill, applied to a merchant in London, to fend the bill to Lutwidge for acceptance : the merchant fent it inclofed to the drawee, who by letter acknowledged the receipt, and wrote thus; " The bill which you fent me I will pay, in cafe the owners of the Queen Ann do not; and they living in Dublin, I muft firft apply to them; I hope to have their anfwer in a week or ten days: I do not expect they will pay it, but I judge it proper to take their advice before I do, with which I requeft you will acquaint Mr. Wilkinfon, and that he may reft fatisfied of the payment." In another letter he writes, " I have not had an opportunity of fending the bill to Ireland, but will take the firft opportunity, and then will remit to the gentlemen concerned, according to my promife." The bill

not

not being paid, an action was brought againft
Lutwidge, as acceptor, in which he infifted that
thefe letters did not amount to an abfolute acceptance, but were only conditional, to pay in cafe
the owners of the Queen Ann did not; and that
his promife to procure payment from them was in
favour of the plaintiff; but the chief juftice thought
it was rather in favour of himfelf; that the letters
were a complete acceptance, and amounted to this;
that he wifhed the holder of the bill to give him
time to write to Ireland, but affured him that at
all events the money fhould be fecured, whether
the owners of the Queen Ann payed it or not.

Raymond.

A BILL was drawn on Mathews, payable to one
Lenox, or order, and by indorfement came into
the hands of Sproat: Sproat's clerk prefented the
bill for acceptance to Mathews, who lived in London, and who told him, "that the drawer had configned a fhip and cargo to him and another perfon
in Briftol; but as he could not then tell whether
the fhip would arrive at London or Briftol, he
could not accept at that time:" the clerk, by the
confent of Mathews, left the bill, and afterwards
called, in company with his mafter, to know
whether Mathews would accept the bill or not;
who, on being preffed, declared, "the bill was a
good one, and would be paid, even if the fhip were
loft."

Sproat v.
Mathews,
1 Term
Rep. 182.

THE court held that this was only a conditional,
not an abfolute acceptance. Mathews had three
events in contemplation; the arrival of the fhip at
Briftol,

Briſtol, her arrival at London, or her being loſt: if the ſhip arrived in London, the cargo being conſigned to him, he would have effects to reimburſe himſelf; if ſhe were loſt, he had the policy of inſurance, by which he could indemnify himſelf by recovering againſt the underwriters: but if ſhe arrived in Briſtol, the cargo was conſigned to another, he would have no effects: in either of the former events he meant to accept the bill; in the latter he did not.

Vid. Doug. 286.

IF the acceptance be in writing, and the drawee intend that it ſhould only be conditional, he muſt be careful to expreſs the condition in writing as well as the acceptance; for if the acceptance ſhould, on the face of it, appear to be abſolute, he cannot take advantage of any verbal condition annexed to it, if the bill ſhould be negociated and come to the hands of a perſon unacquainted with the condition, and even againſt the perſon to whom the verbal condition was expreſſed, the burthen of proof will be on the acceptor.

A CONDITIONAL acceptance, when the conditions on which it depends are performed, becomes abſolute.

Pierſon v. Dunlop, Cowp 571.

NICHOL was the captain of a ſhip of which Pierſon was the owner. The ſhip was freighted with naval ſtores by M'Lintot, who being unable to diſcharge the freight, drew a bill on Dunlop and Co. payable fifteen days after ſight to the order of Nichol, and gave Nichol a certificate or navy bill, aſſigned to Dunlop and Co. as a ſecurity till the

the Bill of Exchange fhould be accepted: Nichol indorfed the bill, and fent it to Pierfon, together with a letter from M'Lintot to Dunlop and Co. in which was inclofed the certificate which M'Lintot defired them to tender at the Navy Office, and at the fame time he advifed them, that he had drawn on them as above. On the 2d of October, 1776, Pierfon fent this letter, with the certificate inclofed, and alfo the Bill of Exchange, to Dunlop and Co. : when the bill was demanded again the next day, the defendants delivered it up, faying, " it would not be accepted till the navy bill was paid;" but they refufed to deliver the navy bill, faying, they would receive the money themfelves. It was held, that this was a conditional acceptance, which, on the receipt of the money, became abfolute. Nichol, the captain, had a lien on the naval ftores for his freight; the certificate was a fecurity for that freight; it was given into his poffeffion as a pledge for the money till the bill fhould be paid. It was not fent to Dunlop and Co. by the poft in the the ufual courfe, but was inclofed to Pierfon as his fecurity. He was therefore not bound to part with it till the bill was accepted. Dunlop and Co. by detaining it, and faying, that the bill would not be accepted till the navy bill fhould be paid, undertook, on that event, to accept and pay the Bill of Exchange.

But if the conditions, on which the agreement to accept a bill is made, be not complied with, that agreement will be difcharged.

As,

As, if a merchant undertake to accept bills to a certain amount, on condition that a cargo of an equal value be configned to him, and an order given for infurance. If the cargo configned do not equal the value, he is not bound to accept.

V. A SMALL matter will frequently amount to an acceptance, according to the circumftances of the cafe: thus, if the merchant fay, leave the bill with me, and to-morrow I will accept it; this is an acceptance, for it gives credit to the bill, and prevents the holder from taking the neceffary fteps againft the drawer.

BUT if the merchant fay, leave the bill with me, and I will look over my books and accounts between the drawer and me; call to-morrow, and accordingly the bill fhall be accepted; this is no complete acceptance, becaufe it depends on the balance of the account, and on the merchant's having effects in his hands to anfwer it, fo that he gives no abfolute credit to the bill.

ANY thing written on the bill by the drawee, not expreffing a direct refufal to accept, as "accepted," "prefented," "feen," will, if unexplained by other circumftances, amount to an acceptance.

So, a direction to a third perfon to pay the money is an acceptance. The drawee of a bill underwrote it thus; "Mr Jackfon, pleafe to pay this bill, and charge it to Mr. Newton's account." It was contended that this was not an acceptance,

for

for that the party did not mean to become the principal debtor. It was only a direction to Jackson, to pay out of a particular fund. But the court held, that the underwriting being a direction to pay the sum, it was of no importance to what account it was to be placed when paid : that was a transaction between the parties themselves, and this was a sufficient acceptance.

A BILL was sent to the drawee for acceptance ; he kept it for ten days before it became due without any objection; and whilst it continued in his hands, he entered it in his bill-book, under a particular number, and wrote the number on the bill, and at the bottom the day when it would become due, and then sent it back, refusing to accept it : it was proved that it was the common practice of the drawee to enter and mark all bills in the same manner, whether he intended to accept them or not : the court seemed to think that these circumstances alone did not amount to an acceptance. _{Powell v. Monnier, 1 Atk. 717. (612.)}

IF a merchant be desired to accept a bill on the account of another, and to draw on a third, in order to reimburse himself, and in consequence he draw a bill on that third person ; the bare act of drawing this bill will not amount to an acceptance of the other, for the party evidently shews he meant only to make himself liable, in case the bill drawn by him should be accepted and paid. _{Smith v. Niffen, 1 Term Rep. 269.}

AN agreement to accept or honour a bill will, in many cases, be equivalent to an acceptance, and whether that agreement be merely verbal or in _{Beawes, 466.}

G   writing.

writing is immaterial: If A. having given or intending to give credit to B. write to C. to know
whether he will accept such bills as shall be drawn
on him on B's account, and C. return for answer
that he will accept them; this is equivalent to an
acceptance, and a subsequent prohibition to draw
on him on B's account will be of no avail, if, in
fact, previous to that prohibition, the credit has
been given.

Pillans v.
Van Mie-
rop, 3 Bur.
1663.

WHITE, a merchant in Ireland, desired to draw
on the plaintiffs, Pillans and Rose, merchants at
Rotterdam, for 800l. payable to one Clifford, and
proposed to give them credit on a good house in
London for their reimbursement, or any other
mode of reimbursement: the plaintiffs, in answer,
desired a confirmed credit on a house of rank in
London, as the condition of their accepting the
bill: White named the house of the defendants as
that house of rank: the plaintiffs honoured the
draft, and paid the money, and then wrote to the
defendants, Van Mierop and Hopkins, merchants in
London, desiring to know whether they would accept
such bills as the plaintiffs should in about a month's
time draw on their house for 800l. on the credit of
White: the defendants agreed to honour the bill;
but, before it was drawn, White failed, and then
the defendants wrote to the plaintiffs, informing
them that White had stopped payment, and desiring them not to draw, as they could not accept
their draught. The plaintiffs however drew, hold-

ing the defendants not at liberty to withdraw their engagement.

On behalf of the defendants it was argued, that the letter in which they promifed to honour the plaintiffs' bill imported a credit given to the plaintiffs in profpect of a future credit to be given by them to White; for the letter of the plaintiffs, to which that of the defendants was an anfwer, only intimated an intention of giving credit to White, on condition of a credit from the defendants; and that therefore this credit might well be countermanded before the advancement of money.—But the real tranfaction between the plaintiffs and White was very different from that reprefented to the defendants; the former had accepted White's bill a confiderable time before the latter had undertaken to honour their draught, and confequently could not be confidered as having been influenced by that engagement. That this tranfaction had been fraudulently concealed from the defendants both by White and the plaintiffs; if it had been difclofed, the defendants would have plainly feen that the plaintiffs doubted of White's fufficiency, by their requiring a further fecurity for a debt already contracted: and that therefore this concealment of circumftances was fufficient to vitiate the contract. It was likewife void for want of confideration, it being like a promife to pay another man's debt contracted before the promife, which was a paft confideration, and therefore no

more

more than a naked agreement, which was not sufficient to maintain an action.

To this it was anfwered, that if indeed there
were any fraud in the tranfaction, that would have
been fufficient to vacate the contract; but it was
manifeft that none exifted here, nor were the defendants deceived into a belief that the credit to
White was future: the plaintiffs' letter imported
only a wifh to be informed, whether the defendants
would accept bills on White's account, which they,
by their anfwer, confented to do. The plaintiffs
did not feem at the time to have doubted of White's
fufficiency, or to have meant to conceal any thing
from the defendants. The draught by White on
the plaintiffs payable to Clifford was no part of the
confideration of the engagement of the defendants;
that, and all the precedent correfpondence, was intirely out of the cafe. By promifing to honour the
plaintiffs' draughts, the defendants admitted that
they either had effects of White in their hands, or
that they had credit on him. There was no pretence for the objection of this being a naked agreement: whatever might be faid in other cafes of a
naked agreement, or the want of confideration,
there was no fuch thing in the cuftom of merchants
with refpect to Bills of Exchange. The true reafon why the acceptance of a Bill of Exchange fhall
bind, is not on account of the acceptor's having, or
being fuppofed to have, effects in his hands, but
from the convenience of trade and commerce: the
acceptance is an obligation to pay, though the
acceptor

acceptor have no effects of the person on whose account the bill is drawn, and though there be no
confideration. The end of the inftitution of bills,
their currency, requires that it fhould be fo. This
cafe is the fame as if White had drawn on Van
Mierop and Hopkins, payable to the plaintiffs: it
would have been immaterial to the plaintiffs whether Van Mierop and Hopkins had effects of
White or not, if they had accepted his bill: what
was done here amounts to the fame thing; to promife to give the bill due honour is, in effect, to accept it: if a man agree to do the formal part, the
law, in the cafe of an acceptance of a bill, confiders
it as actually done: the defendants could not afterwards retract; it would be deftructive to trade and
credit if they might. There is no analogy between
this cafe and a promife to pay another man's debts
already contracted. It is a tranfaction of quite a
different nature. If a confideration were neceffary,
there is here a fufficient one. Any damage to another, or forbearance or fufpenfion of the affertion
of his right, is a fufficient foundation for an undertaking, and will make it binding, though no actual
benefit accrue to the party who undertakes. Here
the engagement of the defendants occafioned a poffibility of lofs to the plaintiffs: it is plain they
would not rely on White's affurance alone, and
therefore they wrote to the defendants to know if
they would honour their draught: by engaging to
do fo, they prevented the plaintiffs from calling on
White to perform his agreement, by giving them

credit

credit on a good houfe in London for a reimburfe-
ment. The fufpenfion of the plaintiffs' right, to
call on White for a compliance with his agreement,
is a confideration fufficient to maintain an action,
if that fufpenfion be only for a day, or for ever fo
fhort a time.

IF a bill be drawn on a fervant, with a direction
to place the money to the account of his mafter,
and the fervant accept it generally, this renders him
liable to anfwer perfonally to an indorfee.

Thomas v.
Bifhop, 2
Str. 955.
B. R. H. 1.
A BILL of Exchange was drawn in this manner:
" At thirty days fight, pay to John Somerville, or
order, 200l. and place the fame to the account of
the York-buildings company, value received by
yours, Charles Mildmay." Directed to Mr. Hum-
phrey Bifhop, cafhier of the York-buildings company, at their houfe in Winchefter-ftreet, London.
" Accepted, H. Bifhop, 13th June, 1732." This
bill was indorfed to Thomas, who brought an action againft Bifhop as the acceptor. At the trial
the defendant proved, that the letter of advice was
addreffed to the company; and that the bill being
brought to their houfe, he was ordered to accept it,
which he did in the fame manner as he had accepted other bills: but it was determined that this
evidence was immaterial. The bill, on the face of
it, imported to be drawn on the defendant; it was
accepted by him generally, not as fervant to the
company, to whofe account he had no right to
charge it, till actual payment by himfelf: and this
being an action by an indorfee, it would be of dangerous

gerous confequence to trade to admit evidence, arifing from extrinfic circumftances, fuch as the letter of advice. This differed widely from the cafe of a bill addreffed to the mafter, and fubfcribed by the fervant. A Bill of Exchange is a contract by the cuftom of merchants, and the whole of that contract muft appear in writing; there is nothing in writing here to bind the company, nor can any action be maintained againft them upon the bill, for the addition of cafhier to the defendant's name, is only to denote the perfon with more certainty; the houfe of the York-buildings company, is to in- form the indorfee where the drawee is to be found, and the direction to whofe account to place the money, is for the ufe of the drawee only. It might have been otherwife, had the action been by the payee, who was privy to the tranfaction, and if it had appeared that he tendered the bill as a bill on the company: but this plaintiff being a ftranger, thofe circumftances could not be confidered.

CHAP.

C H A P. VI.

Transfer of BILLS *and* NOTES.

ACCORDING to the difference in the ſtyle of nego-
'ciability of Bills and Notes, the modes of their
transfer alſo differ.

1 Bur. 452.
3 Bur. 1516.
1 Bl. Rep.
485.

BILLS and Notes payable to bearer are transferred
by delivery: if payable to J. S. or bearer, they are
payable to bearer as if J. S. were not mentioned.

BUT to the transfer of thoſe payable to order, it
is neceſſary, in addition to delivery, that there
ſhould be ſomething by which the payee may appear to expreſs his order. This additional circumſtance is an indorſement, ſo called from being
uſually written on the back, though, without doubt,
an order of transfer would be equally valid, if
written at the bottom or on the face of the inſtrument.

WHERE no regulation is made by act of parliament relative to the negociation of bills or notes, no
particular form of words is neceſſary to make an
indorſement, only the name of the indorſor muſt
appear upon it, and it muſt be written or ſigned by
him, or by ſome perſon authoriſed by him for that
purpoſe.

INDORSE-

INDORSEMENTS are either in full or in blank; a full indorfement is that by which the indorfor orders the money to be paid to fome particular perfon by name. A blank indorfement confifts only of the name of the indorfor.

A BLANK indorfement renders the bill or note afterwards transferable by delivery only, as if it were payable to bearer, for by only writing his name, the indorfor fhews his intention that the inftrument fhould have a general currency, and be transferred by every poffeffor.

Doug. 617. (639.) 611. (633.)

BLANK indorfements are more frequent than thofe in full, becaufe, if every indorfement were in full, the back of the inftrument would be foon filled up, and its negociability would be lefs extenfive.

EXCEPT where reftrained by act of parliament, the transfer of a bill or note may be made at any time after it has iffued, even after the day of payment; and in cafe of the former, where the acceptor refides at a diftance from the drawer, is frequently made before acceptance.

1 Ld. Ray. 575. Vid. 3 Term Rep. 80. Vid. 3 Bur. 1516. 1 Bl. Rep. 485. Doug. 611. (633.) Vid. 1 H. Bl. Rep. 88, 89.

AND where the transfer is by indorfement, that indorfement may be made on a blank note, before the infertion of any date or fum of money, in which cafe, the indorfor is liable for any fum, at any time of payment that may afterwards be inferted; and it is immaterial whether the perfon taking the note on the credit of the indorfement knew whether it was made before the drawing of the note or not; for in fuch a cafe the indorfement is equivalent to a letter of credit for any indefinite fum.

ONE

Ruſſel v.
Langſtaffe,
Doug. 496.
(514.)

ONE Galley having had frequent money tranſactions with Ruſſel, a banker, and having overdrawn his caſh account; Ruſſel ſuſpecting his credit, refuſed to advance him any more money, without the addition of the name of ſome indorſor of whom he ſhould approve: on this Galley applied to Langſtaffe, who indorſed his name on five copper-plate checks, made in the form of Promiſſory Notes, but in blank, that is, without any ſum, date, or time of payment, mentioned in the body of the notes. Galley afterwards filled up the blanks with different ſums and dates, and Ruſſel diſcounted the notes. Galley became a bankrupt, and Ruſſel demanded payment of Langſtaffe, and, on his refuſal, brought an action, in which the court thought he was entitled to recover, though it appeared that he knew the notes were blank at the time of the indorſement.

Bank of
England v.
Newman, 1
Ld. Raym.
442. 12
Mod. 241.
Lambert v.
Pack, 1
Salk. 128.
7th reſolution.

IT is ſaid, that on a transfer by delivery, the perſon making it ceaſes to be a party to the bill or note; that ſuch a transfer is a ſale, and that he who ſells it, does not become a new ſecurity, and is not liable to refund the money if the bill ſhould not be paid.

BUT this can only be true to its full extent when applied to the caſe of a demand by a ſubſequent party when one or more have intervened between him and the party againſt whom he makes the demand: as between the immediate parties to the transfer, this diſtinction muſt be taken, that when the bill or note has been given in payment of a prece-

a precedent debt, or for a vaulable confideration at
the time of the transfer, without being difcounted;
then, though the perfon who has given the money
for the bill or note cannot recover againft the perfon who received it, as indorfor, yet he may certainly recover in an action for money had and received for his ufe, as the transferer muft be underftood to undertake that the bill fhall be duly paid.
But if the bill or note be *difcounted* for the accommodation of the transferer, then the transfer is a fale,
and the doctrine here laid down will apply.

IN a cafe which has lately occurred, and which has
fome relation to this fubject, the circumftances which
appeared on a motion for a new trial were thefe :

THE action was for money lent, money paid by
the plaintiffs to the ufe of the defendants, and money
had and received by the defendants to the ufe of
the plaintiffs. The defendants having a Bill of
Exchange, which came to them by indorfement,
and wifhing to have it difcounted, employed Francis Huet for that purpofe, telling him to carry it to
market and to get cafh for it, but that they would
not indorfe it. F. Huet applied to his brother,
James Huet, to get the bill difcounted, informing
him that it belonged to the defendants, and that
though they did not choofe to indorfe it, yet he
added, as a reafon of his own, that as their number
was on the bill, it was equivalent to an indorfement,
and that he (F. Huet) would indemnify him if he
indorfed. James Huet applied to the plaintiffs,
who difcounted it, relying chiefly on the credit of
the

Fenn v.
Harrifon, 3
Term Rep.
757.

the acceptors, not knowing at the time that the defendants had any concern with it; but they required the indorfement of James Huet, which he gave, becaufe, without that, the plaintiffs refufed to difcount the bill. Afterwards, on the failure of the acceptors, the plaint.fis having heard that the bill had paffed through the hands of the defendants, applied to them for payment, who at firft refufed, but afterwards promifed to take it up; and on their not performing their promife, brought the prefent action to recover the amount, and obtained a verdict.

The application for a new trial was founded on the idea that the promife of the defendants was without confideration, and confequently was a *nudum pactum*.

In oppofition to this application, it was contended, that the promife was binding on the defendants, whether confidered as given by them when under a *moral* obligation to pay, or as having received *a legal and valuable confideration for it*. It could not, it was faid, be denied that fo much money belonging to the plaintiffs had got into the pockets of the defendants, for which the former had received no confideration. This was a fum, therefore, which, in confcience and morality, the defendants were bound to pay to the plaintiffs; that this alone, though there were ftrictly no legal debt, was a fufficient confideration to raife a promife: but the circumftances of the tranfaction amounted to a valuable and legal confideration: the plaintiffs had a right of action againft James Huet, who, as an innocent man,

and

and not involved in the mifconduct of his brother,
had a claim on the defendants; for as James Huet,
in putting his indorfement on the bill, acted by the
direction of his brother, who was the avowed agent
of the defendants, though F. Huet might have exceeded his authority, they muft be bound by his act,
and were therefore liable to James Huet. But it
did not appear that he had ; for the only reftraint
impofed-on him by the defendants was not to indorfe *their names*, becaufe they did not wifh that
their names fhould appear on the bill: but they
did not mean to reftrain *him* from indorfing it, or
any other perfon for him, provided the money could
not be raifed on any other terms, and that had
turned out to be the cafe.

The argument in favour of the defendants
turned principally on the diftinction between
a general and a circumfcribed authority. If
Francis Huet had been the *general* agent of the
defendants, it was admitted, that they would have
been chargeable with his acts; but it appeared
from the facts, that he was conftituted their *particular* agent with a *circumfcribed* authority; the fubftance of which was, that he would *fell* the bill ; for
that they would not make themfelves liable, either
on the bill by their indorfement, or by any other
circuitous mode. F. Huet, it was agreed, would
be liable to James Huet, either as for money paid
to his ufe, or on the exprefs promife to guarantee ;
but there the matter ftopped ; for as to the defendants, he would pay the money in his own wrong,

having

having exceeded his authority: the result must be, that as between these parties, the plaintiffs had no equity, and that the defendants were not under any legal or moral obligation whatever to pay the amount of the bill: this was a new attempt, and it was difficult to say to what extent it might be carried, if it were encouraged: in the case of a Bill of Exchange, it was precisely known what remedy the holder had, if the bill were not paid; his security appeared wholly on the face of the bill itself: the acceptor, the drawer, and the indorsors were all liable in their turns; but they were only liable because they had written their names on the bill. But this was an attempt to make some other persons liable, whose names did not appear on the bill, and that too under circumstances very alarming to mercantile houses through which Bills of Exchange pass. Indorsors, whose names were on the bill, could only be called on, after notice of non-payment, and without delay. But if these defendants were answerable, by what rule was the court to be guided? Were the defendants to be called upon at any distance of time? When a person *refused* to indorse a bill, it could not be implied that he meant to make himself liable on the bill, much less in a more extensive way than if he had indorsed it.—On these grounds the rule was made absolute for a new trial. On the next trial, the evidence was the same as before, in every other respect, but that when the defendants desired F. Huet to get the bill discounted, *they did not say that they would not indorse it.* The jury found a verdict for the plaintiffs; and 4 Term Rep. 177. on a motion for another trial, the court were unanimoufly of opinion that it fhould not be granted, on the ground, that as the defendants had authorifed F. Huet to get the bill difcounted, without reftraining his authority as to the mode of doing it, they were bound by his acts; and that if it were doubtful, from the converfation which paffed between the defendants and F. Huet, at the time when they applied to him to get the bill difcounted, what authority they meant to confer on him in this tranfaction, their fubfequent conduct, in promifing to pay the bill, was decifive.—But the three Judges, Afhhurft, Buller, and Grofe, faid, that had not the evidence given on this trial varied from that given before, they fhould have continued to entertain the fame opinion which they delivered on the former occafion.

THOUGH a blank indorfement be a fufficient transfer, and may enable the perfon in whofe favour it is made to negociate the inftrument, yet it is in his option to take it, either as indorfee or as fervant or agent to the indorfor, and the latter may, notwithftanding his indorfement, declare as holder in an action againft the drawer or acceptor. Nothing is more ufual than for the holder of a bill or note, to indorfe it in blank, and fend it to fome friend for the purpofe of procuring the acceptance or the payment; in this cafe it is in the power of his friend, either to fill up the blank fpace over the indorfor's name with an order to pay

the

Clark v. Pigot, 1 Salk. 125. Dehers v. Harriot, 1 Show. 163. Lambert v. Pack, 1 Salk. 128, 6th refolution. Lucas v. Haynes, 1 Salk. 130. 2 Lord Raym. 871.

the money to himfelf, which fhews his election to take as indorfee, or to write a receipt, which fhews that he is only the agent of the indorfor.

Lucas v. Haynes, 1 Salk. 130. 2 Lord Raym.871.
On this principle, a man to whom a bill was delivered with a blank indorfement, and who carried it for acceptance, was admitted, in an action of trover for the bill againft the drawee, to prove the delivery of it to the latter.

2Bur.1226.
The original contract on negociable bills and notes is to pay to fuch perfon or perfons, as the payee or his indorfees, or their indorfees, fhall direct; and there is as much privity between the laft indorfor and the laft indorfee, as between the drawer and the original payee. When the payee affigns it over, he does it by the law of merchants; for as a thing in action, it is not affignable by the general law. The indorfement is part of the original contract, is incidental to it in the nature of the thing, and muft be underftood to be made in the fame manner as the inftrument was drawn: the indorfee holds it in the fame manner, and with the fame privileges, qualities, and advantages as the original payee, as a tranfferable negociable inftrument, which he may indorfe over to another, and that other to a third, and fo on at pleafure; and therefore an indorfor, where he indorfes it for a valuable confideration, cannot limit his indorfement by any reftriction on the indorfee, fo as to preclude him from transferring it to another as a thing negociable.

On thefe principles it has been feveral times folemnly fettled, that it is no objection to the claim of

an

an indorfee, that the indorfement to him does not contain the words "to order."

In one cafe it appeared that Manning had given a Promiffory Note to Statham or order; Statham affigned it to Witherhead, and Witherhead to More, who, on non-payment at the time, brought an action againft Manning: on a demurrer to the declaration, exception was taken, that the affignment to Witherhead was made without faying to him or order, and that therefore he could not affign it over to More. But it was held by the whole court that the indorfement was fufficient; for if the original note be affignable, then, to whomfoever it may be affigned, he has the whole intereft in it, and may affign it as he pleafes; an affignment to him comprehends his affigns.

More v. Manning, Comyns 311. in C. B. Hil. 6 G. I. cited 2 Bur. 1222.

In another cafe the plaintiff had declared on an indorfement made by William Abercrombie, by which he appointed the payment to be to Louifa Achefon, "or order"; on the bill being produced in evidence, it appeared to be originally made payable to Abercrombie or order, but Abercrombie's indorfement was only this; "pray pay the contents to Louifa Achefon." It was objected "that the indorfement did not agree with the declaration." The court however gave judgment, on the ground of a general propofition in law, that a bill is negociable without the addition of thofe words to the indorfement; the legal import of fuch indorfement being, that the bill was payable to order, and that the plaintiff might on this have indorfed it over to

Achefon v. Fountain, Mich. 9 G. I. B. R. 1 Str. 457, cited 2 Bur. 1223.

H   another,

another, who would have been the proper order of the firft indorfor.

YET, notwithftanding thefe cafes, the fame point was again agitated on the following occafion:

Edie v.
Eaft-India
Company, 2
Bur. 1216.
1 Bl. Rep.
295.

COLONEL CLIVE drew a bill, payable to Mr. Cambell, or order, on the Eaft-India company, who accepted it; Mr. Cambell indorfed it to Mr. Robert Ogilby, but the words " or order" being originally omitted, were afterwards inferted by another hand before the trial: Ogilby indorfed it over to Meffrs. Edie and Laird, or order, and afterwards, before the payment, became infolvent: Edie and Laird brought an action againft the company as acceptors, who refufed payment, on pretence that Ogilby had no right to affign to the plaintiffs: the real queftion was, who fhould bear the lofs, Mr. Cambell or the plaintiffs; for the Eaft-India company, if they did not pay to the plaintiffs, muft pay to Mr. Cambell.

AT the trial, Lord Mansfield permitted the defendants to give evidence of a *ufage among merchants,* that an indorfement to any individual by name, without the words " or order," deftroyed the negociability of the bill, and confined the right of recovery to that individual perfon: this ufage was proved by a number of witneffes; but no inftance was fhewn where the indorfee, to whom a bill was indorfed without adding the words, " or order," ever actually loft the money, fo as to put him on difputing the point. His lordfhip, in his addrefs to the jury, told them, that, laying the ufage out of the

the cafe, by the general law, the indorfement would follow the nature of the original bill, and be an abfolute affignment to the indorfee or his order: but that he left it to them, on the particular evidence of the ufage that had been laid before them : that if they found an ufage fo eftablifhed and fettled amongft merchants and traders as to be clear and plain beyond all doubt, they might find a verdict for the defendant, but that if they were doubtful of the ufage, or if it appeared to them not to be fully and clearly eftablifhed, or to be the other way, then they ought to find for the plaintiff.

THAT the queftion arofe on the infolvency of Ogilby, the firft indorfee; that therefore it ought to be confidered who it was that gave credit to him, for that he who gives the credit ought to run the rifk : that if Mr. Cambell meant to truft Ogilby with the money, it was he who ought to fuffer by him; and that he meant to truft him was clear; for it was acknowledged on all hands, that Ogilby himfelf had a right to receive it of the company, whether he had a right to indorfe the bill to another perfon or not.

THE jury found for the defendants; and on an application for a new trial, the counfel in fupport of the verdict refted principally on the ufage which had been eftablifhed by the evidence; and with refpect to the two cafes before cited, they endeavoured to fhew that they did not apply to the prefent; the firft, they faid, muft have been an indorfement in blank, not to Witherhead by name, and then there could be no doubt of his power to transfer it : the fecond did not decide the prefent queftion, for it was only an objection on account of the declaration varying from the evidence : the plaintiff had clearly a right to recover, without entering into the general queftion, for fhe was the perfon to whom the bill was indorfed, and had not indorfed it over ; and what the court was reported to have faid, " as to her power to have indorfed it to another, who would be the proper order of the firft indorfor," was at leaft extrajudicial, if not added by the reporter himfelf : but the court, on full deliberation, were of opinion, that the law was fettled by thofe two cafes, that fuch an indorfement was good, and gave the indorfee a right of indorf-ing over : that the law having been fo fettled, no evidence of an ufage to it ought to have been ad-mitted ; that the law of merchants is the law of the kingdom, and part of the common law, and when once eftablifhed by judicial determinations, cannot be fhaken.   Where indeed the law of merchants is doubtful, the evidence of a cuftom may be received; but even then it muft be proved by facts, not by opinion only, and muft be confiftent with the ge-neral principles of the law.

2 Bur. 1227.
Doug. 617.
(639.)

YET an indorfement may be reftrictive, and then it operates to preclude the perfon to whom it is made from transferring the inftrument to another, fo as to give him a right of action, either againft the perfon impofing the reftriction, or againft any of the preceding parties ; it may give a bare authority

authority to the indorfee to receive the money for the indorfor; as if it fay, " pray pay the money to fuch a one for my ufe," or ufe fuch other expreffions as neceffarily import that he does not mean to transfer his intereft in the bill or note, but merely to give a power of receiving the money. In fuch a cafe it would be clear that no valuable confideration had been paid; but the intention of reftraint muft appear on the face of the indorfement.

So, if the payee direct by indorfement, that " the within muft be credited to the account of a third perfon." This is not a transfer of the bill to that third perfon, but only an authority to the drawees to give him credit for fo much; the payee does not mean to make himfelf liable as indorfor, or to enable the other to raife money on the bill.

Doug. 617. (640.)

AND, if in fuch a cafe the drawee accept the bill, inftead of cancelling it, and an indorfement be forged and the bill negociated, the party who fhall advance money on it muft fuftain the lofs; and if afterwards a friend of the drawer, by miftake, pay the bill for his honour, the drawer may recover back the money, in an action for money had and received to his ufe; for it was the duty of the party advancing the money on the bill to read the fpecial indorfement, and he muft fuffer for his negligence.

THUS, where a bill was drawn by a houfe in Denmark on a houfe in London, payable to a perfon refiding in Denmark, or his order, and the payee made fuch a fpecial indorfement; the drawees accepted and gave notice to the drawers and to the perfon

Ancher v. Bank of England. Doug. 615. (637.)

fon

son in whose favour the indorsement was made, that
they had received the bill, and placed it to the account of the latter; the clerk of the acceptors
forged an indorsement to himself or order, from
the person to whose account the money was to be
credited, and discounted it at the bank; the acceptors failed before the day of payment, and a
friend of the drawers went to the bank and paid
the bill for their honour: the drawers afterwards
recovered back the money from the bank, on the
ground that this special indorsement restrained the
negociability of the bill, and that the money was
paid by mistake.

IF an indorsement be made in favour of an infant, and he indorse it to another, no recovery can
be had on that indorsement against the infant,
because he cannot render himself liable by his contract; yet, as it is to be presumed, unless the contrary appear on the face of the indorsement, that
every indorsee has given a valuable consideration,
the infant's indorsement cannot be considered as
such a restraint on the negociability of the bill as
to prevent the indorsee's recovery against the acceptor or drawer, or any of the other indorsors.

WHERE the transfer may be by delivery only,
that transfer may be made by any person who, by
any means, whether accident or theft, has obtained
the possession; and any holder may recover against
the drawer, acceptor or indorsor in blank, if he
gave a valuable consideration without knowledge of
the accident.

A BANK

A. BANK note for 21l. 10s. payable to one William Finney, or bearer, on demand, was fent by Finney under cover by the general poft to his correfpondent in Oxfordfhire; the mail on the fame night was robbed, and this note among others taken and carried away by the robber; it afterwards came into the poffeffion of one Miller, an innkeeper, for a full and valuable confideration, in the ufual courfe of his bufinefs, without any notice or knowledge of its having been taken out of the mail. Finney, hearing of the robbery, applied to the bank to ftop the payment of this note, which was ordered, on his entering into fecurity to indemnify the bank: Miller afterwards prefented the note for payment, and delivered it to Race a clerk of the bank, who refufed either to pay it, or to re-deliver it. Miller brought an action of trover againft Race, for the recovery of the note; and a cafe ftating thefe circumftances coming before the court, it was held that the plaintiff was entitled to recover; becaufe there appeared no circumftance of collufion in him; he had taken the note in the ufual courfe of his bufinefs, for a valuable confideration, and the currency of thefe notes and the nature of trade required that the fair holder fhould be protected even againft the true owner, who could only recover them back from the finder, or any other perfon who had given no value for them.

Miller v. Race, 1 Bur. 452.

VAUGHAN, a merchant in London, gave to Bicknell, one of his fhips hufbands, a draught on his banker, Sir Charles Afgill, payable to fhip Fortune,

Grant v. Vaughan, 3 Bur. 1516. 1 Bl Rep. 485.

H 4   or

or bearer : Bicknell loft the draught : the perfon
who found it, or at leaft was in poffeffion, however
he might have obtained that poffeffion, went four
days after the note was payable, to the fhop of
Grant, a tradefman at Portfmouth, and having
bought fome tea, gave him the note in payment,
and defired to have the balance. Grant ftepped
out to make enquiry who Vaughan might be, and
being informed he was a refponfible man, and that
the note was in his hand-writing, gave the change
out of the note, retaining the price of the tea.
Vaughan being apprifed that Bicknell had loft the
note, fent notice to Sir Charles Afgill not to pay it.
Payment being accordingly refufed, Grant brought
his action againft Vaughan as the drawer. The
caufe was tried by a fpecial jury of merchants, who
found for the defendant. On an application for a
new trial, the court held that thefe notes were tranfferable by mere delivery, and however the true
owner may have loft them, the fair poffeffor for a
valuable confideration was intitled to the money,
and therefore granted a new trial.

THE fame principle applies to the cafe of a bill
negociated with a blank indorfement.

Peacock v.
Rhodes et
al. Doug.
611. (613.)

A BILL was drawn at Halifax, by Rhodes and
another, on Smith, Payne, and Smith, bankers in
London, payable to William Ingham, or order,
thirty-one days after date, for value received. Ingham indorfed it in blank; John Daltry received it
from him, and indorfed it in the fame manner, and
delivered it to Jofeph Fifher; it was ftolen from
Fifher

Fisher at York, without any indorsement by him:
Peacock, a mercer at Scarborough, afterwards received it from a man unknown, who called himself
William Brown, and by that name indorsed it to
Peacock, of whom he bought cloth and other articles
in the way of his trade as a mercer, and gave him
that bill in payment, receiving the balance in cash
and small bills: it appeared that Peacock did not
know the drawers, but had, several times before
that, received bills drawn by them, which were duly
paid. Peacock tendered this bill for acceptance
and payment to the drawees, who refused; on
which he brought an action as the indorsee of Ingham against the drawers. A verdict by consent
was found for the plaintiff, subject to the opinion of
the Court of King's Bench, on a special case stating
the preceding facts. The court held that there
was no difference between a bill or note indorsed
blank and one payable to bearer. They both pass
by delivery, and possession proves property in both
cases. The holder of either cannot with propriety
be considered as assignee of the payee. An assignee
must take the thing assigned, subject to all the
equity to which the original party was subject: if
this rule were applied to bills and notes, it would
stop their currency; it would render it necessary
for every indorsee to enquire into all the circumstances, and the manner in which the bill came to
the indorsor; but the law is now clearly settled,
that a holder coming fairly by a bill or note, is not
to be affected with the transaction between the
original

Vid. page
66. original parties, except in such cases as depend on particular acts of parliament.

BUT a transfer by indorsement, where that is necessary, can only be made by him who has a right to make it, and that is strictly only the payee, or the person to whom he or his indorsees have transferred it, or some one claiming in the right of some of these parties.

WHERE a bill or note is drawn in favour of two or more in partnership with one another, an indorsement by one will bind both, if the instrument concern their joint trade: so, where it is in favour of them *or* either of them, an indorsement by one is a sufficient transfer, though they be not in partnership.

Carvick v.
Vickery,
Doug. 630.
(653.) in
the notes. So, where a bill drawn by two is made payable to them or their order, it would seem from principle that either might transfer without the other; for when two persons join in the same bill, they hold themselves out to the world as partners, and, for that purpose, are to be treated as such; and when a bill goes out into the world, the persons to whom it is negociated are to collect the state and relation of the parties from the bill itself. If they appear on the bill as partners, it may be of less public detriment to subject them to the inconvenience of being treated as such, than to permit them to deny that they are so.

BUT there is a universal usage among all the bankers and merchants in London, that in such a case, an indorsement by one of the payees only is void.

If

If a Bill of Exchange or Promissory Note be made or indorsed to a woman while single, and she afterwards marry, the right to idorse it over belongs to her husband, for by the marriage he is intitled to all her personal property.

Connor v. Martin, 1 Str. 516.

If a man become bankrupt, the property of bills and notes of which he is the payee or indorsee, vests in his assignees, and the right to transfer is in them. And if in fact he indorse a bill or note after his bankruptcy, and that be discovered before it be paid, the assignees may recover it back from his indorsee in an action of trover, and if the money be received, they may recover the money in an action for so much money paid to their use.

Beawes, 469, 470.

If he die, it devolves to his personal representatives, his executors, or administrators; and they may indorse it, and their indorsee maintain an action, in the same manner as if the indorsement had been by the testator or intestate. But on their indorsement they are liable personally to the subsequent parties, and not as executors; for they cannot charge the effects of the testator.

Rawlinson v. Stone, 3 Wils. 1. 2 Str. 1260. 2 Barnes, 157, cited 2 Bur. 1225. 1 Term Rep. 487.

They may also be the *indorsees* of a bill or note in their quality of executors or administrators; as where they receive one from their testator or intestate, and in that character they may bring an action on it against the acceptor or any of the other parties.

King, Ex. v. Thorn, 1 Term Rep. 487. Vid. also 10 Mod. 315.

When a bill payable to order is expressed to be for the *use* of another person than the payee, yet the
right

right of transfer is in the payee, and his indorfee may recover againft the drawer or acceptor.

Evans v.
Cramling-
ton, Eaft. 2
Jac. 2.
Carth. 5. 2
Vent. 309.
2 Show.
509.

ONE Cramlington drew a Bill of Exchange on Rider, payable to Price or order, for the ufe of one Calvert. Price indorfed this bill to Evans. Rider accepted the bill, but did not pay it at the day; on which Evans, as indorfee of Price, brought his action againft Cramlington, the drawer. Cramlington pleaded that Calvert, for whofe ufe the money was to be paid, being an officer of Excife, and indebted to the king, an Exchequer procefs had extended in the hands of the defendant, a fum equal to that contained in the bill.

BUT the court held that Calvert had only an equitable right to have the money, and could not have maintained an action againft the acceptor; and the indorfement by Price to Evans being for value received, Price had received the very money to which Calvert had an equitable title; but the fum demanded by Evans was not that fum, but another due to him for value given, in which Calvert was not concerned; and therefore the money in demand was not extendible in the hands of the defendant; and his plea of courfe was bad, and the plaintiff intitled to recover.

Carth. 403.

AN indorfement to the order of a perfon, is of the fame force as an indorfement to that perfon or his order, and he may maintain an action on fuch indorfement in his own name; for among tradefmen this form is common, though it be intended

to

to be made payable to the perfon whofe order is mentioned.

But an indorfement by which *part* only of the Carth.466. money is ordered to be paid, is not valid to charge the drawer or acceptor; becaufe by fuch indorfement he would be liable on one contract to as many actions as the payee or indorfor fhould think fit.

C H A P. VII.

Engagement of the feveral Parties.

By the very act of drawing a bill, a man comes under an implied engagement to the payee and to every fubfequent holder fairly intitled to the poffeffion, that the perfon on whom he draws is capable of binding himfelf by his acceptance; that he is to be found at the place of which he is defcribed to be, if that defcription be mentioned in the bill; that if the bill be duly prefented to him, he will accept it in writing on the bill itfelf according to its tenor; and that he will pay it when it becomes due, if prefented in proper time for that purpofe.

In default of any of thefe particulars, the drawer is liable to an action at the fuit of any of the parties before

before-mentioned, on due diligence being exercifed on their parts, not only for the payment of the original fum mentioned in the bill, but alfo in fome cafes for damages, intereft and cofts: and he is equally anfwerable whether the bill was drawn on his own account, or on that of a third perfon; for the holder of the bill is not to be affected by the circumftances that may exift between the drawer and another: the perfonal credit of the drawer being pledged for the due honour of the bill.

Beawes 469.

IF a man write his name on a blank piece of paper, and deliver it to another, with authority to draw on it a Bill of Exchange to any amount, at any diftance of time, he renders himfelf liable to be called upon as the drawer of any bill fo formed by the perfon to whom he has given the authority.

Bl. Term Rep. C. B. 313.

IF the drawee do not accept, and the holder take the fteps requifite on his part to charge the drawer, it is faid the latter is bound to anfwer the money and damages, or give fufficient fecurity to anfwer them within double the time the firft bill had to run.

G. L. E. 118. 119. cites Mol. 81.

By the manner in which this alternative is ex-preffed, it would feem that the drawer is not under an abfolute obligation to make immediate fatisfaction, and that the other party muft be contented with the latter part of it, at the pleafure of the drawer: fuch may be the law and cuftom in other countries, but it is certainly not fo here; for it has often been determined, that if acceptance be refufed and the bill returned, this is only notice to the

Vid. Mar. 29.

Mitford v. Mayor, Doug. 55.

the drawer of the refufal of the drawee; but that
the period when the debt of the former is to be
confidered as contracted, is the moment he draws
the bill, and an action may be immediately commenced againft him, though the regular time of
payment, according to the tenor of the bill, be
not arrived. For the drawee not having given
credit, which was the ground of the contract, what
the drawer had undertaken has not been performed.

On this principle it has been held, that if a man
draw a bill, and commit an act of bankruptcy, and
afterwards the bill be returned for non-acceptance;
the debt is contracted before the act of bankruptcy,
and may be proved under the commiffion, and
therefore a certificate obtained on that commiffion
will be a bar to an action on the bill, which could
not have been the cafe if the notice of non-acceptance had been the period when the debt was contracted.

Macarty v.
Barrow, 2
Str. 949,
cited 3
Wilf. 16,
17.

When a Bill of Exchange is indorfed by the
perfon to whom it was made payable, as between
the indorfor and indorfee, it is a new Bill of Exchange; as it is alfo between every fubfequent indorfor and indorfee; the indorfor, therefore, with
refpect to all the parties fubfequent to him, ftands
in place of the drawer, being a collateral fecurity
for the acceptance and payment of the bill by the
drawee: his indorfement impofes on him the fame
engagement that the drawing of the bill does on
the drawee; and the period when that engagement
attaches is the time of the indorfement. Thus
whatever

1 Salk.133.
2 Show.
441, 494. 2
Bur. 674.

whatever doubts there may be as to the propriety of permitting a holder of a bill, made to a fictitious payee, to recover from the drawer or acceptor, yet no question on that subject can arise between a real indorsor and a subsequent indorsee.

3 Brown
Rep.Chan.
238.
ex parte
Clarke.

NOTHING will discharge the indorsor from his engagement but the absolute payment of the money; not even a judgment recovered against the drawer, or any previous indorsor, as appears from the following case.

Claxton v.
Smith. 3
Mod. 86.
2 Show.
441, 494.
Skinner
255.

THE plaintiff, as last indorsee of a Bill of Exchange, brought an action against the last indorsor, who pleaded that the plaintiff had sued and recovered against the original drawer, and that the judgment was still in force; to this the plaintiff demurred. In favour of the defendant it was argued, that though the plaintiff might originally bring his action against either the drawer or any of the indorsors, yet, having made his election, he should not therefore be permitted to resort to the others, for that, it was said, would deprive some of them of their remedies, and election was to choose either one or the other, and not every one successively: and this case was compared to that of a trespass done by several, where the party injured, having brought his action against one, and recovered judgment, he cannot afterwards recover damages against any of the others, because the action is founded on uncertain damages, which being ascertained by the first action, cannot be brought in question again.

FOR

For the plaintiff it was argued, that as no exception was taken to the declaration, the whole question was confined to the validity of the plea. No plea can be a good bar to an action which is not in reason a good anfwer to the matter charged in the declaration, nor an evasion of it: the fact in this plea is no anfwer to the charge: the fact alleged is, that a bill was drawn and directed to be paid to the defendant; that he by indorfement ordered the contents to be paid to the plaintiff: the cuftom of merchants is, that he who indorfes or fubfcribes a Bill of Exchange, and by fuch indorfement or fubfcription orders the acceptor to pay the contents to another, becomes chargeable to pay that money himfelf, in cafe the indorfee or payee do not otherwife receive it: it is here alleged that the money is not paid, and it muft be agreed that fuch an allegation is neceffary in every declaration of this kind, and had it been omitted the defendant might have demurred. Every indorfor is chargeable, becaufe he is fuppofed to have received the value at the time of the indorfement: the law implies that, if the indorfee had then afked the indorfor, what if this bill be not paid by the drawee? the anfwer would have been, the drawer is a good man: but what if the drawer fhould fail? then I will pay you; this is as ftrongly implied as if it had been written in exprefs terms: the contract of the indorfor is diftinct from that of the drawer, by implication of law and the cuftom of merchants: he is as a collateral fecurity, that, if the acceptor or

I   the

the drawer do not pay the money, he will: the greater the number of indorfors, the better is the bill efteemed, if before the day of payment, becaufe every name is an additional fecurity, and the indorfee as frequently receives it on the credit of the indorfor, as on that of the drawer or acceptor.

As it is neceffary for the plaintiff to allege the non-payment of the money, in order to charge the defendant; fo to difcharge himfelf, the latter muft fhew that it has been paid; for the nature of his undertaking is fuch, that if the acceptor do not pay it at the day, or afterwards fatisfaction be made by fomebody, he will fee it paid: but what is the defence fet up here? it amounts to no more than this; you have fued the drawer, and recovered a judgment againft him, and he has not paid you, therefore *I* will not pay you; the drawer was bound to pay you as well as *I*, if the acceptor did not, therefore as he has not paid you, fo neither will *I:* every indorfement being a new bill, has two effects; it transfers to the indorfee the indorfor's right of action againft the drawer and acceptor; and it creates an obligation on the indorfor, that the indorfee fhall be fatisfied: can a recovery then againft the drawer, without fatisfaction, difcharge that engagement?

This cafe differs in two very material points from the cafe of trefpafs: in trefpafs the action may be brought jointly againft all the trefpaffers; but here the undertakings of the drawer and indorfor are diftinct, and a joint action cannot be brought

brought againſt them both: again, trover and treſ-
paſs are founded on a wrong, and the damages are
uncertain; and when they are reduced to a certainty
by the verdict and judgment, they are changed
into another nature from an action for a wrong to
an action for a right, and the plaintiff cannot reſort
back to any of the other parties to demand the
uncertainty again: but this is an action founded on
a right, and the recovery againſt one does not alter
the nature of the claim againſt the other: the damages are certain, and the contract ſeveral; and
there is an exact reſemblance between this caſe and
that of two obligors in a bond: there judgment
againſt one is not pleadable to an action againſt
the other; nothing leſs than ſatisfaction will diſcharge the debt; becauſe the undertaking is ſeveral,
each being bound for the payment.

THE ſame reaſon holds in this caſe; by the plaintiff's judgment againſt the drawer, the defendant's
promiſe or contract is not changed, but his undertaking to ſee the debt paid ſtill continues.

As to his having made his election, that doctrine
does not apply here; this is not like the caſe of a
man having two remedies to enforce the performance of one contract, as in the caſe of rent, where
the landlord has two remedies, an action and diſtreſs,
and after he has choſen to purſue one method he is
barred from the other: but here there are not different remedies on the ſame contract, but the ſame
remedy on ſeveral diſtinct contracts; for the drawer,
acceptor, and indorſor, are all chargeable on their

ſeveral

several contracts: would this plea be good in the mouth of the acceptor? it cannot be pretended that it would, for his contract is of quite a different nature from that of the drawer; and that of the indorsor is as distinct as that.

THE great objection is, that we have inverted the course of proceeding, and deprived some of the parties of their remedies, if we should be admitted to resort back to the indorsor; but it is conceived the case is otherwise; for the judgment against the drawer will not be pleadable against the defendant, if he sue him after he has paid us; we have rather pursued the right method in suing the first obligor, the drawer, and not finding satisfaction from him we resort to the defendant.

NOTWITHSTANDING these arguments in favour of the plaintiff, judgment was given for the defendant; but it was afterwards reversed in the Exchequer chamber.

NEITHER is the engagement of an indorsor discharged by an ineffectual *execution* against the drawer or any prior or subsequent indorsor.

Hayling v. Mulhall, 2 Bl. Rep. 1232. A BILL was indorsed by Sheridan, and afterwards by one Boon, and came into the hands of Hayling, who sued Boon, and took him in execution, and afterwards let him out on a letter of licence without paying the debt. He then sued Sheridan, and held him to bail: Sheridan not paying the bill, Hayling brought a third action against Mulhall, one of the bail, who insisted that the debt was satisfied by the imprisonment of Boon. But it was observed by the

the court, that each indorfor is independent of the
reft, and that the bill-holder had a right to fue all
the indorfors till the bill was fatisfied : the law indeed fo highly regards the liberty of the fubject,
that the taking of his body in execution is, with refpect to him, a full fatisfaction of the debt. But it
only operates as a difcharge to the identical perfon fo
imprifoned ; it does not difcharge even his goods
after his death, fince the ftatute of James the firft.
The remedy ftill remains, after the death or difcharge, againft every other indorfor.

On a Promiffory Note, the engagement of the
payee and other indorfors is fimilar to that of the
drawer, payee, and indorfors of a Bill of Exchange,
as far as that engagement can apply, which is for
payment only ; the acceptance being already made
by the bare iffuing of the note.

The engagement of the drawer and indorfors is
however ftill but conditional : in order to intitle
himfelf to call upon them in confequence of it, the
holder undertakes to perform certain requifites on
his part, a failure in which precludes him from his
remedy againft them.

Where the payment of a bill is limited at a certain time after fight, it is evident the holder muft
prefent it for acceptance, otherwife the time of
payment would never come : it does not appear,
however, that any precife time, within which this
prefentment muft be made, has in any cafe been
afcertained : but it muft be done as foon as, under
all the circumftances of the cafe, that can con-

I 3 veniently

veniently be done; and all that has been said on
the presentment of Bills and Notes payable on demand, seems exactly to apply here, that which
might be construed as unnecessary delay in the one
case, having evidently the same tendency to produce inconvenience or loss to the preceding parties
in the other.

Vid. Mar. 12.

WHETHER the holder of a bill, payable at a certain time after the date, be bound to present for
acceptance immediately on the receipt of it, or
whether he may wait till it become due, and then
present it for payment, is a question which seems

Vid. 5 Bur. 2671. 1 Term Rep. 713.

never to have had a direct judicial determination:
in practice however it frequently happens that a
bill is negociated and transferred through many
hands without acceptance, and not presented to
the drawee till the time of payment, and no objection ever made on that account.

Mar. 12,13. Beawes, 454.

WHERE indeed a bill is remitted to a factor or
agent, to procure acceptance, for the benefit of his
principal, it is the duty of the factor to use all diligence to have it accepted, and to give advice to
his principal of the event, that he may take the
proper steps in case of non-acceptance; and the
factor may be liable to make good any loss to his
principal arising from his negligence: but this
does not affect the bill itself, nor the right of the
principal on it.

Blefard and Hirst, 5 Bur. 2670. Goodall v. Dolley, 1 Term Rep. 712.

IF, however, the holder in fact present the bill
for acceptance, and that be refused, he is bound to
give regular notice to all the preceding parties to
whom

whom he intends to refort for non-payment; to the drawer, that he may know how to regulate his conduct with refpect to the drawee, and make other provifion for the payment of the bill; and to the indorfors, that they may feverally have their remedy in time againft the parties on whom they have a right to call: and if, on account of his delay, any lofs accrue by the failure of any of the preceding parties, *he* muft bear the lofs.

THUS, if in the mean time the drawer fail, the holder cannot call on the payee indorfor, becaufe *he* can have no remedy againft the drawer. Blefard v. Hirft, 5 Bur. 2670.

So, alfo, if the drawee fail, the holder cannot recover againft either the drawer or indorfor, becaufe, if he could, a lofs muft fall on one of them, as the drawer can have no remedy againft the drawee. Goodall v. Dolley, 1 Term Rep. 712.

NOR will it make any difference, though the indorfor, from an ignorance of the law, thinking himfelf bound to make good the money, promife afterwards to take up the bill at fome future time. 5Bur.2670.

MUCH lefs can the indorfor be bound by a propofal to difcharge the bill by inftalments, made after the return of the bill for non-payment, under an ignorance of acceptance being refufed; more efpecially if that propofal be rejected by the indorfee. 1 Term Rep. 712.

IF an acceptance varying from the tenor of the bill be offered by the drawee, the holder acquiefcing muft fend the fame notice to the preceding parties, as if acceptance were refufed, otherwife he Mar. 17.

I 4   cannot

cannot have recourse to them; for to admit of such
acceptance without notice is to give credit to the
acceptor.

It is also the duty of the holder of a bill, whether
accepted or not, to present it for payment within a
limited time; for otherwise the law will imply that
payment has been had, and it would be prejudicial
to commerce if a bill might rise up to charge the
drawer at any distance of time, when all accounts
might be adjusted between him and the drawee.

Allen v.
Dockwra, 1
Salk. 127.
Darrack v.
Savage, 1
Show. 155.

But so little was it understood at the beginning of
this century within what time payment was to be
demanded, that cases are reported of actions brought
against the drawer several years after the bills were
due, and without demand from the drawee.   There
is also a difference in the terms in which the time
for presentment is prescribed by the judges: in one

Hill v.
Lewis, at
N. P. 1
Salk.
132, 133.

case it is said, that with respect to foreign bills the
drawee has three days to pay them, and no demand
needs be made till the *expiration* of the three days,
and if within that time he fail, the indorsor is
chargeable, and after the *expiration* of the three
days the indorsee may take the steps necessary to
intitle him to his remedy against the preceding

Taffel v.
Lewis, 1
Ld. Rzym.
743.
Coleman v.
Sayer, 2
Str. 829.
Vid.
Beawes,
461.

parties: but in another place it is laid down that
the time of payment is the last of the three days,
and on that the money must be demanded; and if
the last be Sunday or a great holiday, the demand
must be made on the second.   The last is the rule
adopted now.   But it has been made a question,
whether the demand may be made at any time on
                                                    the

the laſt of the days of grace; or, whether the holder
be bound to wait till the laſt moment of the day?
On one ſide it has been ſaid,* That, in analogy to
the rule with reſpect to the time when rent is payable, the acceptor had till the laſt moment of the
day: but, on the other ſide, it was well anſwered,†
That the rule, as to the time of paying rent, or
that adopted in other ſimilar caſes, could not apply
to this; that the undertaking of the acceptor was,
to pay the bill *on demand, on any part of the third day
of grace;* that this rule was now ſo well eſtabliſhed,
that it would be extremely dangerous to depart from
it.   That with regard to foreign bills, all the books
agreed that the proteſt muſt be made *on* the laſt day
of grace, which ſuppoſed a default in payment, as
a proteſt could not exiſt till default was made; but
if the party had till the laſt moment of the day to
pay the bill, the proteſt could not be made on that
day.   The uſage, therefore, was eſtabliſhed, that
Bills of Exchange are payable at any time on the
laſt day of grace on demand, provided that demand
be made within reaſonable hours.

    In practice the three days of grace have uſually
been allowed on Promiſſory Notes; but it was
not till very lately that the propriety of this practice
was eſtabliſhed by a judicial determination.   The
firſt notice we find taken of this point is in a
ſhort note of a caſe, in which it is ſaid to have been

---

    * By Lord Kenyon, in the caſe of Leftley v. Mills, 4 Term
Rep. 173.
    † By Buller J. id. 174.

determined,

May v.
Cooper,
Fort. 376.

determined, that the three days were *not* to be allowed; and, from the examination of the record, it appears to have come before the court on demurrer.

Deflaux v.
Hood, at
Guildhall.
Bul. N. P.
274.
Ward v.
Honey-
wood,
Doug. 61,
63.

IN a subsequent case Mr. Justice Dennison is said to have ruled that they were not to be allowed, but that case is mentioned with a quere. In another, where the question was, whether the action was not commenced before the cause of action accrued, Mr. Justice Buller is reported to have said, that he doubted whether the allowance was to be made; but as it appeared that, independently of the three days, the action had been commenced too soon, the point was not generally considered. In a subsequent case, this point was incidentally mentioned. That was an action on the statute of usury, in which

Lloyd v.
Skutt, M.
20 G. III.
Doug. 63,
in the
notes.

the plaintiff declared, on a contract, to forbear for four calendar months and three days. The evidence was a Promissory Note payable at four months from the date, and it was objected for the defendant that this was a variance. But Lord Mansfield observing that in a computation of interest made by the defendant himself, and which was in evidence, the three days of grace were allowed, he thought this decisive against him, without determining the general question.

ON principle there seems little reason why the three days of grace should not be allowed. They were originally allowed on Bills of Exchange by custom established by the universal consent of merchants. The statute of Queen Anne, which was made to put Promissory Notes on the same footing

with

with Bills of Exchange, does not certainly in exprefs terms fay that, in this refpect, they fhall be
confidered in the fame light, for then there could
be no doubt; but it renders them negociable in the
fame manner, and gives the *fame* remedy to the
poffeffor : and it is fair to prefume it was intended,
that, as far as the nature of them admitted a comparifon with Bills of Exchange, they fhould have
the fame incidents. The general practice ever
fince the ftatute has been to make the allowance;
every man who makes a Promiffory Note does it
under the conviction that he is not to be called
upon for payment till the third day, or, if that be a
Sunday or a great holiday, till the fecond: he who
takes the note, and every other poffeffor, refpectively, purchafes it under the opinion that they have
no right to call on the drawer till that time.

In a cafe, in which the principal queftion was, Tindal r.
whether the indorfee of a Promiffory Note had Brown,
1 Term
given due notice to the indorfor of its having been Rep. 167.
difhonoured by the maker, the courfe of argument
proceeded on the fuppofition that the three days
grace were allowable; that cafe was argued three
feveral times in the Court of King's Bench, and
afterwards in the Exchequer Chamber: but the
prefent queftion was not even raifed, and it was
taken for granted in all the different ftages of that
caufe, that the negligence of the holder did not
commence until the expiration of the three days
grace; for if that had not been admitted on both
fides,

fides, no queſtion at all could have ariſen, as, if they were not to be allowed, there would indiſputably have been negligence in the holder.

Brown v.
Harraden,
4 Term
Rep. 148.

IN a late caſe, in which this point has been finally ſettled in favour of the allowance of the three days, the declaration ſtated a note drawn by one W. Gurman, on the 15th of September, 1789, for 20l. payable to the defendant, or order, on the 2d of November; it then deduced a title to the plaintiff, and averred a refuſal to pay, by the defendant, on the 2d of November. The defendant pleaded a tender on the 5th of November. The plaintiff replied, that he ſued out a bill of Middleſex, on the 4th of November, and that the defendant did not at any time, before that day, tender the 20l. The rejoinder was, that the bill of Middleſex was ſued out on the 4th of November, and that before that time the defendant was not, by force of the ſtatute, liable to pay. The ſurrejoinder, that he did become liable, by force of the ſtatute, before the ſuing out of the bill of Middleſex; to this there was a demurrer; and the queſtion was, whether the defendant was not intitled to the three days of grace?

May v.
Cooper,
For. 376,
vid. page
122.

IN favour of the plaintiff were cited the caſe above mentioned, which had directly decided the point, and a great many others, which ſeemed to favour the ſame opinion; but to theſe one ſhort anſwer was given, that they were decided at a time when the ſubject was not well underſtood, and were therefore

therefore no authority; and judgement was given in favour of the defendant, on reafons fimilar to thofe above fuggefted. It was alfo obferved, that it had been uniformly the cuftom of the Bank of England, the bankers, and the principal merchants in the city, to make allowance for the three days in difcounting thefe notes; and that if they were not to be allowed, that practice muft be illegal, and they muft all have incurred the penalties of ufury. It was further obferved, that numberlefs queftions would arife on notes, which had been paid by indorfors, in default of payment by the makers, on the ground that the holders had not ufed due diligence.

A PRESENTMENT either for payment or acceptance muft be made at feafonable hours: and feafonable hours are the common hours of bufinefs in the place were the party lives to whom the prefentment is to be made.

IF acceptance or payment be refufed, or the drawee of the bill or maker of the note has become infolvent, or has abfconded, the holder muft give notice to the preceding parties; and in that notice it is not enough to fay that the drawee or maker refufes, is infolvent, or has abfconded; but it muft be added, that the holder does not intend to give him credit. The purpofe of giving notice is not merely that the indorfor fhould know that default has been made, for he is chargeable only in a fecondary degree; but to render him liable, it muft

be

As to Bills, vid. 1 Str. 441, 515. Dagglifh v. Weatherby 2 Bl. Rep. 747. As to Notes, vid. 1 Str. 649. 2 Str. 1087, Tindal v. Brown, 1. Term Rep. 170.

be fhewn that the holder looked to him for payment, and gave him notice that he did fo. A cafe
might eafily be imagined, where the indorfor
might have notice from the holder, and yet would
not be liable; as if that notice contained circumftances which fhewed that the indorfee had given
time and credit to the acceptor or maker.

It is therefore neceffary that notice fhould come
from the indorfee himfelf: it is not fufficient that
the indorfor fhould be informed by fome third perfon, as by the drawee or maker, that he does not
choofe to accept, or cannot pay.

What fhould be confidered as a reafonable time,
within which notice fhould be given either of non-
acceptance or non-payment, has been fubject to
much doubt and uncertainty: it was once held that
a fortnight was a reafonable time, but that is now
much narrowed.

M.21C.II.
per Twif-
den, 1
Mod. 27.

With refpect to acceptance, it is ufual to leave
a bill for that purpofe with the drawee till the next
day, and that is not confidered as giving him
time; it being underftood to be the ufual practice:
but if, on being called on the next day, he delay
or refufe to accept according to the tenor of the
bill, the rule now eftablifhed, where the parties, to
whom notice is to be given, refide at a different
place from the holder and drawee, is, that notice
muft be fent by the next poft. Under the fame
circumftances, the fame rule obtains in the cafe of
non-payment.

Mar. 16.

1 Term
Rep. 169.

So,

So, alfo, in cafe the drawee or maker has abfconded, or cannot be found, notice of thefe circumftances, either in cafe of non-acceptance or non-payment, muft be fent by the firft poft.

But the great difficulty has been to eftablifh any general rule, where the party intitled to notice refides in the fame place, or at a place at a fmall diftance from that in which the holder lives. On this point, as well as on the queftion of what fhall be confidered as a reafonable time for making the *demand* of payment, it has been an objeft of no little controverfy, whether it was the province of the jury or of the judge to decide: till lately, it feems the jury had been permitted to determine on the particular circumftances of each individual cafe what time was reafonably to be allowed, either for making demand or giving notice.

Vid. the cafes at the end of Chap. III. and Doug. 515, 681.

But it having been found that this was productive of endlefs uncertainty and inconvenience, the court on feveral occafions have laid it down as a principle, that what fhall be confidered as a reafonable time in either cafe is a queftion of law: juries have however ftruggled fo hard to maintain their privilege in this refpeft, that in two cafes they have narrowed the time for demand, contrary to the opinion of the court; and on a fecond trial being granted, have in both cafes adhered to their opinion, contrary to the direction of the judge. In one of them, however, an application being made for a third trial, the court would have granted it, had not the plaintiff precluded himfelf by proving his

Metcalf v. Hall, B.R. T. 22 G. III. cited Doug. 515. & 1 Term Rep. 171. Appleton v. Sweetapple. B.R. M. 23 G. III. cited Doug. 515.

his debt under a commiffion of bankrupt which had iffued againft the drawees of the bill between the time of the verdict and the application.

1 Term
Rep. 169.
Tindal v.
Brown, 1
Term Rep.
167.

IN a third cafe, where the ftruggle by the jury was to give a longer time for notice than was neceffary, the court adhered to their principle, and granted no lefs than three trials.

THIS cafe was an action by the indorfees of a Promiffory Note againft the indorfor. The circumftances were thefe: on the 21ft of Auguft, 1784, the note in queftion was made by one Donaldfon for 35l. payable fix weeks after date; on the fifth of October, 1784, the day on which the note became due, allowing for the three days of grace, Howell, the plaintiff's clerk, called at Donaldfon's at ten in the morning, and, not finding him at home, he left word that the note was due, and defired Donaldfon would fend for it at his mafter's, where it lay, and take it up; on the next day, the fixth of October, he called again at Donaldfon's, who told him he would take it up that day within the banking hours, which were from nine to four o'clock; the note not being taken up that day, he called again on Donaldfon on the feventh, and not finding him at home, he was fent to the defendant to tender the note, who refufed to pay it, faying, the plaintiffs had made it their own. Donaldfon proved at the trial, that immediately on his parting with Howell on the fixth, he went to the defendant's houfe, and, not finding him at home, left a meffage with his wife that the note was due; that

that he Donaldſon, could not pay it, but that if the
defendant would take it up, he would make it good
to him.

Iᴛ appeared that all the parties lived at Briſtol,
within twenty minutes walk of each other.

· Oɴ the firſt trial the jury gave a verdict for the
plaintiffs. On an application for a new trial, the
court held that the bill had been diſhonoured on
the fifth, and that notice to the indorſor ſhould
have been given the ſame day; that by not giving
it then, the holder had given credit to the maker
and diſcharged the indorſor, and therefore they
granted a new trial, on the ground that the jury
had taken upon them to decide on a matter of law :
on the ſecond trial the jury gave a ſimilar verdict,
and a third trial was granted. It ſeems therefore
fully eſtabliſhed, that what ſhall be reaſonable time
is a queſtion of law : but it ſeems almoſt impoſſible
to fix any other rule than this, that demand muſt be
made, and notice given, as ſoon as, under all the
circumſtances, it is poſſible ſo to do.

Tʜᴇ reaſon why the law requires notice is, that
it is preſumed that the bill is drawn on account of
the drawee's having effects of the drawer in his
hands; and that if the latter has notice that the bill
is not accepted, or not paid, he may withdraw them
immediately. But if he have no effects in the
other's hands, then he cannot be injured for want
of notice, and if it be proved on the part of the
plaintiff, that, from the time the bill was drawn,
till the time it became due, the drawee never had

1 Term
Rep. 410.

K   any

any effects of the drawer in his hands, notice to the latter is not necessary in order to charge him, for he must know whether he had effects in the hands of the drawee or not: and if he had none, he had no right to draw upon him, and to expect payment from him ; nor can he be injured by the non-payment of the bill, or the want of notice, that it has been dishonoured.

Bickerdike
v. Bollman
1 Term
Rep. 405.
A QUESTION arising on the validity of a commission of bankrupt on account of the insufficiency of the debt due to the petitioning creditor, the facts appeared to be these: the bankrupt being indebted to the petitioning creditors in the sum of 115l. 3s. 8d. on the 15th of September, 1784, drew a bill for 20l. on the defendant, " who, till the time of the bankruptcy and of the bill becoming due, was a creditor of the bankrupt," payable to the petitioning creditors, two months after date, and paid it to them on account of part of their debt : the bill was presented for payment on the 18th of November following, and dishonoured.   No notice however was ever given by the petitioning creditors to the bankrupt, or left at his house; a commission issued against the drawer on the 20th of November, on which he was declared a bankrupt in the afternoon of the 24th; that commission was afterwards superseded, and another commission was issued on the petition of the parties, on the amount of whose debt the present question arose.   If the petitioning creditors, by not giving notice to the bankrupt of his bill being dishonoured, had made the bill their own

own, their debt was reduced within 100l. and then the commiſſion could not be ſupported ; but if notice was not neceſſary, the bill was not payment ; their debt remained as it originally was, and the commiſſion was valid.   On the principles before ſtated, the court held that notice in this caſe was not neceſſary, and therefore the commiſſion was good.

Yet though it appear that the drawer had no effects in the hands of the drawee, no action can be maintained againſt the *indorſor* if no notice was given him of the bill being diſhonoured ; for though the drawer may have received no injury, the indorſor, who muſt be preſumed to have paid a valuable conſideration for the bill, probably has.

1 Term Rep. 714.

Though in the caſe where the drawer has effects in the hands of the drawee, the want of notice cannot be waved by a ſubſequent promiſe by him to diſcharge the bill ; yet where he had no effects, it may ; though it appear that in fact he ſuſtained an injury for want of ſuch notice : ſuch a ſubſequent promiſe is an acknowledgment that he had no right to draw on the drawee, and if he has in fact ſuſtained damage, it is his own fault.

Rogers v. Stephens, 2 Term Rep. 713.

But where damage in ſuch a caſe has been ſuſtained, and no ſubſequent promiſe appears, it may be very doubtful whether want of notice can be waved.

Stephens, reſiding at Newfoundland, drew a bill in favour of Rogers on Birbeck and Blake in London, value received for the uſe of William Calvert at Liverpool ; Rogers preſented the bill for acceptance,

Rogers v. Stephens, 2 Term Rep. 714.

K 2   tance,

tance, which was refused, and afterwards for payment, which was also refused; but he sent no
notice to the drawer of the refusal to accept: he
afterwards brought an action against Stephens as
the drawer, at the trial of which, the defence set
up was the want of notice of non-acceptance, which
was rebutted by shewing that the drawee never had
any effects of the drawer in his hands, and by a
subsequent promise appearing of the drawer to the
plaintiff's agent; on which account a verdict, by
Lord Ken- the direction of the judge, was given for the
yon. plaintiff.

On an application for a new trial, the defendant's
counsel stated, that, in addition to the above circumstances, they had evidence to shew that the
defendant really had been injured for want of notice; that they thought such evidence had been
offered and refused, and that his lordship had
given his opinion on an admission of its truth: but
his lordship said he had no note or recollection of
any evidence of that kind having been tendered.
The circumstances were these: the defendant and
Calvert had had dealings together previous to the
departure of the former for Newfoundland, and he
had a right to draw on Calvert at the time when
the bill was drawn, having advanced money on his
account to the amount of the bill. Under these
circumstances Calvert had directed the defendant
to draw on Birbeck and Blake as his agents, instead
of drawing on him. The defendant accordingly
drew the bill, on a supposition that Calvert really
had

had effects in their hands to anfwer it. It turned out however that he had none, but that was not known to the defendant; who, on his return to England, relying on his bill having been duly honoured as he had had no notice to the contrary, had fettled his accounts with Calvert, and had delivered up to him goods and effects which he held in his hands of greater value than the amount of the bill; and that Calvert had fince become infolvent.

REASONING on thefe facts, the counfel for the defendant contended that the principle, on which it had been held that no notice was neceffary to be given to the drawer of the non-acceptance of his bill when he had no effects in the hands of the drawee, was decifive that it ought to have been given in the prefent cafe. Befide the prefumption of fraud againft a man who draws a bill on another who, he knows, has no effects to anfwer it, one of the principal grounds affigned by the court for their opinion was, that no injury could arife to the drawer for want of notice. That reafon therefore could not apply, where the drawer acted fairly and had actually fuftained an injury for want of notice. That cafe too is an exception to the general rule; nothing is better eftablifhed than that the holder of a Bill of Exchange, of which acceptance is refufed, is in general bound to give notice of fuch refufal to the drawer; if from any collateral circumftances he take upon himfelf to withhold it, he acts at his peril. If it appear that the drawer could receive no injury from

K 3   the

the want of it, he is indemnified by the event; but still he is guilty of neglect, the consequences of which to him are only avoided by that circumstance. The very form of this bill was sufficient notice to the holder that it was to be paid out of Calvert's effects; for it is said to be for his use. So that there was more reason than usual to imagine that want of notice might be prejudicial to the defendant. Considering the question even in a general point of view, it would be highly detrimental to commerce, if it were to be laid down as a general rule without exception, that the objection arising from want of notice in these cases might be done away by shewing that the drawee had no effects of the drawer in his hands at the time. Nothing is more common than for merchants abroad, who are about to ship goods to their consignees or factors in England, to draw Bills of Exchange on them, before the goods come into their hands; in which cases, the most material injury might arise to those traders from want of notice that the bills had not been accepted, since they might be deprived by that means of the opportunity of stopping their goods in their way.

To this it was answered, that admitting the full force of the evidence before stated, it could not vary this case; for that as between these parties, it was not necessary for the holder of a bill to look to any other persons than those who are liable on the face of the bill itself. He cannot enter into the particular grounds which induce the drawer to

draw

draw the bill, or the drawee to refufe his acceptance; it would lead to endlefs uncertainty if he
were bound to do fo. If one man choofe to draw
a bill, having no funds of his own in the hands of
the drawee, but relying on the cafualty of the ftock
of another who has mifled him, he has his remedy
againft that perfon, but that makes no alteration
in the law relative to the holder of fuch a bill. The
rule of law is clear, and operates with a double af-
pect in this cafe; for fuppofing the plaintiff was
bound to take notice that this was in reality the
bill of Calvert, and not of the defendant Stephens,
which it purports to be, ftill the rule would apply
againft the latter, for it appears that Calvert himfelf had no effects in the hands of the drawees.

So much of this reafoning, however, as applies
to the particular cafe, appears fallacious, for the
real queftion was not whether Calvert himfelf could
have drawn on the prefent drawees, but whether
the defendant, having a clear right to draw on Calvert, and being directed by him to draw on his
agents, not knowing that they had no effects of Calvert's, was entitled to notice from the holder of his
bill being difhonoured.

But on this occafion, the court did not think
proper to decide on the general queftion; firft, becaufe the circumftances here mentioned did not
appear to have been offered in evidence at the trial;
and fecondly, becaufe if they had, whatever might
have been the effect of them in favour of the defendant, he had precluded himfelf from taking ad-

K 4   vantage

vantage of it, by his subsequent promise to discharge the bill.

In the manner in which notice either of non-acceptance or non-payment is given, there is a remarkable difference between inland and foreign
bills: in the former, no particular form of words
is necessary to intitle the holder to recover against
the drawer or indorsors, the amount of the bill on
failure of the drawee or acceptor; it is sufficient if
it appear that the holder means to give no credit
to the latter, but to hold the former to their re-
sponsibility.

But in foreign bills other formalities are required: if the person to whom the bill is addressed, on
presentment, will not accept it, the holder is to
carry it to a person vested with a public character,
who is to go to the drawee and demand acceptance
in the same manner as before, and if he then refuse,
the officer is there to make a minute on the bill itself, consisting of his initials, the month, the day,
and the year, with his charges for minuting. He
must afterwards draw up a solemn declaration, that
the bill has been presented for acceptance, which
was refused, and that the holder intends to recover
all damages which he, or the deliverer of the money
to the drawer, or any other, may sustain on account
of the non-acceptance: the minute is in common
language termed the noting of the bill, the solemn
declaration the protest, and the person whose office
it is to do these acts a public notary: and to his
protestation all foreign courts give credit.

*1 Term
Rep. 170.*

*Mal. 264.
Mar. 16.*

In

IN making a proteſt, therefore, there are three things to be done ;—the noting, demanding, and drawing up the proteſt:—But the noting is unknown in the law, as diſtinguiſhed from the proteſt; it is merely a preliminary ſtep, and has grown into practice only in modern times. The party making the demand muſt have authority to receive the money, and in caſe that be refuſed, the drawing up of the proteſt is mere matter of form, the demand being the material part: The demand of payment of a *foreign* bill muſt be made by the notary public himſelf, and not by his clerk ; and even in the caſe of an *inland* bill, it is doubtful whether the demand, as the foundation of the proteſt made in conſequence of the ſtatute hereafter mentioned, can be made by the notary's clerk or by any other than the notary himſelf.

Leftley v. Mills, 4 Term Rep. 170.

THIS proteſt muſt be made within the regular hours of buſineſs, and in ſufficient time to have it ſent to the holder's correſpondent by the very next poſt after acceptance refuſed ; for if it be not ſent by that time, with a letter of advice, the holder will be conſtrued to have diſcharged the drawer and the other parties intitled to notice: and noting alone is not ſufficient; there muſt abſolutely be a proteſt to render the preceding parties liable.

Gooſtrey v. Mead, Bul. N. P. 271. 2 Term Rep. 713.

BUT in this caſe the holder is not to ſend the bill itſelf to his correſpondent; he muſt retain it, in order to demand payment of the drawee when it becomes due.

WHEN

Beawes,
460.

WHEN the bill becomes due, whether it was accepted or not, it is again to be prefented for payment within the days of grace, and if payment be refufed, it muft be prefented for non-payment, and the bill itfelf, together with the proteft, fent to the holder's correfpondent, unlefs he fhall be ordered by him to retain the bill, with a profpect of obtaining its difcharge from the acceptor.

Beawes,
461.

FOR no drawer or indorfor is bound to make reftitution on fight of the proteft alone; nor, where one of the fet has been accepted, on fight of the proteft and unaccepted bill, but he muft give fatisfactory fecurity to the remitter on his producing the proteft only, to make payment when that and the accepted bill fhall be prefented.

Mal. 265.

WHERE the drawee cannot be found at the place mentioned in the bill, or has abfconded, proteft is to be made for non-acceptance in the fame manner as if acceptance had been refufed on prefentment.

Mar. 17,
18.

So alfo, if the drawee offer an acceptance differing from the tenor of the bill, and the holder be inclined to admit it without giving up his claim on the other parties, he muft proteft it for that caufe; as if the drawee offer an acceptance for part, the holder may permit him to accept in that way; but he muft caufe it to be protefted for non-acceptance of the whole, and fend the proteft to his correfpondent, that he may endeavour to procure fecurity for the remaining fum. When the bill becomes due, the holder muft prefent it for payment

payment, and may receive the fum for which it was accepted, and write a receipt for fo much on the bill; but he muft proteft it for non-payment of the reft, and fend back the proteft with the bill.

Beside the proteft for non-acceptance, and non-payment, there may alfo be a proteft for better fe-curity; this is ufual, when a merchant, who has accepted a bill, happens to become infolvent, or is publicly reported to have failed in his credit, or abfents himfelf from 'Change before the bill he has accepted has become due, or when the holder has any reafon to fuppofe it will not be paid: in fuch cafes he may caufe a notary to demand better fecu-rity, and on that being refufed, make proteft for want of it; which proteft muft, as in other cafes, be fent away by the next poft, that the remitter or drawer may take the proper means to procure better fecurity.

Where the original bill is loft, and another can-not be had of the drawer, a proteft may be made on a copy, efpecially where the refufal of payment is not for want of the original bill, but merely for another caufe.

A. drew a firft and fecond Bill of Exchange, payable by himfelf in Dublin, to B. or order, for value received of him. B. after the bill was due, negociated it with the plaintiff. The plaintiff on the fame day indorfed it to D. living in Dublin, in thefe words, " Pay to D. value on my account." The firft of thefe bills was at the fame time fent away to D. and was loft on the way, and the drawer being

Mar. 27. 1 Lord Rayni.743.

Dehers v. Harriott, 1 Show. 164.

being gone to Ireland, no third bill could be had,
and left the fecond fhould mifcarry as well as the
firft, an exact copy of the fecond bill was fent to D.
and demand of payment being made, it was refufed,
becaufe the money had been attached in the hands
of the party who was to pay the bill; the proteft
was made on the copy, and at the trial the original
fecond bill, along with the proteft on the copy, was
produced and held good.

THE effect of proteft for non-acceptance or non-
payment is to charge the drawer or indorfors, not
only with the payment of the principal fum, but
with damages, intereft, and cofts; but where the
bill is accepted, it is fo far from difcharging the
acceptor, that it renders him liable to refund every
lofs fuftained by his non-payment. Here however
it muft be obferved, that the cofts mentioned to be
given by the proteft, are not cofts of fuit, but other
expences incurred: cofts of fuit, where the fuit may
be without proteft, are of courfe given.

BESIDE the intereft and cofts, the damages, incurred by non-acceptance or non-payment, confift
ufually of the exchange, re-exchange, provifion,
and poftage, together with the expences of proteft.
The exchange is reckoned according to the courfe
at fight, at that time and place where the proteft is
made, to the place where the payment fhould be
made by the drawer; but if payment be not made
there, then the fum is again increafed, by the addition of commiffion and poftage; and the courfe of
exchange is now reckoned on the whole fum, according

*Mar. 13,
14.*

*Beawes,
461.*

cording as it obtains at that time and place, on fight to the place where the bill is paid; and the acceptor muft pay the re-exchange and all charges, although the parcel was not effectually negociated and re-drawn, that is, re-exchange, provifion, and poftage muft be twice paid, &c. as provifion twice for the exchange and re-exchange; the charges being only for poftage and protefts, unlefs the acceptor, by delays and excufes, force the holder on fome neceffary charges to recover, which the acceptor is obliged to pay; but no extraordinary ones, fuch as travelling, will be allowed. And if the acceptor under the before mentioned circumftances refufe immediate payment to the returned bill, a legal intereft may be charged him, from the day the bill was due to the time of its difcharge; though he fhall not be obliged to make good any other lofs or damage which the poffeffor may pretend he has fuftained from want of punctual payment, by being fruftrated in his defigns of entering into fome beneficial engagement, or the lofs of a convenient opportunity of advantageoufly employing the fum detained. *Str. 649.*

Beawes, 461.

WHEREVER intereft is allowed, and a new action cannot be brought for it, which is the cafe on Bills of Exchange and Promiffory Notes, the intereft is to be calculated up to the time of figning final judgment. *2 Bur. 1086,1087.*

WHERE a bill indorfed over is not duly paid, the indorfee may charge the indorfor with intereft, exchange, and other incidental expences, beyond the *Auriol v. Thomas, 2 Term Rep. 52.*

the amount of 5 per cent. if such charges be reasonable, warranted by usage, and not made a colour for usury: thus the constant course has been with respect to bills returned, protested, from India, to allow 10s. per pagoda, which includes interest, exchange, and all other charges; and this notwithstanding the current price of exchange at which the bill was discounted, may have been greatly below 10s. as at 6s. 6d. and the indorsee will also be intitled to interest at 5 per cent. from a reasonable time after notice given to the indorsor of the bill having been returned unpaid.

The principal difference between foreign and inland Bills of Exchange, at common law, seems to have been this. A protest for non-acceptance or non-payment of a foreign bill was, as it still is, essentially necessary to charge the drawer on the default of the drawee; nothing, not even the principal sum, could, or can at this time, be recovered against him without a protest: no other form of notice having been admitted by the custom of merchants as sufficient. But inland bills having been introduced at a late period, in imitation of foreign ones, did not immediately adopt all their incidents: simple notice, within a reasonable time of the default of the drawee, was held sufficient to charge the drawer; but it does not appear that in any instance they were favoured with the solemnity of a protest: the disadvantage arising from thence was this, that notice entitled the holder to recover only the sum in the original bill, which in many

cases

cafes might be a very ferious difadvantage : to remedy this inconvenience in fome degree, it was
enacted " that after the twentieth of June, 1698, 9 & 10 W.
III. c. 17.
" all and every Bill or Bills of Exchange drawn in,
" or dated at and from, any trading city or town,
" or any other place in the kingdom of England,
" dominion of Wales, or town of Berwick upon
" Tweed, of the fum of 5l. fterling or upwards, on
" any perfon or perfons of, or in London, or any
" other trading city, town, or any other place, *in*
" *which faid Bill or Bills of Exchange fhall be ex-*
" *preffed the faid value to be received,* and is and
" fhall be drawn payable at a certain number of
" days, weeks, or months after *date* thereof, that
" from and after prefentation and acceptance of
" the faid Bill or Bills of Exchange, *which ac-*
" *ceptance fhall be by underwriting the fame under the*
" *party's hand fo accepting,* and *after* the *expiration*
" of three days after the faid bill or bills fhall be-
" come due, the party to whom the faid bill or
" bills are made payable, his fervant, agent or
" affigns, may and fhall caufe the faid bill or bills
" to be protefted by a notary public, and in default
" of fuch notary public, by any other fubftantial
" perfon of the city, town, or place, in the prefence
" of two or more credible witneffes, refufal or neg-
" lect being firft made of due payment of the
" fame : which proteft fhall be made and written
" under a fair written copy of the faid Bill of Ex-
" change, in the words or form following :

Know

Know all men, that I A. B. on the
day of ·   at the usual place of abode
of the said   have demanded payment of the bill, of which the above is a copy,
which the said   *   did not pay,
wherefore I the said   do hereby
protest the said bill.   Dated this·   day
of

" WHICH protest so made, shall within *fourteen*
" days after the making thereof, be sent; or *other-*
" *wise* due notice shall be given, to the party *from*
" *whom* the said bill or bills *were received*, ·who is,
" on producing such protest, to repay the said bill
" or bills, together with all interest and charges,
" from the day such bill or bills were protested ;
" for which protest shall be paid a sum not exceed-
" ing the sum of sixpence ; and in default or neg-
" lect of such protest made and sent, or due notice
" given within the days before limited, *the person*
" *so failing or neglecting thereof, is and shall be liable*
" *to all costs, damages, and interest, which do and shall*
" *accrue thereby.*"

Harris v.   IN an action against the drawer of an inland bill
Benton,
2 Str. 910.   after an acceptance, no interest will be allowed on
this statute, without a protest.

BUT this statute only giving the protest in cases
where the acceptance was by writing on the bill,
persons on whom bills were drawn, knowing that
ultimately the damages arising on the protest for
non-

non-payment, muſt fall on themſelves, refuſed to accept in that form, and would give only a verbal promiſe, which rendered the proviſions of the act perfectly nugatory: in order to remedy this inconvenience, it was enacted by a ſubſequent ſtatute, " that from and after the firſt of May, 1705, in " caſe, upon preſenting any ſuch Bill or Bills of " Exchange, the party or parties, on whom the " ſame ſhall be drawn, ſhall refuſe to accept the " ſame, by underwriting the ſame, as aforeſaid, the " party to whom the ſaid bill or bills are made " payable, his ſervant, agent, or aſſigns, may and " ſhall cauſe the ſaid bill or bills to be proteſted for " non-acceptance, as in caſe of foreign Bills of " Exchange, any thing in the former act, or any " other law to the contrary notwithſtanding: for " which proteſt there ſhall be paid two ſhillings, " and no more."

3 & 4 Ann,
c. 9.

" PROVIDED that the proteſt hereby required for " non-acceptance ſhall be made by ſuch perſons as " are appointed by the former act to proteſt inland " Bills of Exchange for non-payment."

s. 6.

" PROVIDED always, that no acceptance of any " ſuch inland Bill of Exchange ſhall be ſufficient to " charge any perſon *whatſoever*, unleſs the ſame be " underwritten or indorſed in writing thereupon: " and if ſuch bill be not accepted by ſuch under-" writing or indorſement in writing, no *drawer* of " any ſuch inland bill ſhall be liable to pay any " coſts, damages, or intereſt thereupon, unleſs ſuch " proteſt be made for non-acceptance thereof, and

s. 5.

L

" within

" within *fourteen* days after such protest, the same
" be sent, or otherwise notice thereof be given to
" the party from whom such bill *was received*, or
" left in writing at the place of his or her usual
" abode; and if such bill be accepted and not paid
" *before* the *expiration* of three days after the said
" bill shall become due and payable, then no *drawer*
" of such bill shall be compellable to pay any costs,
" damages, or interest thereupon, unless a protest be
" made and sent in manner and form above men-
" tioned: nevertheless, every drawer of such bill
" shall be liable to make payment of costs, damages,
" and interest upon such inland bill, *if any one protest*
" *be made of non-acceptance or non-payment thereof,*
" *and notice thereof be sent, given, or left, as aforesaid.*"

S. 6.   " PROVIDED, that no such protest shall be ne-
" cessary, either for non-acceptance or non-pay-
" ment, *unless the value be acknowledged and expressed*
" *in such bill to be received, and unless such bill be*
" *drawn for the payment of twenty pounds sterling or*
" *upwards.*"

S. 8.   " PROVIDED that nothing herein contained shall
" extend to discharge any remedy, that any person
" may have against the drawer, acceptor, or in-
" dorsor of such bill."

THESE acts are in many respects obscure, and
the comments on them in many of the early reporters equally so. It was soon discovered, that
from the general wording of both, and the provision in the eighth section of the latter, notwithstanding these statutes, the holder might still, by
                                                  giving

'6 Mod. 80,
81. 1 Salk.
131. 3 Salk.
69.
Brough v.
Perkins, 2
Ld. Raym.
992.

giving reafonable notice without proteft, recover
againft the acceptor, the drawer, or indorfor, the
amount of the original bill; and that a written ac- Vid. Page 70.
ceptance was not neceffary to charge the acceptor:
for that the word *damages* in thefe acts does not
mean the original fum, that being recoverable before, but the lofs accruing from the delay: and
that the claufe, which provides that no "acceptance Vid. Page 70, 71.
" not expreffed in writing on the bill fhould be
" fufficient to charge any perfon whatever," relates
only to the non-recovery of *thefe* damages without
a proteft for non-acceptance. So far is perfectly
intelligible. The fame thing cannot be faid of
what follows: " If the drawer for want of proteft
" or reafonable notice fuffer any damage, that fhall
" be borne by him to whom the bill is made, and
" if the damage amount to the whole fum men-
" tioned in the bill, the payee fhall not recover:
" the act feems only to *take* from the plaintiff his
" *intereft and damages*, where he has *not* made a
" proteft, or to give the *drawer* a remedy againft
" him by way of action for the cofts and damages."
This evidently is intended as an explanation of
that part of the firft ftatute which provides, that
" the perfon failing to proteft is and fhall be *liable*
" to all cofts, damages, and intereft, which fhall
" accrue thereby." But it is manifeft this provifion
could never be meant to *take* from a plaintiff that
to which he was *not before intitled*: neither can it be
imagined that it was intended to give an action to
the drawer on account of damages which he could

L 2   not

not suſtain, but by being made anſwerable for the loſs of another: to enable him to reſiſt the claim of that other, who had not entitled himſelf to recover, by neglecting to follow the directions of the act, was ſufficient to protect the drawer againſt all poſſible loſs. The clauſe is certainly inaccurate; the word *liable* is equivocal; but the meaning is maniſeſtly this, that the perſon neglecting to proteſt, ſhall not be entitled to call on the drawer for his extraordinary damages, intereſt, and coſts, but muſt bear them himſelf.

THE profeſſed intention of theſe acts was to put inland Bills of Exchange on the ſame footing with foreign ones; ſo far as relates to the recovery of damages, intereſt, and coſts, by means of the proteſt, they have done it; but there are ſeveral minute particulars in which, from an attentive peruſal of the acts, it will appear they ſtill differ.

Page 62. To the conſtitution of a Bill of Exchange, we have ſeen, it is not neceſſary that the words " value received" ſhould be inſerted, and the want of theſe in a foreign bill cannot deprive the holder of the benefit of a proteſt; but that benefit in caſe of non-payment is not given to inland bills which want theſe words; and therefore they cannot be proteſted for non-payment: and the ſecond act provides that " where theſe words are wanting, or " the value is leſs than twenty pounds, no proteſt " is *neceſſary* either for non-acceptance or non-" payment." What may be the true meaning and operation of this proviſion is far from being clear:

by

by the natural conftruction of the words, it might
be imagined the legiflature meant to give damages
on bills of thefe defcriptions, without impofing on
the holder the *neceffity* of protefting: but that fuppofition is not confiftent with the general purview
of the two acts, fo that the fafeft conftruction feems
to be, that inland bills without the words " value
received," or under twenty pounds, fhall continue
as at common law, and fhall not be *intitled* to the
privilege of a proteft either for non-acceptance or
non-payment.

In foreign bills, there is no diftinction between
thofe payable at fuch a time after *date*, and after
fight; but the ftatute confines the benefit of proteft
on inland ones to thofe payable after *date;* fo that
in *firictnefs* there can be no proteft on thofe payable
after fight: and this has been lately fo adjudged.

Leftley v.
Mills, 4
TermRep.
170.

In foreign bills, where the acceptance is in words
only, or in fome collateral writing, a proteft may
be made for non-payment, as well as if the acceptance had been in writing on the bill: but the
ftatute of William confines the proteft for non-
payment to thofe bills on which the acceptance is
written; and therefore, in order to have the benefit
of a proteft for non-payment, where the acceptance
is collateral, the holder muft proteft for non-acceptance; unlefs it be fuppofed that this claufe is
repealed, by that provifion in the ftatute of Queen
Anne, which fays, " neverthelefs, every drawer of
" fuch bill fhall be liable to make payment of cofts,
" damages, and intereft on fuch inland bill, *if any*

Vid. Mar.
17.

L 3

" one

" *one protest be made of non-acceptance or non-payment,*
" *and notice thereof be sent, given, or left as aforesaid:*"
which indeed seems to be the only construction
that can ascribe any meaning to the clause: for if
this be not the true construction, then this provision
can mean nothing more than that, where only acceptance is refused, but the money paid when due,
there a protest for non-acceptance alone is sufficient; and that where the bill is accepted, but
not duly paid, then a protest for non-payment is
sufficient; which would be to suppose that the legislature meant nothing at all.

If, indeed, this clause be not a repeal of the
clause in the former statute, the general practice of
merchants in the city of London is unwarranted;
for a protest is hardly ever made for non-acceptance of an inland bill; it is only noted for non-
acceptance, and if not paid when due, it is frequently protested for non-payment: however, notice must be given of the non-acceptance and
noting, otherwise, according to the cases before
cited, the holder takes the risk upon himself.

The preceding clauses of the sixth section of this
statute of Queen Anne creates indeed a difficulty in
supporting this construction of the latter clause; for
if this be a repeal of the clause in the statute of
King William, it is very difficult to say whether it
may be considered as a repeal of those also; and it
would be too much to say that the legislature has
made a provision in the former part of a single
section of an act of parliament, and in the latter
part

part repealed it: the only way I can fee of solving this difficulty is, to take the whole fection together, and to endeavour to give it one cumulative conftruction, confiruing the preceding claufes in the alternative, and then it may be confidered as running thus: "If fuch bill be not accepted by underwriting or indorfement, when prefented for acceptance, and, when prefented for payment, be not paid; then if it be not protefted either for nonacceptance or for non-payment, the drawer fhall not be liable for damages, intereft, and cofts."

IF this be the true conftruction of this claufe, there appears to be another difference ftill fubfifting between foreign and inland Bills of Exchange; for where acceptance and payment are both refufed on foreign bills, it feems neceffary that there fhould be a proteft for each; at leaft it is decided that in fuch a cafe, a proteft for non-payment only is not fufficient. Vid. ante page 137, 138.

ANOTHER difference between foreign and inland bills with refpect to the proteft is, that the former muft be prefented for payment *before* the expiration of the laft day of grace, and in time to have the proteft fent off the fame night, if the poft then fets out: but on inland bills the proteft for non-payment cannot be made till *after* the expiration of the three days, and notice may be fent at any time within *fourteen* days after the proteft. Vid. Leftley v. Mills, 4 Term Rep. 170.

IT is alfo remarkable that in inland bills, where damages, intereft, and cofts are to be recovered, there is more indulgence in the time allowed for

notice

notice of non-payment than where only the principal fum is to be recovered; for when there is no protest for non-payment, prefentment for payment muft be made fo early on the laft day of grace that the holder may give notice of non-payment by the next pot.

Vid. ante page 126.

S. 1.

THAT part of the ftatute of Queen Anne which puts Promiffory Notes on the fame footing with inland Bills of Exchange, makes no exprefs provifion for protefting them for non-payment; but there can be no doubt that the fame privilege is impliedly conferred on them, and in practice fuch a proteft is frequently made.

Beqwes, 456.

WHEN a bill is drawn for the account of a third perfon, and is accepted according to its tenor for his account, and he fails without making provifion for its payment, the acceptor muft difcharge the bill, and can have no redrefs againft the drawer.

Id. ibid.

BUT if the drawee do not choofe to accept on the account of him for whofe account he is advifed the bill is drawn, he may accept for the account and honour of the drawer.

OR, if a bill made payable to order, be indorfed by a fubftantial man before acceptance be demanded, the drawee, if he have any doubt about the drawer, or of him on whofe account it is

Id. ibid.

drawn, may accept it for the honour of the indorfor; but in this cafe he muft firft have a formal proteft made for non-acceptance, and fhould fend it without delay to the indorfor for whofe honour he has accepted it.

SUCH

Such acceptances as thefe are called acceptances Id. 458. *fupra* proteft; and have this effect with refpect to the fecurity of the acceptor, that they give him a right to call on the party for whofe honour he accepts; and in the cafe of an acceptance for the honour of the indorfor, on him and all the parties before him; whereas a fimple acceptance, according to the tenor of the bill, gives him a remedy only againft the drawer, or againft him on whofe account the bill is drawn, as the cafe may be.

The method of accepting *fupra* proteft is this; the acceptor muft perfonally appear with witneffes before a notary, (whether the fame who protefted the bill or not, is of no importance) and declare that he accepts fuch protefted bill in honour of the drawer or indorfor, &c. and that he will fatisfy the fame at the appointed time; and then he muft fubfcribe the bill thus, " Accepted *fupra* proteft, in honour of T. B. &c."

But this acceptance *fupra* proteft may be fo Id. 457. worded, that though it be intended for the honour of the drawer, yet it may equally bind the indorfor, and in fuch a cafe it muft be fent to the latter.

If the perfon on whom the bill is drawn refufe Id. ibid. to accept it, any *third* perfon after proteft for nonacceptance may accept *fupra* proteft for the honour of the bill or of the drawer, or of any particular indorfor: if he accept for the honour of the bill or of the drawer, he is bound to all the indorfees as well as to the holder: if in honour of a particular indorfor, then to all fubfequent indorfees.

Any

Id. 457,
458.

ANY one accepting a bill *supra* proteft, though without the orders or knowledge of the perfon for whofe honour he accepted it, has a remedy againft that perfon, who is bound to fatisfy him as if he had acted intirely by his directions, for his commiffion, poftage, and other charges.

Id. 457.

IF a bill be protefted for non-acceptance, and after it has been accepted *supra* proteft by a third perfon, the drawee, on receiving frefh advice and orders, determine to accept and pay it, the acceptor *supra* proteft may permit him, though the holder cannot be obliged to free him from his acceptance; and if the two acceptors agree, the drawee muft pay the other his commiffion, charges, &c. as it was by his acceptance that the bill was prevented from being returned protefted.

Id. 458.

IF the acceptor of a bill for the honour of the drawer or indorfor, receive his approbation of the acceptance, then he may fafely pay the bill without any proteft for non-payment. But if the perfon, for whofe honour the bill was accepted, either return no anfwer to the advice, or exprefs a difapprobation of the acceptance, then the acceptor *supra* proteft muft caufe a formal proteft to be drawn up for non-payment againft him to whom the bill was directed, and on his continuing to refufe payment, muft then pay it for him.

Id. ibid.

WHEN a bill is protefted for non-payment, any man may pay it under proteft, for the drawer's or indorfor's honour, even he who made or he who fuffered the proteft; but he muft previoufly declare

clare before a notary, for whofe honour he difcharges it; and of this the notary muft give an account to the parties concerned, either jointly with
the proteft, or in a feparate inftrument.

HE who difcharges a bill protefted for non-pay- Beawes,
ment, in honour of the drawer, has his remedy 459·
againft the latter, but not againft the indorfors;
but he who difcharges a bill protefted for non-
payment, in honour of an indorfor, has his remedy
not only againft that indorfor, but againft all that
were before him, including the drawer; but he has
no right againft fubfequent indorfors.

A MAN, after having given a fimple acceptance Id. 458,
to a bill, cannot fatisfy it under proteft, in honour
of an indorfor, becaufe as acceptor, he has already
bound himfelf to that indorfor; but a drawee, not
having yet accepted the bill, may difcharge it for
the honour of the indorfor or drawee, as if he were
a third perfon unconcerned.

YET it is faid that the poffeffor of a bill, pro- Id. ibid,
tefted for non-payment, is not bound to admit of
its difcharge from a third perfon under proteft,
either in honour of the drawee or of any indorfor,
unlefs he declare and prove that the honour of that
bill was particularly recommended to him : and if
the protefted bill be indorfed by the poffeffor's correfpondent, and was remitted by him, then the
poffeffor ought not to admit of any payment in
honour of the indorfements, but under the exprefs
condition, that the payer fhall have no redrefs
againft the faid correfpondent.

WHAT

WHAT is faid with refpect to the *payment* of a bill *fupra* proteft is applicable to that of a Promiffory Note.

Id. 455.

THE effect of the acceptance is to give credit to the bill, and to render the acceptor liable according to the tenor of his acceptance; the very act of accepting implies an acknowledgment that he has effects of the drawer in his hands.

Symonds v. Parminter, 1 Will. 185.

IF therefore the drawee accept a bill generally, and by reafon of his non-payment, the drawer is obliged to pay it, the latter, as drawer, may maintain an action againft him, not only for the principal fum, but, in cafe of a proteft, for damages, intereft, and cofts.

IF indeed the drawee have no effects of the drawer in his hands, and notwithftanding accept the bill, he has his remedy, if he pay it, againft the drawer; but with regard to every body befides, the acceptor is confidered as the original debtor, and to be entitled to have recourfe againft him, it is not neceffary for the holder to fhew notice given to him of non-payment ·by any other perfon.

Doug. 249.

Mar. 17. Beawes, 454.

WHEN a bill is once accepted abfolutely, it cannot in any cafe be revoked, and the acceptor is at all events bound, though he hear of the drawer's having failed the next moment, even if the failure was before the acceptance.

BUT the acceptor may be difcharged by an exprefs declaration of the holder, or by fomething equivalent to fuch declaration.

BLACK

BLACK held, as indorfee, a bill drawn by one *Black v. Peele, cited Doug. 237. (249.)* Dallas, and accepted by Peele. Black arrefted Peele, but finding that no confideration had been given for the acceptance, his attorney took fecurity from Dallas, and fent word to Peele " that he had fettled with Dallas, and he needed not to trouble himfelf any further.'' Dallas afterwards became bankrupt, and then Black demanded payment of Peele. The caufe was tried firft before Lord Mansfield, and afterwards by Chief Juftice de Grey, who both held that the acceptor was difcharged.

IN another cafe a book of the plaintiff's was *Walpole v. Pulteney, cited Doug. 237. (249.)* produced in which the bill was entered, and over againft it this memorial, " Mr. Pulteney's acceptance annulled.'' The jury however gave a verdict for the plaintiff; but the Court of Exchequer granted a new trial, on the ground that this was an implied difcharge; and on the fecond trial before Chief Baron Skinner, one Alexander, who had indorfed the bill to the plaintiff, was produced as a witnefs on the part of the defendant, and fwore that Walpole had pofitively agreed to confider Pulteney's acceptance as at an end ; on which the jury found for the defendant. Walpole had kept the bill from 1772 to 1775 without calling on Pulteney.

BUT no circumftances of indulgence fhewn to the acceptor by the holder, nor any attempt by him to recover of the drawer, will amount to an exprefs declaration of difcharge.

DUNSTER

DUNSTER accepted a bill merely to lend his credit, and to accommodate Wheate, the drawer. Fitzgerald, the payee, indorfed it to Dingwall, and delivered it to him in payment for jewels. After it became due, the plaintiff, underftanding that the acceptor never had any confideration for it, and that Wheate was the real debtor, wrote to one Ready, Wheate's Attorney, on the 6th of February, and on the 4th of November, 1775, preffing him for the payment. Dunfter, on the 13th of February, 1775, wrote a letter to Dingwall, thanking him in ftrong terms for not proceeding againft *him*, but mentioning in the fame letter, that he had been informed by a perfon who had been fent from him to Dingwall on the bufinefs, that Wheate had taken up the bill, and given another to Dingwall's fatisfaction. It did not appear that Dingwall took any notice of that letter. But he for fome time received intereft on the bill from Wheate, and alfo the principal due by another bill, made at the fame time, and drawn and accepted by the fame parties, and under like circumftances. The plaintiff fuffered feveral years to elapfe without calling on Dunfter, or treating him as his debtor.

THE queftion was, whether the plaintiff, by his conduct, had difcharged the acceptor; and the court unanimoufly held that he had done nothing from which it could be concluded he meant to abandon his claim againft him. He had done right in applying to Wheate for payment, as he was apprifed that he was in fact the debtor, and

Dunfter

Dunſter was ſo far ſenſible of his kjndneſs, as to thank him for his indulgence in a letter; had the ſuggeſtion in that letter been true, relative to the plaintiff's having delivered up the bill to Wheate, that might have made a material difference: but the plaintiff having returned no anſwer to the letter, and the fact not having been attempted to be proved at the trial, it was probable the aſſertion was not warranted. This caſe had no reſemblance to the two preceding caſes which had been cited in argument.

NEITHER will any length of time ſhort of the ſtatute of limitations, nor the receipt of part of the money from the drawer or indorſor, nor a promiſe by indorſement on the bill by the drawer to pay the reſidue, diſcharge the holder's remedy againſt the acceptor.

A BILL was drawn by one brother and accepted by another. When it became due, the payee received of the drawer 3l. 15s. 4d. and at the ſame time the following indorſement was made on the bill: "Received on account of this bill 3l. 15s. 4d:" "Balance remaining due 26l. 4s. 8d. I promiſe to pay Mr. Thomas Ellis, within three months from the date of this." Signed by James Galindo, who was the drawer. The balance was never paid, and at the diſtance of three years an action was brought againſt the acceptor; the cauſe was tried before Lord Mansfield, who thought the acceptor was diſcharged, and non-ſuited the plaintiff. The ground of his lordſhip's opinion probably was, that the

Ellis v. Galindo, Doug. 238. (250.) in the notes.

the indorfement was as a new bill accepted by the plaintiff in payment of the old; and on an application for a new trial, his lordfhip faid he did not think that this cafe at all interfered with the determination in Dingwall and Dunfter. The plaintiff's counfel contended that the indorfement was made to prevent an imputation of neglect, becaufe delay in coming againft an acceptor may difcharge a drawer or indorfor. The court all feemed to think that this was a queftion of intention, and ought therefore to have been left to the jury, but they refufed a new trial on account of the fmallnefs of the fum.

Bacon v. Searles, 1 H.Bl.Rep. C. B. 88.

But when the holder of a bill receives part of the money from the drawer, he cannot recover more than the refidue from the acceptor; and where the drawer pays the whole, the acceptor is completely difcharged.

Burrows v. Jemino, in Canc. M. 13 G. Str. 733.

And where a merchant, having accepted a bill in a foreign country, has been difcharged by the laws of that country, he cannot afterwards be fued here on his acceptance, though the circumftances under which he was difcharged there, would not difcharge him here; becaufe he muft be taken by his acceptance to have entered into fuch engagement only as was from thence implied by the laws of the country in which he refided.

By the law of Leghorn, if a bill had been accepted and the drawer had failed, and the acceptor had not fufficient effects of the drawer in his hands at the time of acceptance, the acceptance became void,

void. This happening to be the cafe of one Burrows, he inftituted a fuit at Leghorn, to difcharge
himfelf of his acceptance, which was accordingly
vacated by a fentence in the court there. He
afterwards returned to England, and was fued here
on his acceptance; on which he filed a bill in
Chancery for an injunction and relief. Lord
Chancellor King was clearly of opinion that this
caufe was to be determined according to the laws
of the place where the bill was negociated; and
the acceptance having been vacated by a competent jurifdiction, that fentence was conclufive, and
bound the court here.

IF the drawee offer a conditional acceptance,
and the holder, inftead of acquiefcing, do fomething which fhews that he does not admit fuch
acceptance, the drawee is not bound, even if the
event afterwards happen on which the acceptance
was to depend.

A BILL payable to one Lenox, or order, forty Sproat v.
days after fight, was drawn on the defendant; Mathews,
Lenox indorfed it to the plaintiff: Allen, the plain- Rep. 182.
tiff's clerk, prefented the bill to the defendant, who
lived in London, for acceptance : the defendant
told him that the drawer had configned a fhip and
cargo to him and another perfon at Briftol, but as
he could not then tell whether the fhip would
arrive at London or Briftol, he could not accept at
that time : on which Allen faid that he would leave
the bill upon this condition, that in the event of
the defendant's not accepting it as from the day

M   when

when it was prefented, he fhould be at liberty to note it for non-acceptance as from that time : to this the defendant affented, and the bill was accordingly left at his houfe till a future day, when Allen called again in company with the plaintiff, to know whether the defendant would accept the bill or not, who, on being preffed to accept it, faid that the bill was a good one, and would be paid, even if the fhip were loft. Allen immediately on this carried the bill to a notary public, and had it noted for non-acceptance from the time when it was firft left with the defendant. The fhip afterwards arrived fafe at the port of London, and the defendant difpofed of the cargo. This being a conditional acceptance, the conduct of the plaintiff was held to have been a waiver of it, and to have precluded him from holding the defendant to his engagement.

THOUGH an agreement to accept, on condition of a certain fund being configned to the acceptor for the difcharge of the bill, may amount to an acceptance on the performance of the conditions, yet if the indorfee take the fund out of the hands of the drawee, he difcharges him from his engagement.

Mafon v.
Hunt,
Doug. 284.
(257.)
ROWLAND HUNT, in Dominica, agreed with a houfe there, that his partner, Thomas Hunt, in London, fhould, on a cargo of tobacco being configned to him, with the bills of lading, and an order for infurance, accept fuch bills as that houfe fhould draw on him, at the rate of 80l. per hhd. from ninety days to fix months fight : infurance for the
sum

fum of 3600l. was ordered on forty hhds. of tobacco, which Thomas Hunt procured for a premium of 303l. He afterwards received a letter, advifing him of fix Bills of Exchange being drawn on him for 3200l. in confequence of Rowland Hunt's agreement, payable to one of the partners of the houfe, on account of forty hhds. of tobacco, and indorfed by him to Mafon. The bills arrived, and were prefented for acceptance. Thomas Hunt re-fufed to accept them, on an apprehenfion that the tobacco was not worth the money at which it was valued. After a negociation of fome days, Mafon took the bill of lading for the forty hhds. and the policy of infurance out of the hands of Thomas Hunt. The tobacco afterwards arriving, was re-ceived and fold by the plaintiff Mafon, and pro-duced only 1400l. The occafion of this difference between the real produce and the valued price did not appear. Under the direction of Lord Manf-field, a verdict was given for the defendant, and on an application for a new trial, his lordfhip expref-fed himfelf thus: An agreement to accept, may in many inftances amount to an acceptance: but an agreement is ftill but an agreement, and if it be conditional, and a third perfon, knowing of the conditions annexed to the agreement, take the bill, he takes it fubject to fuch agreement. Here there were many things fpecified as the conditions of the acceptance—the number of hhds. to be delivered —of a certain value rated by the hhd.—the in-furance—the bills of lading—the confignment.

On

On the face of the agreement, I thought at the trial, and still incline to think, that the meaning of the parties was, that tobacco should be confignèd which should be worth 80l. per hhd.: this fell immenfely fhort of that fum. It is plain the *Hunts* never *meant* to be in advance, and I think fo great a difference in the value fuch a fraud as to intitle the defendants to relief againft the agreement. But as to this the reft of the court have doubted, chiefly becaufe there is no evidence to fhew how the decreafe in the value arofe; whether from the inferiority of the quality, or the fluctuation in the market. But the reft of the court are extremely clear that the fubfequent conduct of the plaintiff makes an end of the whole, and I think the reafons are unanfwerable. As to that part of the cafe, it ftands thus:. The Hunts fay, " we are not bound: " This is an impofition:—The tobacco is of in- " ferior value. The letter reprefents it as worth " 80l. the infurance makes it 90l. per hhd. and it " turns out not to be worth 40l." If Mafon had meant to fay, " you are liable, and fhall pay the " bills," what would his conduct have been?—he would have left the policy of infurance and the bills of lading in their hands, and fued them upon the acceptance. The temptation to accept was the commiffion on the confignment, and they were to have the fecurity of the goods and the infurance. But the plaintiff undoes all this, and fays, then I will take all from you, fecurity, commiffion, &c. This was faying, " I will ftand in your place,

but

but not fo as to be anfwerable for more than the produce of the tobacco." It is impoffible the defendants could mean to accept, without any benefit or fecurity. We are all clear that this made an end of the agreement.

THOUGH the receipt of part from the drawer or indorfor be no difcharge to the acceptor for more than the part received, yet the receipt of part from the acceptor of a bill, or the maker of a note, is a difcharge to the drawer and indorfors in the one cafe, and to the indorfors in the other, unlefs due notice be given of the non-payment of the refidue; for the receipt of part from the maker or acceptor without notice, is conftrued to be a giving of credit for the remainder, and the undertaking of the preceding parties is only conditional, to pay in default of the original debtor, on due notice given : but where due notice is given that the bill is not duly paid, the receipt of part of the money from an acceptor or maker will not difcharge the drawer or indorfors; for it is for their advantage that as much fhould be received from others as may be.

1 Ld Raym. 744. Kellock v. Robinfon, 2 Str. 745. cited 1 Wilf. 48.

Bul. N. P. 271. cites Johnfon v. Kenyon, C. B. Hil. 5 G. III.

THE receipt of part from an indorfor, is no difcharge of the drawer or preceding indorfor, for more than the part received.

Vid. Johnfon v. Kenyon, Wilf. 262.

IF the drawer of a note, or the acceptor of a bill, be fued by the indorfee, and the bail for the drawer or acceptor pay the debt and cofts, this abfolutely difcharges the indorfor as much as if the principal had paid the note or the bill ; and the bail cannot

M 3   afterwards

afterwards recover againſt the indorſor in the name of the indorſee.

Hull v. Pit-
field, 1
Wilſ. 46.

ONE Scraiſton drew a note, by which he promiſed to pay to one Pitfield, or order, the ſum of 200l. and indorſed it to Hull. Hull brought an action againſt Scraiſton, in which he held him to ſpecial bail; Hull recovered interlocutory judgment againſt Scraiſton, on which his bail paid the debt and coſts, amounting to 220l. 15s. Hull executed an inſtrument between himſelf on the one part, and the bail on the other, reciting the note, and that he had recovered interlocutory judgment on it againſt Scraiſton: that the bail had purchaſed the note, and paid the debt and coſts, in conſideration of which Hull aſſigned over to them the note and the interlocutory judgment, with a power of attorney to make uſe of Hull's name to ſue the indorſor, and covenanted in the common manner, not to do any act to hinder the bail from recovering the money on the note. An action was afterwards brought in Hull's name againſt Pitfield the indorſor, on which theſe circumſtances were ſtated, and the court held the indorſor was diſcharged by the payment by the bail in the former action, as much as if the drawer had paid the money himſelf.

THOUGH, in order to intitle himſelf to call on any of the preceding parties, in default of the acceptor of a Bill of Exchange, or of the maker of a Promiſſory Note, it be neceſſary that the holder ſhould give due notice of ſuch default to the party to whom he means to reſort, yet notice to that party

party alone is fufficient as againft him: it is not neceffary that any attempt fhould be made to recover the money of any of the other collateral undertakers; or in cafe of fuch attempt being made, to give notice of its being without effect. Thus, in order to intitle himfelf to recover againft an indorfor, it is not neceffary for the indorfee to fhew an attempt to recover againft the drawer of a Bill of Exchange, or the payee indorfor of a Promiffory Note.

CONTRADICTORY opinions on this point, however, being found in an early reporter, the court, on a fubfequent cafe of an action by an indorfee of a *foreign* Bill of Exchange againft the indorfor, where it was objected that no demand was made on the drawer, thought it neceffary to take time to confider the fubject, and, on mature deliberation, delivered their opinion, that no fuch demand was neceffary to be fhewn. " The defign of the law of " merchants," they faid, " in diftinguifhing thefe " from all other contracts, by making them affign- " able, was for the convenience of commerce, that " they might pafs from hand to hand in the way of " trade, in the fame manner as if they were fpecie; " now to require a demand on the drawer, would " be laying fuch a clog on thefe bills, as would " deter every body from taking them:—the drawer " lives abroad, perhaps in the Indies, where the in- " dorfee has no correfpondent to whom he can " fend the bill for a demand, or if he could, yet " the delay would be fo great, that nobody would

1 Salk. 131. 133.

Bromley v. Frazier, 1 Str. 441.

M 4 " meddle

" meddle with them. Suppofe it were the cafe of
" feveral indorfements, muft the laft indorfee travel
" round the world before he can fix his action on
" the man from whom he received the bill? In
" common experience every body knows, that the
" more indorfements a bill has, the greater credit
" it bears; whereas, if thofe demands were all
" neceffary to be made, it muft naturally diminifh
" the value, by how much more difficult it would
" render the calling in of the money. And as to
" the notion that has prevailed, that the indorfor
" warrants only in default of the drawer, there is
" no colour for it, for every indorfor is in the na-
" ture of a new drawer, and at *nifi prius* the in-
" dorfee is never put to prove the hand of the firft
" drawer, where the action is againft an indorfor.
" The requiring of a proteft for non-acceptance is
" not becaufe a proteft amounts to a demand, for
" it is no more than giving notice to the drawer to
" get his effects out of the hands of the drawee,
" who, by the others drawing, is fuppofed to have
" fufficient wherewith to fatisfy the bill."

THIS cafe fettled the law with refpect to foreign
Bills of Exchange; but as to inland bills, great
doubts ftill remained. Thefe were occafioned by
the inaccurate and confufed manner in which fome
cafes were reported, in which it did not appear
whether the queftion arofe on Bills of Exchange or
Promiffory Notes, and from confounding the term
drawer as applied to the latter with the fame term
as applied to the former. There could be no
doubt,

doubt, but that to recover againſt the indorſor of a note, due diligence muſt be ſhewn to have been uſed to obtain payment from the drawer; but in the analogy between the two inſtruments, the drawer of the note does not reſemble the drawer but the acceptor of the bill : for want of attention to this diſtinction, reporters have been led to repreſent ſix chief juſtices to have been of different opinions on this point. Holt, Eyre, and Raymond are ſaid to have held, that a demand on the drawer of a bill was neceſſary; and Macclesfield, Pratt, and King, that it was not.

THE principal caſe to which a reference is made to prove that Holt was of opinion, that in actions on Bills of Exchange, it is neceſſary to prove a demand on the drawer, is reported in three different books; Lord Raymond, Salkeld, and 12 Modern. Lambert v. Oakes.

IN Lord Raymond, it appears manifeſtly that the queſtion aroſe upon a Promiſſory Note. " R. " ſigned a *note* under his hand, payable to Oakes, " or his order; Oakes indorſed it to Lambert; on " which Lambert brought the action for the money " againſt Oakes. Per Holt, C. J:—He ought to " prove that he had demanded, or done his endea- " vour to demand this money of R. before he can " ſue Oakes upon the indorſement. The ſame law " if the bill were drawn on any other perſon, pay- " able to Oakes, or order." That is, a demand muſt be made of the perſon on whom the bill is drawn. And other parts of the caſe manifeſtly 1 Lord Raym 443.

ſhew

shew this to have been the *meaning*. For my Lord
C. J. Holt is reported to have said, " the indorse-
" ment will subject the indorsor to an action; be-
" cause it makes a new contract, in case the person
" *on whom it is drawn* does not pay it." Again,
" if the indorsee does not demand the money pay-
" able by the bill, of the person *upon whom* it is
" drawn, in convenient time, and afterwards he
" fails, the indorsor is not liable."

127, there
called Lam-
bert v.
Pack.

In Salkeld, the case is confounded: it is stated
to be a Bill of Exchange, and " that the demand
" must be made on the *drawer*, or him upon whom
" it was drawn." Holt had said, that a demand
must be made of the *maker* of a Promissory Note,
(calling him the *drawer*;) and in the case of a Bill
of Exchange, of *him* upon whom the bill is drawn.
The report jumbles both together, as applied only
to a Bill of Exchange, misled, very probably, by
the equivocal meaning of the term *drawer*, and by
the chief justice's reasoning in the case of a Promissory Note, from the law upon Bills of Exchange.

244.

In 12 Modern—The case is mistaken too, and
stated as upon a Bill of Exchange, and as a determination that there must be a demand upon the
drawer of the Bill of Exchange. And yet the
report itself shews demonstrably, that what was said
by Holt, was applied to the *maker* of a Promissory
Note, (calling him the *drawer*.) For the report
makes him argue thus:—" So, if the bill was
" drawn on any *other* person, payable to Oakes,
" or order:" which shews that the case in judgment

ment was " not a bill drawn on *another* perfon, but " payable to Oakes by R. *himfelf*."

EVERY inconvenience fuggefted in the cafe of foreign Bills of Exchange, holds in a great degree, and every other argument holds equally, in the cafe of inland bills: the indorfee does not truft to the credit of the original drawer: he does not know whether fuch a perfon exifts, or where he lives, or whether his name may have been forged. The indorfor is his drawer, and the perfon to whom he originally trufted in cafe the drawer fhould not pay the money. And it is worth while to obferve, that the act of William the third requires notice of the proteft to be given to the perfon *from whom* the bill was received. He may have another remedy againft the firft drawer as affignee to the indorfor, and ftanding in his place.

ON thefe principles it is now finally fettled, that to entitle the indorfee to recover againft the indor-for of an *inland* Bill of Exchange, it is not neceffary to demand the money of the firft drawer.

Heylin v. Adamfon, 2 Bur. 669.

ANCIENTLY a diftinction feems to have been taken between the cafe of a Bill of Exchange, given in payment of a precedent debt, and that of one given for a debt contracted at the time the bill was given. In the latter cafe the perfon who received it muft have ufed due diligence to recover the money of him on whom it was drawn; otherwife he could not refort to the party from whom he received it, and charge him on the original contract. But in the former cafe, the bill was not confidered

as

as payment, unless the money was paid by the
drawee, and no diligence seems to have been necessary in the holder to obtain that payment, nor
any notice to the person from whom he received it
of the failure in payment; that this was once held
to be the law, the following case is a proof.

Clarke v.
Mundal,
3 Wil. & M.
cor. Holt,
C. J. at
Guildhall.
1 Salk. 124.
3 Salk. 68.

ONE Mundal, having a Bill of Exchange payable to him, indorsed it to Clarke, to whom he
was indebted : Clarke afterwards brought an action
on the original contract against Mundal, who, in
his defence, gave in evidence this bill indorsed to
Clarke, who had kept it so long in his hands after
it became payable, that it ought to be considered
as money paid : but the chief justice refused to
receive this as evidence of payment, but took
the distinction above-mentioned, saying, that if
A sells goods to B, and B is to give a bill in satisfaction, B is discharged, though the bill be never
paid, for the bill is payment : that however in the
case of a precedent debt, if part of the money on
the bill were paid, it should go in discharge of so
much.

S. 7.

BUT by the statute of Queen Anne before mentioned it is enacted, " that if any person accept a
" Bill of Exchange for and in satisfaction of any
" former debt, or sum of money formerly due to
" him, this shall be accounted and esteemed a full
" and complete payment of such debt, if such
" person accepting of any such bill for his debt do
" not take his due course to obtain payment of it,
" by endeavouring to get the same accepted and
                                               " paid,

" paid, and make his proteſt according to the
" directions of the act, either for non-acceptance
" or non-payment."

IF a Bill of Exchange be loſt by him with whom Beawes,
it was left for acceptance, or if by miſtake he have $^{476.}$
given it to a wrong perſon, or on any other account
the holder cannot obtain a return of his bill, either
accepted or unaccepted, he who loſt it muſt give
the perſon to whom it was payable, or to his order,
a note of hand for the payment of its amount, on
the day it becomes due, on delivery of the ſecond
if it arrive in time, or if not, on the ſame note,
which in all caſes is to have the law and privileges
of a Bill of Exchange; and if the acceptor refuſe
this, the holder muſt immediately proteſt for non-
acceptance, and when due muſt demand the money, (though he have neither note nor bill) and if
that be refuſed, a proteſt muſt be regularly made
for non-payment.

MARIUS adviſes, that as ſoon as the poſſeſſor of Mar.19,20.
a bill miſſes it, he ſhould have immediate recourſe
to the acceptor, and in the preſence of a notary and
two witneſſes, acquaint him with its being loſt;
and ſignify to him that at his peril he pay it to
none but thoſe with his order: and he adds, that
no one ſhould refuſe payment of a bill he has accepted merely becauſe it it miſſing: as he aſſerts,
that proteſt being made for non-payment, on offer
of a ſufficient ſecurity and indemnification, will
oblige the acceptor to make good all loſſes, re-
exchange,

exchange, and charges, as having wilfully occafioned them.

S. 3.

So, by the ſtatute of William, it is provided,
that "in caſe any *ſuch* inland Bill or Bills of Ex-
" change," as mentioned in the former part of the
act, " ſhall happen to be loſt or miſcarried within
" the time before limited for payment of the ſame,
" then the drawer of the ſaid bill or bills is and
" ſhall be obliged to give another bill or bills of
" the ſame tenor with thoſe firſt given, the perſon
" or perſons to whom they are and ſhall be ſo de-
" livered giving ſecurity, if demanded, to the ſaid
" drawer, to indemnify him againſt all perſons
" whatſoever, in caſe the ſaid Bill or Bills of Ex-
" change ſo alledged to be loſt or miſcarried ſhall
" be found again."

But if a bill loſt by the poſſeſſor ſhould afterwards come into the poſſeſſion of any perſon who
ſhall have paid a full and valuable conſideration
for it, without knowledge of the circumſtance of
its having been loſt, the drawer and the acceptor,
Vid. page
104—106.
if the bill was accepted, and the drawer, if it was
not, muſt pay it when due to ſuch a fair poſſeſſor:
ſo that Marius's law ſeems very doubtful, and the
proviſion of the ſtatute may in many caſes be uſeleſs
to the loſer of the bill.

1 Salk. 126.
1 Ld.
Raym. 738.
But againſt the perſon who finds the bill, the
real owner may maintain an action of trover.

CHAP.

C H A P. VIII.

Of the Remedy on a BILL *or* NOTE.

BEFORE the doctrine of Bills of Exchange was well underſtood, and the nature and extent of the cuſtoms relative to them fully recognized by the courts, the remedy on them was ſought in different forms of action, according to the opinions which were entertained of the applicability of theſe ſeveral forms to the reſpective ſituations of the parties.

OF caſes, however, where a remedy was ſought in any other form of action than that founded on the cuſtom reſpecting Bills of Exchange, or on the ſtatute reſpecting Promiſſory Notes, the reports are but few; and of theſe few ſome are ſo inaccurate, and in others the judges expreſs themſelves in terms ſo vague, that it is not eaſy to deduce from them any general rule.

IN one book it is laid down that the *payee* of a bill cannot maintain an action of debt againſt the acceptor, becauſe there is no privity between them, becauſe the acceptance does not create a duty, any more than a promiſe by a ſtranger to pay, if the creditor forbear his debt, which renders the ſtranger liable, but not in an action of debt, and
becauſe

Hardr.
485, 487.

because on a search for precedents, no one could be found of an action of debt on the acceptance of a Bill of Exchange.

Brown v. London, 1 Mod. 285. 1 Vent. 152. 1 Freem. 14. 1 Lev. 298. D. 11. Mod. 190. Comb. 204. In another case, reported in several books, it is laid down that an *indebitatus assumpsit* will not lie on the acceptance of a Bill of Exchange; perhaps on the same principle that it was determined that debt would not lie, for an allusion is made to the former case.

1 Salk. 125. 12 Mod. 37. In other books, it is laid down in general terms that an *indebitatus assumpsit* will not lie on a bill.

12 Mod. 345. In one of these, however, in another place, it is held that the payee of a bill, which imports to have been given for value received, may maintain *indebitatis assumpsit* against the drawer.

Skinn. 346. And in another it is said, that it will *only* lie against the drawer, on a bill which appears to have been given for value received.

Welsh v. Craig, or Creagh, Str. 680. 8 Mod. 373. On a Promissory Note a case is reported in two books, but in a manner so inaccurate, that it can only be collected, that in that particular case it was determined that debt would not lie; for it does not appear between what parties the action was, though the assertion is general that debt will not lie on a Promissory Note.

1 Mod. Ent. 312. pl. 13. It is said in another place, that debt will lie against the maker of the note, though not against the indorsor.

Morg. Prec. 548. And a very able pleader has given a precedent of a declaration in debt by the administratrix of the payee of a note against the maker.

It

It has been alfo held by Lord Mansfield, that the indorfee of a note might maintain *indebitatus affumpfit* upon it, againft the perfon who indorfed it to him.

Keffebower
v. Tims,
B. R. E.
22 G. III.
Bailey 47.

The conclufion, refulting from the whole, feems to be this; that where a privity exifts between the parties, there an action of debt or *indebitatus affumpfit* may be maintained; but that where it does not exift, neither of thefe actions will lie.

A privity exifts between the payee and the drawer of a Bill of Exchange, the payee and drawer of a Promiffory Note; the indorfee and his immediate indorfor of either the one or the other, and perhaps between the drawer and acceptor of a bill; provided that in all thefe cafes, a confideration paffed refpectively between the parties.

But it feems to be confidered, that no privity exifts between the indorfee and acceptor of a bill or the maker of a note, or between an indorfee and a remote indorfor of either.

The action which is now ufually brought on a Bill of Exchange is a fpecial action on the cafe, founded on the cuftom of merchants. That cuftom was not at firft recognized by the court, unlefs it was fpecially fet forth; and therefore it was deemed neceffary to fet forth, by way of inducement, fo much of it as applied to the particular cafe, and impofed on the defendant a liability to pay.

D. per
Powel, J.
1 Ld. Raym
21.

Vid.
1 Wilf. 189.

Thus in an action by an indorfee againft the acceptor, it was neceffary to ftate a cuftom among merchants, that " if any merchant drew a Bill of

N   " Exchange,

" Exchange, and directed it to his correspondent,
" and by that bill requested his correspondent to
" pay a sum of money to a third person, or to his
" order, and the correspondent accepted the bill,
" then if the person to whom or to whose order the
" money was to be paid indorsed the bill, the ac-
" ceptor, on the bill's being presented to him for
" payment, by the person to whom it was indorsed
" when it became due, by the custom of merchants,
" became liable to pay the money to the indorsee:"
then the particular circumstances of the case were
stated as coming under that part of the general
custom on which the action was brought.

Vid. Rich-
ardson's
Practice,
C. B.
vol.2.p.74. So, in an action by an indorsee against the drawer
for non-payment by the acceptor, it was necessary
to state that " there was a certain custom among
" merchants, that if a merchant drew a Bill of
" Exchange, and directed it to his correspondent,
" and by that bill requested him to pay a sum of
" money to a third person, or his order, and the
" correspondent accepted the bill, then if the per-
" son to whom, or to whose order the money was
" to be paid, indorsed the bill, and the indorsee
" presented the bill to the acceptor when due, who
" refused payment, then if the indorsee protested it,
" and returned it to the drawer, together with the
" protest, the drawer, by the custom of merchants,
" was liable to pay the principal sum, with da-
" mages arising from non-payment at the time;"
and then to state the circumstances in the particular case, to shew that it fell within the custom.

So,

So, if a man fubfcribed a bill for himfelf and partner; in an action againft them on this fub- fcription, it was thought prudent to ftate a cuftom, "that if two were partners, jointly merchandizing "together, and if one of them fubfcribed a bill for "the payment of money by him and his partner, "mentioned there, to another, and his order, then "both the partners were bound to that perfon; "and that if the perfon to whom this bill was "payable, indorfed it to another, then thofe part- "ners ought to pay fuch bill, on notice, to him to "whom it was fo indorfed:" and then to ftate the facts coming under this cuftom.

Vid. Pink- ney v. Hall, 1 Ld. Raym. 175.

WHERE the action was on an inland Bill of Ex- change, it was ufual to lay the cuftom as exifting between the two cities where the drawer and ac- ceptor lived; and if both lived in the fame place, to allege its exiftence between merchants and others refiding in that place.

Vid. 3 Mod. 86.

Vid. 4Mod.242.

BUT when the cuftom of merchants was recog- niged by the judges as part of the law of the land, and they declared they would take notice of it as fuch *ex officio*, it became unneceffary to recite the cuftom at full length; a fimple allegation that "the "drawer, mentioning him by his name, *according to* "*the cuftom of merchants*, drew his Bill of Ex- "change, &c." was fufficient.

3Mod.226. Carth. 83, 270. 1 Show. 130.

AND if the plaintiff, ftill adhering to former pre- cedents, thought proper to recite the cuftom in general terms, and did not bring his cafe within the cuftom fo fet forth; yet if by the law of mer-

chants,

chants, as recognized by the court, the cafe as
ftated intitled him to his action, he might recover,
and the fetting forth of the cuftom was reckoned
furplufage and rejected.

Mogadara
v. Holt,
1 Show.
317.
Thus, where the plaintiff fet forth a cuftom of
merchants, that if the merchant to whom the bill
is directed accept it after indorfement, and fail of
payment to the indorfee *at the time*, in fuch cafe,
on the bill's being protefted for non-payment, and
notice of it given to the drawer, the latter becomes
liable to pay the fame, with damage to the indorfee: and the cafe fet forth was, that the indorfee
had prefented it to the drawee *a month after the time*
of payment, who accepted it, but failed to pay it,
on which it was protefted, and notice given to the
drawer : though this cafe does not come within
the cuftom fet forth, yet becaufe by the law of merchants an action might be fuftained on this cafe, the
declaration was held good, and the cuftom rejected
as furplufage.

2 Ld.
Raym.
1342.
On the ftatement of any material fact, it is ftill
ufual to allude to the cuftom, by alleging that it
was done " according to the cuftom from time im-
" memorial ufed and approved among merchants:"
but even that is unneceffary, it being fufficient if
the facts ftated come within the cuftom as recognized.

3 and 4
Ann. c. 9.
As the action on a Bill of Exchange is founded
on the cuftom of merchants, fo that on a Promiffory Note is founded on the ftatute, and ufually
refers to it ; though, it is conceived, fuch reference

4   is

is as unneceffary in this cafe, as that to the cuftom in the other.

In both cafes, however, it is neceffary that all thofe circumftances fhould either be exprefsly ftated, or clearly and inevitably implied, which, according to the characters of the parties to the action, muft neceffarily concur in order to intitle the plaintiff to recover.

In all cafes arifing on a Bill of Exchange, it is neceffary to ftate that the drawer made his bill, and directed it to the drawee, and thereby directed him to pay.

In all thofe arifing on a Promiffory Note, that the maker made his Promiffory Note, and thereby promifed to pay.

In ftating the Bill or the Note, regard muft be had to the legal operation of each refpectively. *1 Bur. 324, 325.*

It has been decided that the legal operation of a bill or of a note, payable to a fictitious payee, is, that it is payable to the bearer, and therefore, if that decifion be right, it is proper, in the ftatement of fuch a bill, to allege that the drawer thereby requefted the drawee to pay fo much money to the bearer; in the ftatement of fuch a note, that the maker thereby promifed to pay fuch a fum to the bearer. *Vere v. Lewis, 3 Term Rep. 183. Minet v. Gibfon, Id. 485. Collins v. Emet, Bl. Term Rep. C. B. 313.*

Or in fuch a cafe, the plaintiff may ftate all the fpecial circumftances, and if the verdict correfpond with them, he will be entitled to recover.

Thus,

THUS, where the plaintiff ftated that the defendant, on the 5th of April, 1788, drew a Bill of
Exchange, directed to Livefay and Co. by which
he required them, three month after date, to pay to
Mr. George Chapman, or order, 1551l. value received,
and delivered the faid bill to them, and " autho-
" rifed them to negociate and indorfe the fame
" in the name of George Chapman, and thereby to
" raife money thereon," for the ufe of the faid
perfons fo ufing the names, ftile, and firm of Livefay
and Co.; and then averred, that when the faid bill
was fo made as aforefaid, or at any time afterwards,
" there was no fuch perfon as George Chapman,
" the fuppofed payee" in the faid Bill of Exchange,
but that the faid name was merely fictitious," to
wit, at London &c. which faid Bill of Exchange
afterwards, to wit, &c. by one " Andrew Good-
" rick, being a perfon thereunto in that behalf law-
" fully authorifed by Livefay and Co. upon fight
" thereof was accepted," according to the ufage
and cuftom aforefaid.   And the faid perfons fo
ufing the names of Livefay and Co. being fo authorifed as aforefaid, afterwards, and before the payment of the fum of money therein contained, or of
any part thereof, and before the time thereby appointed for fuch payment, to wit, &c. " negociated
" and indorfed the faid Bill of Exchange, in and
" with the name of the faid George Chapman, and
" by that indorfement, in the name of the faid
" George Chapman, appointed the contents of the
faid

" faid Bill of Exchange to be paid to the faid
" plaintiffs, and thereby raifed money thereon, for
" the ufe of the faid perfons fo ufing the names, &c.
" of Livefay and Co." and then and there delivered
the faid Bill of Exchange fo indorfed to the faid
plaintiffs, " who, thereupon, on the credit thereof,
" advanced to the faid perfons," fo ufing the name,
&c. of Livefay and Co. the fum of money in the
bill mentioned.

The circumftances ftated in a fpecial verdict on
this cafe were thefe, that Emett, who was a partner
with Livefay and Co. in the the fpinning of cotton
at Clithero, wrote his name on a piece of blank
paper, with a fhilling ftamp on it; and delivered it to Livefay and Co. for the purpofe of
drawing a Bill of Excgange, for fuch fum, payable
at fuch time, and to fuch perfon or perfons as they
fhould think fit.

That Livefay and Co. on the 5th of April, 1788,
drew on this paper, above the name of Emett, a
certain writing, directed to Livefay and Co. in
the words and figures followind, viz. " *Clithero*,
" April 5, 1788. £. 1,551. Three months after
" date pay to *Mr. George Chapman, or order*, fifteen
" hundred and fifty-one pounds, value received,
" as advifed, John Emett." That the occafion
and manner of giving this paper writing were as
follow: on the 5th of April, Livefay and Co. were
indebted to Thomas Jeffery in the fum of 1,512l.
9s. on a Bill of Exchange, which became due that
day, and which had been previoufly given for goods
fold

fold by Jeffery to them.   One Richard Collis,
clerk to Jeffery, on that day applied to the house of
Livefay and Co. for payment of that bill; he there
faw Anftie, one of the partners, who informed him
that they could not conveniently then pay the
money, but requefted him to take a bill on their
houfe for the fum, at three months date, and the
intereft in the mean time, and gave him the blank
paper above mentioned, with the name of Emett
written on it, to be filled up by one of the clerks of
the houfe.

THAT one Ludlow, a clerk of Livefay and Co.
filled up the paper in the manner as above fet
forth; that immediately afterwards it was carried
to Andrew Goodrick, another clerk of the houfe,
who was authorifed by Livefay and Co. to accept
it, which he accordingly did, in the names of
Livefay and Co. : that with the authority of Livefay
and Co. the name of George Chapman was then
indorfed on the faid paper writing, which being
fo filled up, accepted, and indorfed, was then delivered to the faid Collis, who then delivered up
the bill for 1,512l. 9s. to the faid Livefay and Co.
That the faid Thomas Jeffery afterwards negociated
the faid paper writing with the plaintiffs, and received the full amount from them, only deducting a
difcount, at $4\frac{1}{2}$ per cent. and delivered the fame to
the faid plaintiffs. That the fame was duly prefented
for payment to Livefay and Co. who refufed to pay
it, of which Emett had due notice. That there
was no fuch perfon as George Chapman, the fuppofed

pofed payee of the faid paper writing, being merely fictitious; that Emett gave no further or other authority than as before fet forth, and knew nothing of this tranfaction. That the plaintiffs had then no knowledge that the faid George Chapman was a fictitious perfon, or of the circumftances under which the faid paper writing was drawn, accepted, and indorfed, but that the faid Thomas Jeffery had full knowledge of the whole of the faid tranfactions.

In pronouncing the judgment of the Court of Common Pleas on this cafe, Lord Loughborough faid, the fpecial circumftances above ftated in the declaration, would, in his opinion, have been fufficient to have intitled the plaintiff to recover, if the cafe ftated in the fpecial verdict had not, in two or three inftances, varied from them.

A Bill or Note payable to the order of a man, may, in an action by him, be ftated as payable to himfelf, for that is its legal import : or it may be ftated in the very words of it, with an averment that he made no order.

If a note purport to be given by two, and be figned only by one, a declaration generally as on a note by that one who figned it will be good; for the legal operation of fuch a note is, that he who figned it promifed to pay. *Semb. 1 Bur. 323.*

On a note to pay jointly *and* feverally, a declaration againft one in the terms of the note will be good. *Burchell v. Slocock, 2 Ld. Raym. 1545.*

Where

Butler v.
Maliffey,
Str. 76.
Neale v.
Ovington,
2 Ld.
Raym.
1544.
2 Str. 819.

WHERE a note is given by two, to pay jointly *or* feverally, the payee may fue both or either ; if he fue both, he may declare on the note in the words of it jointly *or* feverally : but if he fue either of them fingly, it was formerly held that he could not declare in that way, but that he muft ftate the note as given only by one, and that the joint *or* feveral note would be good evidence to fupport fuch a declaration.

Rees v.
Abbot,
Cowp. 832.

BUT the doctrine in the latter cafe has been fince overruled, and it is now held, that in an action on a joint *or* feveral Promiffory Note, againft one, a declaration that he and another made their Promiffory Note, by which they *jointly or feverally* promifed to pay, is good : for if *or* muft be underftood as a disjunctive, the election whether the note fhall be joint or feveral, is in the perfon to whom it is given, and by fuing one, he fhews his election to confider it as a feveral note : but in this cafe, the true conftruction of the word *or* is, that it is fynonimous with *and.* They both promife that *they* or *one* of them fhall pay ; therefore the liability is on *both*, and on *each.* The nature of the tranfaction forces this conftruction.

Ibid. per
Buller, J.

AND if the note had been joint only, and it had been ftated as a feveral one, no advantage could have been taken of this but by a plea in abatement.

1 Str. 22.

WHERE the payment of a bill or note is limited at a certain time after the date, it muft be ftated as being made on the day of the date, that it may appear

pear on the face of the declaration, at what time it became due; if the bill have no date, as on the day when it iffued, or the firft day the plaintiff had knowledge of its exiftence; for an inftrument not dated muft be confidered as dated at the time of the delivery.

2 Ld. Raym. 1082.

BUT in ftating the bill or note, it is not necef-fary to allege that it bore date, though that be generally done; it is fufficient that the date appear by implication, which it does from the allegation, that on fuch a day the drawer made the bill or note.

2 Show. 422.

IT muft be alleged, that the bill or note was made at fome certain place: if the action be on a bill dated abroad, that muft be the place where it was actually made; but where it is neceffary to prove, at the trial, the making of the bill, which is only in an action againft the drawer, then in ftrict-nefs that place in England or Wales where the action is laid, ought to be fubjoined under a videlicet, in deference to the antient rule of pleading with refpect to the *venue:* by the precedents, however, that ftrictnefs feems now to be difregarded, and the place of the videlicet fupplied in a fubfequent part of the declaration, by an allegation that the drawer had notice of the default of the drawee at the place where the action is laid, or that he there undertook to pay.

Vid.Morg. Prec. 47.

INLAND Bills and Notes may be ftated to have been made at any place where the plaintiff choofes to lay his action, becaufe the action on them is tranfitory, transitory, and may be stated to have arisen any where.

Bailey 54.

But it is said, that " on a bill dated at any place " in England or Wales, and payable abroad at "usance, the bill should be stated to have been " made at the place where it bears date;" for what reason this should be done in this case, any more than in any other, does not appear: if the usance between any place abroad and the different towns of this country differed, it might be supposed that exactness in stating the very place from whence the bill bears date might be material to ascertain what the usance is: but as the usance between other countries and any one place in the kingdom is the same as between those same countries and any other place, that reason fails: it would also fail, if the usance varied as reckoned from different places of this kingdom to the same place abroad; for it is an established rule, that where a bill is payable at

Buckley v. Campbell, 1 Salk. 13.

usance, it must be averred what that usance is, because usances differing according to the places between which they are reckoned, the court cannot in any instance take notice *ex officio* what they are; and that averment ascertaining the time when the bill is payable, it seems immaterial from what place the bill is stated to be dated.

Erskine v. Murray, 2 Ld. Raym. 1542, 1543. Taylor v. Dobbins, M. 7. G. 1. B. R. 2. Ld. Raym. 1543.

In stating the drawing of a bill or note, it is unnecessary to say that the drawer subscribed it with his own hand writing, though that is generally done; the allegation that he made his Bill of Exchange or Promissory Note, and, in the case of the former,

former, that he directed the bill to the drawee, by
which he requested him to pay, and in the cafe of
the latter, that by fuch note he promifed to pay,
fufficiently implies that his name was fomewhere
on the inftrument, and that he or fomebody by his
authority wrote it; otherwife it could not with
propriety be faid that he requefted in the one cafe
or promifed in the other.

Elliot v.
Cooper,
2 Ld.
Raym.
1376.

If the bill was in fact drawn by a fervant, by the
authority of a mafter, it is fufficient to ftate it as
drawn by the mafter himfelf, unlefs the fubfcription be alleged, and then it muft be ftated
according to the truth of the cafe, that the fervant,
by the authority of his mafter, drew and fubfcribed
the bill on his mafter's account.

Vid.
12 Mod,
346.

The fame obfervations apply to the cafe of an
indorfement or acceptance by the fervant, by the
authority, and on the account of his mafter.

Vid.
12 Mod,
564.

Where partners are concerned in the drawing,
negociating, or accepting of a bill or note, the
ufual way of introducing the partnerfhip, is to
mention it by way of inducement, and to ftate that
one of them, according to the cuftom of merchants,
fubfcribed, accepted, or indorfed the bill for the
partnerfhip account: but the allufion to the cuftom
is not abfolutely neceffary; nor is it abfolutely neceffary that it fhould be directly charged that the
partner acting for the reft fubfcribed, accepted, or
indorfed for the partnerfhip; it is fufficient if, on
the whole, it appear to have been fo.

Vid.Morg.
Prec. 43.

ab. 2. Ld.
Raym. act,
1484.

Where

Effington v
Eaſt,
2 Ld.
Raym. 810
1 Salk.130.
Wegerflofe
v. Keene,
1 Str. 224.
WHERE a bill is drawn in ſets, and the action is brought on the firſt, the uſual way of ſtating the requeſt to the drawee is, " that he requeſted him " to pay that firſt of exchange, (ſecond and third " not paid) following the very form of the bill;" and then it is not neceſſary, in the ſubſequent part of the declaration, to aver that the ſecond and third were not paid, for if either of them was paid, that would be a ſufficient defence at the trial.

DELIVERY being neceſſary to give the bill an operation, it muſt be ſtated that the drawer delivered it to the payee.

Vid. page
109, 110.
As the holder, in order to intitle himſelf to recover againſt the drawer or indorſor, is not bound to preſent the bill for acceptance, when it is payable at a certain time after the date, ſo in that caſe it is not neceſſary to ſtate any acceptance; but if it was payable at a certain time after ſight, it is neceſſary to ſtate that the bill was preſented for acceptance, and, if the truth will permit, that it was accepted; or that the drawee could not be found, or refuſed to accept.

Erefkine v.
Murray,
2 Str. 817.
2 Ld.
Raym.
1542.
IN an action againſt the acceptor, it muſt be alleged that he accepted the bill, for the acceptance is the foundation of the action; but the manner of acceptance needs not to be alleged.

AND if the acceptance be alleged generally without any ſpecification of time, evidence of acceptance after time of payment will maintain the declaration, though the acceptance be alleged to
have

have been according to the tenor and effect of the
bill, for this shall be construed as a general promise
to pay the money, and the words " according to
" the tenor and effect of the bill" shall be rejected
as surplusage; but if the acceptance be alleged to
have been *before* the time of payment, perhaps evidence of an acceptance after will not do.

    IF the bill or note was payable to order, and the
action by an indorsee, such indorsements must be
stated as to shew his title; an indorsement by the
payee must at all events be stated, because without
that, it cannot appear that he made any order, on
the existence of which depends the title of the indorsee.   If the first indorsement was special, to any
person by name, in an action by an indorsee after
him, his indorsement must for the same reason be
stated : so also must all special indorsements.

    BUT if the indorsement was in blank, and the
action be against the drawer, acceptor, or payee,
no other indorsement is necessary to be stated than
that of the payee: in an action against a subsequent indorsor, his indorsement at least must be
added : in an action on a bill or note payable to
bearer, no indorsement needs be stated, because it
is transferable without indorsement

    As a bill may be negociated at any time after it
issues, it is immaterial on what day the indorsement is stated to have been; but if it be stated to
have been before the time the bill or note became
due, an indorsement afterwards will probably be
                                  considered

1 Ld.
Raym.
364, 365,
574, 575.
1 Salk.
127, 129.
Carth. 459.

Vid. page
89, 90, 99.

Vid. supra.

considered as a variance. It is not essential to state
a delivery by the indorsor; that he indorsed the
bill or note, implies that he delivered it.

Rushton v.
Alpinall,
Doug. 679.
(654.)
In an action against the drawer or indorsor of a
bill, or against the indorsor of a note, it is absolutely necessary, on account of non-payment of the
bill or note, to state a demand of payment from the
acceptor of the bill or the maker of the note, and
due notice of refusal given to the party against
whom the action is brought; for these circumstances are absolutely necessary to intitle the plaintiff
to maintain his action; and a verdict will not help
him on a writ of error : the general rule of pleading
in this case is, that where the plaintiff omits alto-
gether to state his title or cause or action, it is not
necessary to prove it at the trial, and therefore there
is no room for presumption that there was actual
proof; where a demand on the acceptor, or notice
to the defendant, are not laid, there is no necessity
to prove them; and if it were to be presumed that
they were proved, no proof can make good a declaration, which contains no ground of action on
the face of it ; and though it be alleged that the
defendant promised, that will not help the case;
the promise is an inference of law, and the declaration must contain premises from whence that inference may be drawn.

BUT if the title be only imperfectly stated, with
the omission only of some circumstances necessary
to complete the title, they shall after a verdict be
                                               presumed

presumed to have been proved ; and in some cases no advantage can be taken of the want of them on a general demurrer.

THUS due notice of the dishonour of a foreign bill can only be by protest; yet the omitting to allege a protest in the declaration is only matter of form; notice being alleged generally, it shall be presumed to have been given with all the ne-cessary formalities, and if these be not proved at the trial, the plaintiff cannot recover.

Salomons v. Stavely, B.R.M.24 G. III. Doug. 684 in the notes.

IT is not necessary, in an action against an indor-for, to state that the indorfee demanded the money of the drawer of a bill, or the first indorfor of a note, because such demand is not necessary to be made in order to complete the title of the indorfee.

Vid. ante, page 119, 120.

WHETHER the drawer of a bill, or the indorfor of a bill or of a note, receiving the bill or the note in the regular course of negociation before it has become due, can maintain an action on it, against the acceptor or maker, in the character of indorfee, feems undecided; no cafe of that kind is reported in any book that I have had an opportunity of confulting: that fuch actions have been brought has been incidentally faid from the bench : there feems no good reafon why they may not be main-tained : but the only cafe in which it is directly held, that the drawer may maintain an action in the character of indorfee, is no authority to eftablifh this point: for there it appears that the bill was protefted for non-payment before the indorfement; and a more recent cafe, determined on principle,

Per J.Afh-hurft, Tr. 14 G. III. Louviere v. Laubray, 10Mod.36.

Beck v. Robley Tr. 14 G. III. B. R. Bl. Term Rep. C. B. 89 in the notes.

O   clearly

clearly shews that a drawer or indorsor cannot maintain an action against the acceptor in the character of indorsee, where the indorsement is after the refusal of payment; because, when a bill is returned unpaid, either on the drawer or indorsor, its negociability is at an end.

Vid.
Symonds v.
Parminter,
1 Will. 185.
Vid. Morg.
Prec. 43,
44, 50.

THE action, therefore, in which the drawer or indorsor, after payment of the money in default of the acceptor, may recover, the first against the acceptor, and the latter against any of the preceding parties, must be brought in their original capacity as drawer or indorsor, and not as indorsee.

IN this action, after stating the drawing of the bill, the delivery, the necessary indorsements, the presentment for acceptance, and the acceptance or refusal to accept, it must be further stated, that at the proper time it was presented to the acceptor for payment, who refused, or that the acceptor could not be found; and if on a foreign bill, a protest for non-payment may be stated; then that it was returned to the plaintiff, and that the defendant had notice of the premises.

2 Show.
180.

1 Will. 185.

IT may also be stated, that the plaintiff paid the contents of the bill, and, in the case of a protest, the costs, interest, and damages arising from the delay; but this does not seem absolutely necessary; that the bill was returned to the plaintiff implies payment by him.

Vid. Morg.
Prec. 44.

ONE who has indorsed a bill or note cannot, in general, maintain an action on a re-indorsement to him, against the party to whom he indorsed it.

BISHOP

BISHOP declared, on a Promiffory Note, made by one Collins, payable to Bifhop or order, and afterwards indorfed by him to the defendant Hayward, who afterwards re-indorfed it to Bifhop. On the general iffue a verdict was given for the plaintiff: a motion was made in arreft of judgment, on the ground that there was no caufe of action ftated on the record. The court obferved, that the confequence of fupporting this verdict would be, that the plaintiff, without having any real demand on the defendant, might recover againft him by the judgment of the court, without allowing to the defendant a poffibility of defending himfelf. That on the trial it was only neceffary for him to prove that the note in queftion was given, as ftated in the declaration, payable to the plaintiff; that it was indorfed by him to the defendant; and re-indorfed by the latter to the plaintiff. The defendant could not deny thefe facts, and on proving them he had proved his whole declaration, and therefore intitled to a verdict. But the court were bound to fee whether, on his own ftatement of the cafe, the plaintiff had fhewn fufficient to intitle him to judgment. There might be circumftances, which, if difclofed on the record, might intitle the plaintiff to recover againft the defendant on this note, as if he had ftated that his own name was originally ufed for form only; and that it was underftood by all the parties, that the note, though nominally made payable to the plaintiff, was in reality to be paid to the defendant; but then the note fhould have been declared on according to its

legal

legal import. Here nothing appeared but that the plaintiff, being the original indorfer of the note, called on the defendant, who appeared on the record to be a fubfequent indorfee. Nothing could be clearer in law, than that an indorfee might refort to any of the preceding indorfors for payment; but the prefent action was an attempt to reverfe this rule. The court could in this cafe prefume nothing that was not ftated on the record; the cafes where prefumption was admitted were where the plaintiff ftated a title defective in form, not where he had fhewn a title defective in itfelf, which was the cafe here.

Bifhop v.
Hayward,
4 Term
Rep.,470.

IF the drawee, without having effects of the drawer, accept and duly pay the bill, without having it protefted, he may recover back the money in an action for money paid, laid out, and expended to the ufe of the drawer.

Vid. Smith
v. Niffen, 1
Term Rep.
269.

ANY one who has accepted and paid the bill under proteft for the honour of the drawer or indorfor, may have a fpecial action on the cuftom againft the perfon for whofe honour he accepted and paid.—So alfo may he who has paid under proteft for the honour of the acceptor; and if in accepting or paying for the honour of any one, he, who does it, retain the drawer or acceptor, and all others obliged to him in due form of law, he may fue the drawer, acceptor, or any of the prior indorfors.

Vid. ante,
page 152.

Starkey v.
Cheefeman,
1 Ld.
Raym.538.
1 Salk.128.
Carth.409.

IT is not neceffary, in any action on a Bill of Exchange or Promiffory Note, to ftate an exprefs promife by the defendant: the law implies a promife

mife where the party is liable; and therefore it is
fufficient, after ftating the circumftances, to fay,
that by thefe he became liable to pay.

But it is ufual to allege an exprefs promife after
ftating the liability, that no exception may be
taken to the addition of other counts in affumpfit,
which are ufually added; for it is faid that where 1Vent.153.
the declaration was upon the cuftom, and likewife 24. Vid.1 Salk.
on an *indebitatus affumpfit*, the judgment was arrefted, which could not have been the cafe had an
exprefs promife been added to the count on the
cuftom, becaufe it is an eftablifhed rule in pleading, 1 Term
that wherever the fame plea may be pleaded, and Rep. 276.
the fame judgment given on different counts, they
may be joined in the fame declaration.

Instead of bringing an action on the cuftom or Vid. ante,
on the ftatute, the plaintiff may in many cafes ufe page 58.
a bill or note, only as evidence in another action; Harris, 3
and where the inftrument wants fome of the re- Term Rep.
quifites to form a good bill or note, the only ufe 174.
he can make of it is to give it in evidence; or if
the count on the inftrument be defective, he may
give it in evidence, in fupport of fome of the other
counts for money had and received, or money lent
and advanced, according to the circumftances of
the tranfaction.

A Bill is prefumptive evidence of money lent Vid.
by the payee to the drawer, and a Note of money Grant v.
lent by the payee to the maker, and both confe- Bur. 1516.
quently of money had and received to the ufe of

O 3 the

Vid. 3
Term Rep.
183.

the holder, whether they be payable to the bearer, or to the order of the payee.

Vid. ante,
page 90.

HE who transfers a bill or note without indorfement gives no additional credit to the inftrument, and therefore he cannot be fued on the inftrument itfelf, nor is liable to anfwer in any fpecies of action to any holder but him to whom he immediately transferred it, and to him only for the confideration on which it was given, whether for work and labour, goods fold and delivered, money lent and advanced, or any other legal confideration.

Vid. Chamberlyn v.
Delarive,
2 Wilf. 353.

BUT if the party who took the bill or note did not ufe due diligence to obtain payment from the acceptor or maker, nor give due notice of their default to the party from whom he received it; the latter may either plead, or give in evidence, the bill or note, to an action on the original confideration.

Vid. ante,
page 112,
116.

THE holder of the bill or note may fue all the parties who are liable to pay the money, either at the fame time or in fucceffion, and he may recover judgment againft all, if fatisfaction be not made by the payment of the money before judgment obtained againft all; and proceedings will not be ftaid in any one action but on payment of the debt and cofts in that action, and the cofts in all the others in which he has not obtained judgment.

Vid. Golding v.
Grace,
2 Bl. Rep.
749.

2 Vefey,
115.

BUT though he may have judgment againft all, yet he can recover but one fatisfaction; yet though

he

he be paid by one, he may fue out execution for the cofts in the feveral actions againft the others.

AND if he have recovered judgment in more than one action, a tender of the principal recovered in one, and the cofts in all the reft, will prevent him from taking out execution; and it will be confidered as a contempt of the court, if he take out execution againft more than one.

Windham v. Wither. Idem v. Trull, 1 Str. 515.

MACDONALD drew a Bill of Exchange for 20l. on Bovington, who accepted it; the bill afterwards came into the hands of Thompfon, who recovered judgment againft Bovington, and charged him in execution. Bovington having obtained his difcharge under the Lords' act in that fuit, Thompfon fued Macdonald, the drawer, and recovered the amount of the bill, on which Macdonald fued Bovington, on his acceptance, and charged him in execution. On a rule to difcharge Bovington out of cuftody, it was contended, that he had fatisfied the debt, by being charged in execution at the fuit of Thompfon, and that he was not liable to be fued again for the fame fum. But the court faid, that nothing could be more clear than that this was not a fatisfaction of the debt as between thefe parties, though it was as between the defendant and Thompfon: that to the holder it was a mere *formal* fatisfaction, and not like actual payment: that the prefent plaintiff, having been obliged to pay the amount of the bill fince the defendant was charged in execution at the fuit of Thompfon, had a right to have recourfe to this defendant as acceptor; for

that

Macdonald
v. Boving-
ton, 4
Term Rep.
825.
that by this payment a new caufe of action arofe
againft the defendant, without regard to what had
paffed in the former action.

THE plea generally pleaded to this action is that
of non-affumpfit: but the defendant may, if the
truth will warrant him, plead *non-affumpfit infra fex
annos;* for by ftatute 21 Jac. I. c. 16. actions on the
cafe, except upon *accounts* between merchants, muft
be brought within fix years: and by the exprefs
S. 2.
provifion of the ftatute of Queen Anne, all actions
on Promiffory Notes muft be brought within the
fame time as is limited by the ftatute of James,
with refpect to actions on the cafe.

BUT an acknowledgment of the debt, or a promife to pay, made within fix years of the commencement of the action, will take the cafe out of
the ftatute.

8 W. 3 M.
5 Mod.
314.
To an action on the cafe on a Bill of Exchange
againft the defendant as acceptor, he pleaded, that
after acceptance he gave a bond in difcharge of it;
it was held that this plea was bad, becaufe it
amounted to the general iffue; for the debt on the
bill being extinguifhed by the bond, the defendant
ought to have pleaded non-affumpfit, and to have
given the bond in evidence.

2 P. Will.
89, 407.
1 Atk. 107.
IF any of the parties whofe names appear on the
bill or note become bankrupt, the holder may come
in under the commiffion; and if he have received
no part of the money from any of the others, may
be admitted to prove the whole fum mentioned,
and receive a dividend on the whole.

IF

IF afterwards any of the others become bankrupt, he may prove the remaining fum, and receive a dividend on that.

IF all become bankrupt, before the holder has received any part of his debt, he may prove the whole fum under each commiffion; and though he afterwards receive a dividend under one, his dividend under a fecond fhall be calculated according to the whole fum originally proved, not on what remains due after deducting the fum received under the firft commiffion; but if the fum fo calculated exceed the fum remaining due, he fhall only receive fo much as is equal to that remaining fum: the fame rule is to be obferved with refpect to the calculation of the dividend under each commiffion, till the holder fhall have received 20s. in the pound on his whole debt.

THE general rule with refpect to debts carrying intereft, in cafe of bankruptcy, is that all intereft ceafes from the date of the commiffion; but if there be an eftate fufficient to pay twenty fhillings in the pound, and a furplus, intereft fhall then revive, and be paid up to the final difcharge of the debt.

IF a man accept a bill without confideration, and the drawees, after negociating it, become bankrupts, and the holder, inftead of coming in under the commiffion, choofe to refort to the acceptor for the whole fum, which he pays after the bankruptcy, this is fuch a debt as the acceptor cannot prove under the commiffion, and he may therefore recover againft the drawers, notwithftanding their certificate.

1 Atk. 110.
2 Vef. 114, 115.

1 Atk. 75, 244.

Vid. Chilton v. Wiffen and Cromwell, 3 Wilf. 13.

certificate. So if the payee of a Promissory Note pay the amount of it to an indorsee, after the bankruptcy of the maker, he may recover against the maker, notwithstanding his bankruptcy and certificate.

Vid. Howis
v. Wiggins
4 Term
Rep. 714.

C H A P.   IX.

Of the Proof necessary at the Trial, and of the Defence that may be set up there.

A Great part of what may be said under this head necessarily rises out of the general doctrine explained in the preceding chapters, and will therefore in substance be little more than a repetition, though different in form.

The plaintiff must in all cases prove so much of what is necessary to intitle him to his action, and of what must be stated in his declaration, as is not from the nature of the thing and the situation of the parties necessarily admitted.

In an action against the acceptor, it is a general rule that the drawer's hand is admitted, because the acceptor is suposed to be acquainted with the writing of his correspondent, and by his acceptance he holds out to every one who shall afterwards be the

1 Ld.
Raym. 444.
Jenys v.
Fowler,
Str. 946.
Price v.
Neal, 3
Bur. 1354.
1 Bl. 390.

the holder, that the bill is truly drawn : it has indeed been lately fuggefted from high authority,
that this rule has probably not been eftablifhed on
the moft mature confideration, and that if it fhould
ever come to be the fubject of future difcuffion,
there might be fome reafon to alter it; cafes, it
was faid, might be imagined, where the knowledge
of the drawer's hand might more naturally be fuppofed in other parties than in the drawee : that the
payee generally received the bill from the drawer,
who was his correfpondent, and that therefore the
prefumption was, that he knew as well as the acceptor, or perhaps better, whether the bill was in
fact drawn by the perfon by whom, on the face of
it, it imported to be drawn, and that from the privity between them, the fame knowledge might be
imputed to his affignee.—But thefe obfervations
feem by no means fatisfactory. By accepting a
bill, the drawee evidently fhews, that he has no
doubt of its being in the hand of the perfon appearing as the drawer; he may have had advice of
an intention to draw upon him; he may have effects of the drawer in his hands, or he has fome
good reafon for honouring his bills; the payee, on
the contrary, may in many cafes be entirely unknown to the drawer; the bill may have been remitted to him by a correfpondent, whofe name
does not appear upon it; or if in fact the remitter
be the payee, who of courfe knows the drawer's
hand, he cannot, along with the bill, tranfmit that
knowledge to the indorfee, who is the perfon that

Ld. Thur-
low in the
Houfe of
Lords, in
the cafe of
the fictiti-
ous indor-
fements.

3   has

has it prefented for acceptance; much lefs can any
of the fubfequent holders be fuppofed to have any
knowledge of the hand of the drawer; it would
therefore be productive of much inconvenience, if
in an action againft the acceptor, the plaintiff were
to be held to the proof of the drawer's hand: on
the event of the bill's not being really drawn by
the perfon whofe name appears upon it · as the
drawer, the true queftion is, *to whom* is negligence
or want of caution to be imputed? to the *holder*,
who, in moft cafes, if he has any knowledge of the
drawer's hand, has that knowledge from accident,
and not from the nature of the tranfaction? or to
the *acceptor*, who, by his acceptance, impliedly tells
the perfon prefenting it, that he undertakes for the
bill's being a true one? To the *acceptor* certainly:
And therefore, if the bill be in fact forged, 'tis he
who muft fuftain the lofs.

Vid. Price
v. Neale,
3 Bur.
1354.

IN an action againft the acceptor, therefore, where
the acceptance was on fight of the bill, whether in
writing on the bill or by parol, it is not neceffary
to prove the hand writing of the drawer. But if
the acceptance was without fight of the bill, the
acceptor is not precluded from difputing the hand
of the drawer; if in truth the hand writing of the
latter was forged, the acceptor could not fet off, in
account with him, the money paid on that bill;
and as he did not fee the bill at the time of acceptance, he has not entered impliedly into any engagement, that the very bill on which the fuit is
founded, was drawn by his correfpondent, and con-

Vid. page
72.

fequently

fequently no negligence can be imputed to him, in not having taken due precaution to be fatisfied that the bill was in the hand writting of the drawer.: in fuch a cafe, therefore, it is neceffary that in an action againft the acceptor, the fignature of the drawer fhould be proved: that of the acceptor himfelf muft of courfe be proved, and that of every perfon through whom the plaintiff, from the nature of the tranfaction, muft neceffarily derive his title.

On a bill payable to bearer, there is no perfon through whom the holder derives his title; in an action againft the acceptor, therefore, he has only to prove the hand writing of the acceptor himfelf. Vid. page 88, 89.

But to a bill payable to order, the holder can have no title, unlefs the payee have actually expreffed his order by indorfement. The engagement of the acceptor is not to pay to every one who fhall happen to be the bearer, but to thofe only who fhall be entitled by the order of the payee: It has therefore long been a general rule, that in an action againft the acceptor of a bill payable to order, the plaintiff muft prove the hand writing of the payee or firft indorfor: if his indorfement be fpecial to " another perfon,". or to " another, or his order," the fame rule, on the fame principle, applies to the indorfement of that other perfon, as it does to the indorfement fpecifically made of every fubfequent indorfor, between the payee and plaintiff. If the indorfement of the payee be general, the proof of his hand writing is fufficient; that of any other of the indorfors is not requifite, though all the fubfequent

quent indorfements be ftated in the declaration; for by indorfing generally, the payee has fhewn his order to be, that the bill fhould be payable to any *Vid. page* fubfequent holder; and accordingly it has been *89.* fhewn, that any fuch fubfequent holder may declare as the indorfee of the firft indorfor, or of that indorfor who firft indorfes in blank: but in this cafe, in order to render the evidence correfpondent to the declaration, all the fubfequent names muft be ftruck out, either at the time of the trial or before.

Vid. ante, BUT the plaintiff, in the cafe of a transfer by de-*88, 89.* livery, which may be either when a bill is payable to bearer, or when a bill payable to order is in-*Miller v.* dorfed blank, may be called upon to prove that he *Race,* *1 Bur. 452.* gave a good confideration for it, without the know-*Peacock v.* *Rhodes,* ledge of its having been ftolen, or of any of the *Doug. 633.* names of the blank indorfors having been forged.

NOTWITHSTANDING this general rule, that, in an action againft an acceptor of a bill payable to order, the hand writting of the firft indorfor muft be *Hankey v.* proved at the trial, a cafe is reported, where it is *Wilfon,* *Sayer 223.* faid to have been held, that fuch proof is not always neceffary: by the report it appears, that it was proved that the defendant had accepted the bill; that there was no *actual* proof, that the name of *one* of the indorfors was of his hand writing; that the name of *that* indorfor, and thofe of all the other indorfors, was upon the bill at the time of the acceptance, and *that at that time the defendant promifed to pay the bill*: this evidence was left to the jury, who found a verdict for the plaintiff.—The
                                                        queftion

queſtion being agitated, whether, upon this evidence, the matter ought to have been left to the
jury, the court held that it ought, and are reported
to have expreſſed themſelves thus : " It is in general
" neceſſary to give actual proof, that the name of
" every indorſor is of his hand writing; but it is
" not neceſſary to do this in every caſe : in the
" preſent it was a matter proper for the determina-
" tion of the jury, whether the acceptance of the
" bill, when the names of all the indorſors were
" upon it, *together with the promiſe of the defendant*
" *to pay it,* did not amount to an *admiſſion,* that the
" name of *every* indorſor is of his hand writing,
" that admiſſion ſuperſeding the neceſſity of actual
" proof."

BUT the authority of this caſe appears to be very
doubtful ; unleſs all the indorſements were ſpecial,
which they are not ſtated to have been, the general
rule as laid down by the court extends too far; the
report, therefore, is at leaſt inaccurate. It is difficult to conceive how a promiſe to pay the bill,
made at the time of the acceptance, can be conſidered as an admiſſion of the hand writing of the
indorſors ; and it has been lately decided that ſuch Smith v.
Chelter,
admiſſion is not to be preſumed from the circum- 1 Term
Rep. 654.
ſtance of the indorſements being on the bill at the
time of the acceptance. The acceptor only looks
on the face of the bill, which purports to be in the
hand writing of the drawer, which he is therefore
precluded from afterwards diſputing ; he never
looks, or at leaſt is not ſuppoſed to look, at the
back

back of the bill; and if he did, he cannot be prefumed to admit the hand writing of the indorfors,
becaufe his privity is not with them,—it is only
with the drawer.

Vid. ante, page 75, 76. WHERE the acceptance is conditional, the event
on which the condition depends muft be proved to
have taken place before the commencement of the
action.

Vid. Collins v. Emett, Bl. Term Rep. 313. IN an action by an indorfee againft the drawer,
the fame rules obtain with refpect to proof of the
hand writing of the indorfors, as in an action againft
the acceptor.

Vid. page 117. THAT of the drawer himfelf muft of courfe be
proved : It muft alfo be proved, that the plaintiff
has purfued that diligence with refpect to the
drawee, and given fuch notice to the drawer, of the
default of the former, as are fhewn in a former
chapter, to be neceffary on his part to intitle him
to have recourfe to the latter.

FROM the rule that, in an action againft the
drawer or acceptor of a bill payable to order, there
muft be proof of the fignature of the firft indorfor,
and of all thofe to whom an indorfement has been
fpecially made, has arifen the queftion which has
fo long agitated the commercial world on the fubject of indorfements, in the name of fictitious
payees.

Stone v. Freeland, B. R. Sittings at Guildhall, after Eafter Term, 1769. A BILL payable to the order of a fictitious perfon,
and indorfed in the fictitious name, is not a novelty
among merchants and traders. A cafe of that kind
appears to have been brought to trial upwards of
twenty

twenty years ago. It was an action by the indorfee againft the acceptor of a Bill of Exchange,
payable to Butler and Co. and their order, and indorfed in that name. The plaintiff was fo far from
proving it to have been indorfed by any perfons ufing
that firm, that his own witneffes faid, they believed it
was indorfed by Cox the drawer. It alfo appeared,
that there was a houfe of Butler and Co. with
whom Cox had dealings, but it was proved that the
bill in queftion had never been in their hands; it
was admitted that the bill was a true one, and that
the defendant had regularly accepted it; it ap- 3 Term
Rep. 176.
peared further, that the acceptor had *exprefsly pro-*
mifed to pay, at the time the holder had difcounted
the bill; but it was infifted, that the indorfement
being fictitious, the plaintiff had failed in making
out an effential part of his title. Lord Mansfield
obferved, that the intent of the bill was only to
enable *Cox* to raife money, and the reafon why it
was not made payable to his order, was, that there
were other bills at that time payable to his order,
and if this had been fo too, there would have been
too many in the fame name in circulation at the
fame time, which would have had the appearance
of fictitious credit; that names were often ufed of
perfons who never exifted: the defendant, by his
acceptance, *and promifing exprefsly to pay the bill*,
had enabled Cox to put it in circulation, and
having fo done, he fhould not avail himfelf of an
objection that the plaintiff had not completely made
out his title.

P   BUT

But in the years 1786, 1787, and 1788, two or three houfes, connected together in trade, entering into engagements far beyond their capital, and apprehending that the credit of their own names would not be fufficient to procure currency to their bills, adopted, in a very extenfive degree, a practice which before had been found convenient on a fmaller fcale. So long as the acceptors or drawers could either procure money to anfwer their bills, or had credit enough with the holder to have them renewed, the fubject of thefe fictitious indorfements never came in queftion. But when the parties could no longer fupport their credit, and a commiffion of bankruptcy became neceffary, the other creditors felt it their intereft to refift the claims of the holders of thefe bills, and infifted that they fhould not be admitted to prove their debts, becaufe they could not comply with the general rule of law, which requires proof of the hand-writing of the firft indorfor. The queftion came before the Lord Chancellor, by petition: He directed trials at law, and feveral have been had; three againft the acceptor in the King's Bench, and one againft the drawer in the Common Pleas; though not all exprefsly by that direction.

Tatlock v. Harris, 3 Term Rep. 174.

In the firft cafe againft the acceptor, befide the general counts for money *paid* by the plaintiffs to the defendant's ufe, and *money had and received* by the defendant to the plaintiffs' ufe, there were alfo two fpecial counts laid on the bill itfelf: The firft was in the terms of the bill, " that the defendant

5   " and

" and others drew a Bill of Exchange on the defen-
" dant, payable to *Grigſon and Co.* or order, three
" months after date, which the defendant accepted;
" and that Grigſon and Co. indorſed it to Lewis
" and Potter, who indorſed it to the plaintiffs."
The ſecond count ſtated it to be " a bill drawn as
" above, in favour of certain perſons trading under
" the firm of Lewis and Potter, or order, and in-
" dorſed by Lewis and Potter to the plaintiffs."

THE circumſtances proved at the trial were theſe:

THAT there was a houſe of trade at Nottingham
under the firm of Harris, Harris, and Plant, of
which the defendant was one of the partners, and
that the defendant *alone* carried on buſineſs in
Wood-ſtreet, and reſided in London; that the body
of the bill, as well as the ſignatures of the drawers
and acceptor, were in the hand-writing of the defendant; that no ſuch houſe of trade as that of Grigſon
and Co. was concerned in the tranſaction, but that
the defendant had drawn the bill payable to Grigſon
and Co. at the requeſt of Lewis and Potter; that
the indorſement in the names of Grigſon and Co.
was fictitious, and that before the bill became due
the defendant knew that to be the caſe, but it did
not expreſsly appear whether he knew it at the
time the bill was drawn; that the indorſement of
Lewis and Potter was in the hand-writing of one
of the partners of that houſe, and that they received
the bill from the defendant and delivered it to the
plaintiffs: that the value of the bill was paid to
the houſe of Lewis and Potter in draughts on

P 2   bankers,

bankers, which were afterwards paid in cafh; and that the defendant had credit given him in account with the houfe of Lewis and Potter for the value of the bill.

To this evidence the defendant's counfel demurred, as not fupporting any count in the declaration.

LORD KENYON, in giving the opinion of the court, faid, that in deciding on this particular cafe they did not wifh to have it underftood that they meant to infringe on the rule as applicable to cafes in general; for that generally fpeaking there was no doubt but the indorfee of a Bill of Exchange, payable to order, muft, in deriving his title, prove the hand-writing of the firft indorfor. But that this decifion proceeded on the fpecial circumftances of this particular cafe, that the defendant, at the time of entering into this engagement, knew there were no fuch perfons as Grigfon and Co. and therefore that in point of formal derivation of title, that which is ufually done could not be done in this cafe. That, on the firft count of this declaration, the opinion of the court did not proceed, neither was it neceffary to fay any thing on the the fecond; though if it had been neceffary to refort to that, he himfelf had an opinion on it. But the counts on which the judgment of the court was given, were thofe for *money paid*, and *money had and received*. In Lord Raymond's time it had been decided, that a general *indebitatus affumpfit* might be maintained to recover money for the value of a

Ld. Kenyon.

Ward v. Evans, 2 Ld. Raymond, 930.

Bill

Bill of Exchange which was not paid. That cafe, indeed, had been on a bill payable to bearer, but the doctrine of that cafe was a fufficient foundation for the opinion of the court in the prefent, and had been recognized in a fubfequent cafe by each of the judges of this court, " That to give fuch a bill is, " as it were, an affignment of fo much property, " which becomes money had and received, to the " ufe of the holder of the bill."   Here the defendant, being a debtor to the houfe of Lewis and Potter, drew a bill, which he delivered to them, and drew it in terms which could not be proved in a formal manner: He was not only privy to the tranfaction, but the very negociator of it; and by drawing it, he put himfelf in a *fituation* to pay, what he was in confcience *bound* to pay; therefore it was an *appropriation* of fo much money to be paid to the perfon who fhould become the holder of the bill.

Grant v. Vaughan.

In the next cafe, the firft count ftated the Bill of Exchange to be drawn by Livefay and Co. on the defendants, in favour of Lawrence Afhworth, who was alfo a fictitious perfon, and by him indorfed to the plaintiffs.   The fecond count ftated the bill to be payable to the *bearer;* the third payable to the order of the drawers, and indorfed by them to the plaintiffs ; then followed the money counts.

Vere v. Lewis, 3 Term Rep. 183.

An attempt was made on behalf of the defendants to diftinguifh this cafe from the former, becaufe there was no evidence that, in point of fact, they received any value for the bill, and that therefore they could not be liable on the *money* counts: But the court said, that the acceptance of the defendants was alone evidence that they had received value from the drawers, and that on the demurrer to evidence, the court might draw the same inference which would have been drawn by the jury.

Ld. Kenyon C. J. Afhhurft J. and Buller J.

Three of the court alfo *thought*, that the plaintiffs might recover on the fecond count, which ftated the bill as drawn payable to *bearer*.

Minet v. Gibfon, 3 Term Rep. 483.

THE next cafe againft the acceptor having alfo a count, in which the bill was ftated to be drawn payable to bearer, and the court being of opinion that it was decided by the laft, gave judgment for the plaintiff without hearing any argument, and added, they underftood it had been agreed to turn it into the fhape of a fpecial verdict, that it might be carried up to the Houfe of Lords.

Collins v. Emett, Bl. Term Rep. C. B. 313.

ON the authority of thefe two laft cafes againft the acceptor in the King's Bench, was decided the cafe againft the drawer in the Common Pleas, the circumftances of which are ftated at full length in the laft chapter, judgment being given for the plaintiff on the count which ftated the bill as being drawn payable to bearer.

THE cafe of Minet and Gibfon after having been folemnly argued before the Houfe of Lords, was at laft decided in favour of the holder of the Bill by the opinion of a majority of the judges.—The circumftances ftated in the fpecial verdict were thefe:

LIVESAY and Co. made a certain inftrument in writing, directed to the defendants, requiring them, three

three months after date, to pay to J. White, or
order, 721l. 5s.; Livefay and Co. knew, at the
time of making it, that no fuch perfon exifted as
J. White, mentioned in the bill; an indorfement
in writing was afterwards made by Livefay and Co.
purporting to be the indorfement of J. White, and
requiring the contents of the bill to be paid to
Livefay and Co. or their order: Livefay and Co.
afterwards indorfed (by A. Goodrich, by procuration of Livefay and Co.) to the plaintiffs for a
full and valuable confideration, when the plaintiffs
became the holders of the bill; the defendants
afterwards accepted, with the full knowledge that
no fuch perfon as J. White, mentioned in the bill,
exifted, and that the name of J. White, fo indorfed
thereon, was not in the hand-writing of any perfon
of that name. The defendants at the time of
making and accepting the bill had not, nor had
they at any time fince, any money, goods, or effects,
of or belonging to Livefay and Co. or of the plaintiffs, in their hands.

BESIDE the money counts, the declaration contained feven fpecial counts on the bill.—The firft
ftated that Livefay and Co. made a Bill of Exchange, directed to the defendants, requiring them,
three months after date, to pay 721l. 5s. to John
White, or order; Livefay and Co. well knowing
that no fuch perfon as J. White exifted; on which
bill an indorfement was made, purporting to be the
indorfement of J. White named in the bill, requiring the contents to be paid to Livefay and Co.

or order; that Livefay and Co. (by one Abfolom Goodrich, by procuration of Livefay and Co.) indorfed to the plaintiffs; and that the defendants accepted it, knowing that no fuch perfon as J. White exifted, and that the name of J. White fo indorfed was not the hand-writing of any perfon of that name.

THE fecond count, after ftating the drawing of the bill, as in the firft, proceeded thus: Livefay and Co. knowing that J. White was not a perfon dealing with, or known to Livefay and Co. and ufing the name of J. White on the bill as a *nominal* perfon only, and intending not to deliver the fame to him, or to procure the fame to be actually indorfed by him; on which bill a certain indorfement was made, requiring the payment to be made to Livefay and Co.; and that Livefay and Co. indorfed to the plaintiffs, without having delivered the bill to J. White, and without any actual indorfement or affignment of the bill by White.

THE third count ftated, that the bill was made payable to themfelves, Livefay and Co. by the name and defcription of J. White.

THE fourth treated it as a common bill, payable to J. White, or order, and ftated that J. White indorfed it to the plaintiffs.

THE fifth as payable to *bearer;* and that the plaintiffs were the bearers.

THE fixth payable to J. White, or order; with an averment that, when the bill was made, there was no fuch perfon as J. White, the fuppofed payee,

but

but that the name was merely fictitious ; by reafon whereof the fum mentioned in the bill became and was payable to the bearer thereof, according to the effect and meaning of the bill ; averring alfo, that the plaintiffs were the bearers and proprietors thereof.

THE feventh count ftated, that there was a part-nerfhip, or houfe, of certain perfons ufing trade, as well in the name and firm of Livefay and Co. as in the name and firm of J. White; that the laft-mentioned perfons made a certain other bill, (the hand of one of them on their joint account, and in their copartnerfhip name and firm of Livefay and Co. being thereto fubfcribed) and directed it to the defendants, requiring them, three months after date, to pay to the faid laft mentioned copartners, by the name of J. White, or order, 721l. 5s. ; and that the faid laft-mentioned copartners afterwards, by a cer-tain indorfement in writing, appointed the contents to be paid to the plaintiffs, and delivered the bill, fo indorfed, to them.

ONE obfervation naturally prefents itfelf to the mind on the infpection of this record : The two firft counts ftate in fubftance all the circumftances found by the fpecial verdict, yet judgment was given for the plaintiffs, not on one of thefe, but on the fifth count, which ftates the bill as payable to bearer : It appears fingular that a court of juftice fhould decide, that a man fhould have a right to recover on a general count, fupported by fpecial circumftances given in evidence, and that thefe very

very circumſtances, when ſtated ſpecially on the record, ſhould not be conſidered as ſufficient to ſuſtain the action.—It ſeems impoſſible to account for this apparent inconſiſtency in any other way than by adverting to the declaration in the caſe of Vere and Lewis, and the judgment given upon it; in that there is no count which ſtates the circumſtances ſpecially; but the court being of opinion that the plaintiff was entitled to recover, thought the count, which ſtated the bill as payable to bearer, was a ſufficient foundation for their judgment; and a like count appearing in the caſe of Minet and Gibſon, they gave judgment on that, without adverting to the two counts, which ſtated the ſpecial circumſtances of the caſe.

THIS inconſiſtency being pointed out by the counſel for the plaintiff in error, in the Houſe of Lords, as one ground of impeaching the judgment of the court below, it was obſerved in anſwer, that there being in fact but one cauſe of action, the plaintiff could have judgment only on one count, and conſequently judgment was neceſſarily entered for the defendant on all the reſt; and if upon the whole record there appeared a ſufficient cauſe of action, but the judgment was entered on the wrong count, the court of error would rectify it.

INDEPENDENTLY of the rule which requires the proof of the hand-writing of the firſt indorſor, one preliminary objection has been made to the holder's right of recovery in any form of action againſt the drawer or acceptor: The very act of indorſing on
a bill

a bill a name which belongs to nobody, is, it is faid, in itſelf a felony; it has a general tendency to defraud, though the fraud be pointed againſt no particular individual; and in all caſes which have ariſen, has actually defrauded the holder of the bill, by impoſing on him the idea of a fecurity which does not exiſt. The act too of fending the bill into circulation with a fictitious name on it, it is faid, is a felony in him who is privy to the tranſaction.

WHETHER each or either of theſe acts be in reality a felony admits of confiderable doubt; and is one point on which the opinion of the judges was required by the Houſe of Lords. On the fuppoſition that that opinion was to be given in the affirmative, the advocates on the part of the defendant to the action inſiſted, that the holder of the bill could not recover againſt either the drawer or the acceptor, becauſe he could not make title, through the medium of a felony, in another; that a felony contaminated a tranſaction, and the civil remedy was completely merged in it by the policy of the law, to prevent, as much as poſſible, crimes from going unpuniſhed. The caſe of Peacock and Rhodes, they faid, could not be cited in oppoſition to this doctrine; for in that caſe the bill having been regularly indorſed by th payee, and having, though after having been ſtolen, come to the hands of the plaintiff for a good confideration, he was only under the neceſſity of proving the hand-writing of the firſt indorſor, and was bound to make no part of his title through the perſon who ſtole

the

Vid. 3 Term Rep. 176. Bl. Term Rep. C. B. 319.

Doug. 611

the bill: but here the plaintiff deriving his title
through the indorfement, which was a forgery, was
neceffarily barred of his action. To this it was
anfwered, that this propofition with refpect to the
effect of the felony was not true to fuch an extent;
it was true, indeed, that a civil action could not
be maintained, where the caufe of action was
grounded wholly on an act of felony; as if one ftole
a horfe or money, the owner could not maintain
trover, or money had and received againft him, becaufe the civil remedy was merged in the felony:
if the horfe came into the hands of another perfon,
under circumftances which would not amount to a
change of property, the original owner might recover him from that perfon; though, therefore,
the felony might be an anfwer to an action againft
either the drawer or acceptor, where it appeared
the defendant was guilty of the felony, yet that
would not preclude the plaintiff from recovering
againft the other if he did not appear to be guilty.

THE advocates on the other fide of the queftion
in the Houfe of Lords, profeffing not to impeach
the judgment of the Common Pleas, in the cafe of
Collins and Emett, in which the defendant was
perfectly innocent of the fuppofed felony, were
fatisfied to maintain, that where the fact of the
felony could be fixed on the defendant, that was a
bar to a civil action.

IN a tranfaction of this kind it is apprehended,
that whoever in fact makes the fictitious indorfement, both the drawer and acceptor muft in general
be

be guilty of publiſhing the bill with that indorſement on it, knowing it to be fictitious.

In ſuch a caſe, whether this amounts to a felony
is certainly a preliminary queſtion; for though,
independently of that queſtion, the plaintiff might
be entitled to recover, yet if in fact it ſhall be decided to be felony, he muſt neceſſarily be precluded
from his action, becauſe, if he were to recover at
all, he muſt recover againſt the felon himſelf.

But it may happen that the acceptor may not
know that the bill he accepts is attended by any
circumſtance different from thoſe attending Bills in
the uſual courſe of buſineſs; as where the bill is
brought him for acceptance by a third perſon,
either before the indorſement is made or afterwards,
without intimation of the payee's being fictitious:
The drawer too, even in *common* caſes, may be ſo
far unaffected with the felony, that he may not be
guilty of publiſhing the bill with a falſe indorſement on it, knowing it to be falſe, for it may be
carried out of his hands before the indorſement is
made: and in ſome caſes, as in that of Collins and
Emett, the perſon appearing as the drawer may be
perfectly ignorant of the tranſaction.

In any of theſe caſes, therefore, in which the defendant may appear to have acted without knowledge of the circumſtances, the queſtion of felony
cannot be conſidered as preliminary to the deciſion
on the plaintiff's right of action: If the adherence
to the rule which requires proof of the hand-writing
of

of the firſt indorſor be ſo rigid, that the plaintiff can in *no* form of action recover without it, that is, of itſelf, ſufficient without the intervention of the felony: If an action in *any* form can be ſuſtained, in which that rule may be diſpenſed with, then it is not through the felony that the plaintiff derives his title, and conſequently he cannot be affected by the deciſion of that queſtion.

If this reaſoning be well founded, it follows that whatever that deciſion might have been, the *general* was queſtion ſtill open to diſcuſſion; if in the affirmative, then in thoſe caſes only where the defendant is innocent; if in the negative, then in all caſes.

3 Term
Rep. 178,
181.
In ſupport of the judgment on the fifth count, which ſtates the bill as being drawn payable to bearer, it had been urged that in ſtating an agreement or a deed in pleading, it is ſufficient to ſtate the legal operation of it, though there might be a verbal variance between that and the inſtrument Co. Lit.
45, a. itſelf: as where a leaſe is made jointly by B. tenant for life of C. and him in remainder or reverſion in fee; during the life of C. this may be ſtated as the leaſe of tenant for life, and the confirmation of him in remainder or reverſion, that being then the legal operation of the deed; and, for the ſame reaſon, after the death of C. it may be ſtated as the leaſe of the perſon in remainder or reverſion, and the confirmation of B.

Bl. Term
Rep. C. B.
321.
So here, it was ſaid, though the bill appeared on the face of it, to be payable to order, yet as no-body

body exifted who could give fuch order, the engagement muft be to pay the bill, which was, in
effect, to render it payable to the bearer.

If, however, recourfe muft be had to the intention of the parties, it would feem that it is only in
the cafe of a *blank* indorfement in the name of the
fictitious payee, that the bill muft be confidered as
in effect payable to bearer; where the indorfement
is *fpecial*, as it was in the prefent cafe, the intention
to be attributed to the parties is, that it fhould be
payable to the order of him to whofe order it is
made payable by the fictitious indorfement, and
then the third count would have been better adapt-
ed to fupport the judgment than the fifth.

But it was objected that this argument was not
applicable to the prefent cafe; for though it muft
be admitted that a deed muft be ftated according to
its legal operation; yet that operation muft appear
on the face of the deed itfelf, without any collateral
circumftances to explain it, *contrary* to the evident
meaning of the words.

With refpect to the joint leafe of tenant for life,
and him in remainder or reverfion, if the feveral
interefts which they had in the land did not appear
in the deed, yet the operative words of the leafe were
not of that fixed and determinate meaning that
they could not admit of a different conftruction, if
collateral circumftances required it, in order to
give them effect: But the words " payable to order"
and " payable to bearer" were fo peculiarly appro-
priated to the diftinct fpecies of bills in which they
were

were refpectively ufed, that the one could by no
poffibility be conftrued to mean the other.

A STILL ftronger objection to the judgment's
being fupported on this count, arifes from a queftion put to the counfel by the Lord Chancellor,
" Whether an action could be maintained on this
" bill againft an indorfor?" That an action may be
maintained againft an indorfor of fuch a bill can
admit of no doubt: It is, from the frame of it,
payable to order, and transferable by indorfement;
and in an action againft an indorfor, no queftion
could arife about the fictitious payee, becaufe, as
will be feen hereafter, in that action the plaintiff derives no part of his title, through any of the parties
to the bill who precede the defendant: But a bill
payable to bearer, being transferable by delivery,
cannot regularly be indorfed ; and it feems, from
the queftion, to have been fuppofed that no action
could be maintained againft the indorfor; though
no doubt was entertained but that it might, even
when it was held, that a bill payable to bearer could
not be the fubject of an action by the indorfee,
againft the acceptor or drawer. If, therefore, the
judgment were affirmed on this count, it would
follow that the fame inftrument muft, in one cafe
be confidered as a bill payable to bearer, and in
another as a bill payable to order, both of which
it cannot be: But the difficulty fuggefted with refpect to the period when the bill fhall be faid to
ceafe to operate as payable to bearer, and affume
the character of a bill payable to order, admits of

an

an eafy folution : As againft the drawer and acceptor it operates as the one; as againft the indorfor it operates as the other.

So general feems to be the opinion that there ought to be a ftrict adherence to the rule which has given rife to this queftion, that the count which ftates the bill in its own terms, appears to have been abandoned on all fides : The plaintiff's counfel in the cafe of Tatlock and Harris abandoned it : the advocates on the fame fide in the Houfe of Lords abandoned it : The Court of King's Bench profeffed, that on it their opinion did not proceed ; and the Lord Chancellor, in his addrefs to the Houfe on the fubject of the queftions to be referred for the opinion of the judges, feemed to think it could not be fupported by the fpecial verdict.

ONE general objection was made to all thofe counts which were founded on the bill itfelf : It is only in favour of the cuftom of merchants that the practice is founded of declaring on thofe inftru-ments as fpecialties ; and if fuch a bill was not within the cuftom of merchants, then the plaintiff could not recover on thofe counts : That fuch a bill was not within the cuftom of merchants, it was argued, appeared from this, that in no book on the fubject was there to be found any allufion to a bill of this kind ; the ufage had provided, and the law had acknowledged two forts of bills, which were fufficient to anfwer every purpofe of trade, where the parties had no finifter view ; if it was wifhed to facilitate the circulation of the bill, it might be

Q   made

made payable to bearer; if to confine it within
certain limits, it might be made payable to order;
but this was a new invention to enable men to raife
money by a fraud, and it could not be pretended
that this was within the cuſtom of merchants.

To this it was anſwered, that the cuſtom of merchants is not to be confined to thoſe particulars
which are to be found in any mercantile book; nor
is the novelty of the thing a ſufficient reaſon to re-
ject it; it had not been all at once that every thing
which makes a part of the law and cuſtom of merchants at this day was eſtabliſhed; it was not without conſiderable ſtruggles that bills payable to bearer
obtained the ſame privileges as thoſe payable to
order: new facts laid the foundation of new rules;
and unleſs the deciſion on the queſtion of felony
could preclude all further diſcuſſion, there could
be no inconvenience in its being determined now
for the firſt time, that where a bill was drawn in
the name of a fictitious payee and accepted, the
drawer and acceptor ſhould, by the cuſtom of merchants, be anſwerable for the money to a holder by
a fair conſideration.

THAT ſuch a holder, in ſubſtantial juſtice, ought
to recover againſt either the drawer or the acceptor,
there can be no doubt: He has parted with his
property on the faith of their ſecurity; and it is not
very gracious in them to tell him, that becauſe, by
their contrivance perhaps, he has one ſecurity leſs
than he ſuppoſed, he ſhall not have the advantage
of thoſe which really exiſt.

SUCH

Such was the substance of the arguments on both sides of this important cause, and the points proposed for the opinion of the judges were these:

First, Whether the publication of the bill by the defendant with the fictitious indorsement on it, he knowing at the time that it was fictitious, a-mounted to a felony?

Secondly, If that were not a felony, whether the facts found by the special verdict, supported the judgment on the count, which stated the bill as payable to bearer?

Thirdly, If judgment on that count could not be supported, whether it could be supported by any other count founded on the bill as a specialty?

Fourthly, Whether, on any of the other counts which stated all the particular circumstances of the case, the plaintiff was entitled to recover?

It was also suggested by the Lord Chancellor, that if on the first point, the opinion of the judges should be in favour of the defendant in error, and on the others against him, another question might still be considered, whether, when the defendant to the action was privy to the fraud, the plaintiff might not recover in an action of deceipt?

On the first question, with respect to the felony, all the judges who delivered their opinions, agreed that the matter found in the special verdict was sufficient to relieve them from the necessity of pro-nouncing the drawers or the acceptors guilty of forgery; because, as it did not appear on the face

Q 2   of

of the fpecial verdict, the policy of the law would not fuffer the judges to infer it.

ON the next queftion, whether, on the matter found in the fpecial verdict, the bill mentioned in the fifth count could be deemed in law a bill payable to bearer?—fix * of their Lordfhips were of opinion that it might. On the queftion, whether the verdict could fupport any other count?—four † were of opinion that it would fupport the firft. Two other judges ‡, together with the Lord Chancellor, were of opinion that the judgment could not be fupported on any count.

THE arguments of the four who thought that the judgment might be fupported either on the fifth or firft count, were nearly fimilar, and to this effect:

THE bill in queftion imported to be a Bill of Exchange, payable to John White, or his order, but it never was, and it never could be fo, becaufe no fuch perfon as John White exifted. This was a fact known to the acceptors as well as to the drawers; it might therefore not be too much to fay that the intention of the acceptors was, that it fhould be payable to the bearer; they knew it had no indorfement on it by John White; they knew it came into the hands of Minet and Fector from Livefey, Hargrave, and Co.—It was fent into the world as

* Hotham, Thompfon, Perryn, Barons,—Gould, Juftice,—and Lords Kenyon and Loughborough.

† Hotham, Thompfon, Perryn, Gould.

‡ Eyre, Chief Baron,—and Heath, Juftice.

a bill

a bill payable to bearer.—The great principle on which their Lordſhips went was, that parties to a bill ſhould not, any more than parties to any deed or inſtrument, take advantage of their own wrongful act. The plaintiffs in error having accepted this bill with the privity that John White was a fictitious payee, and that the holders could not derive a title through him, the law would preſume that they intended that ceremony ſhould be waved. That this bill might be paid, the law would conclude that it was the undertaking and intention of the acceptors to pay it to any *bonâ fide* holder; or, in other words, it ſhould be conſidered as a bill payable to bearer.

Such a conſtruction, they conceived, would be moſt conformable to the effect which ought to be given to all commercial tranſactions, to true policy, and the principles of ſubſtantial juſtice. It was not poſſible for theſe partners in fraud to ſay, " we " have accepted this bill, but we meant nothing by " it, but to cheat all mankind." The law would hold them more ſtrongly to their engagement, on the ground of their own fraud, and would conſider the bill as capable of being transferred by delivery. They ſhould not be permitted to ſay, that the bill was not according to the law and cuſtom of merchants. The acceptors had put themſelves in a ſituation which made it obligatory on them to pay the bill, either in the very terms of it, or according to its legal operation, as in the preſent caſe, where the name of John White muſt be looked

Q 3   upon

upon as nothing,—as a non-entity,—and the bill
muſt be conſidered as payable to a real exiſting perſon, that is, to the bearer.

THEY were of opinion that the judgment of the
Court of King's Bench would afford a proper ſecurity to paper circulation; that it would tend to
the ſupport of public credit, and prove moſt beneficial to the great intereſts of commerce.

ON this queſtion, therefore, they were of opinion,
that on the matter found in the ſpecial verdict, the
bill, as mentioned in the fifth count, might be conſidered as a bill payable to bearer.

ON the queſtion, Whether the matter in the ſpecial verdict would ſupport any other count in the
declaration?—they were of opinion that it would
alſo ſupport the firſt count, by conſidering the bill
as a new bill, by the ſubſequent indorſement of
Liveſey, Hargrave, and Co.—Every indorſement
was in the nature of a new bill, and had the ſame
effect as if they had originally drawn the bill, without the name of John White, payable to themſelves
or their own order. The acceptance was ſubſequent to this indorſement, which muſt therefore be
coupled with the knowledge which the acceptors
had, or were bound to have, of this ſecond indorſement by the drawers; in this view they conſidered
the acceptors as liable under the firſt count.

THE argument of the Chief Baron was to this
effect:—That there was not a pretence for ſaying
that the matter of the ſpecial verdict could ſupport
any of the counts, except the firſt, ſecond, fifth,
and

and fixth : that therefore the enquiry was reduced
to this, whether this fpecial verdict would fupport
any one of thefe four counts.   This included every
thing that remained on the fecond and third queftions.—The Court of King's Bench, he faid, were of
opinion, that neither the firft, fecond, nor fixth
count, could be fupported in point of law ; and this
would be material on the argument on the fecond
queftion.

His Lordfhip entered particularly into the diftinct natures of the two kinds of bills, and the difference in the manner of transfer, the one being
transferable by indorfement, and the other by delivery, which gave rife to the difference in the
manner in which the holders of thefe refpective inftruments muft make out their titles.

It had been contended on the other fide, that
this was a bill payable to bearer. In his Lordfhip's
apprehenfion, it was a mere nullity : it was not
furely a very found argument to fay, that this muft
be a bill payable to bearer, becaufe it could be payable to no other man.   The affignable quality of a
bill was a thing created in the original frame and
conftitution of the inftrument ; and the party to
whom it was offered had only to read it.   If the
intent of the parties was to be collected from what
appeared on the face of the inftrument; they muft
confider it as a bill to pafs by indorfement.   Where
then was the authority for faying, that it was according to the effect and meaning of the bill, that

Q 4   the

the contents fhould become payable to the bearer?
—Every bill fhould be taken to be what, on the
face of it, it imported to be, and ought not to be
governed by any extrinfic circumftances.—It had
been ftated, that there was an analogy between Bills
of Exchange and deeds, and that the fame fort of
conftruction was applicable to both. But it ought
to be obferved, that deeds, by the common law,
had a certain operation and conftruction. Bills of
Exchange were inftruments which derived their
effect from the cuftom of merchants. Yet, admitting that there was fome analogy between Bills of
Exchange and deeds, would it from thence follow
that a bill payable to order, could be conftrued into a bill payable to bearer?

THERE were certain words in deeds which had a
certain fenfe and known conftruction, according to
their plain, obvious, and common import. If
judges went one ftep beyond this, they did not *con-
ftrue* men's deeds, but *made* them. It was fallacious
to apply the rules of common law to the law of
merchants. It had been faid that Bills of Exchange ought to be fupported: they certainly
fhould; but if a man would demand payment of a
Bill of Exchange according to the law of merchants,
he ought to bring his cafe within that law.

THE plaintiffs had declared on this bill as a Bill
of Exchange, and ftated their title to it to be by
affignment; the cuftom of merchants directed that
this affignment fhould be by indorfement; and if
the payee were a real perfon, it could not be tranf-
ferred

ferred in any other manner. If a man claimed to
be intitled to a Bill of Exchange drawn in favour of
a real payee, and not having an indorfement by
that payee, he could not recover on it as a Bill of
Exchange, though he had paid a full confideration
for it. But, in the prefent cafe, it was faid, that
John White was a fictitious name, and that his indorfement was likewife fictitious; this fact, it was
faid, was known to the acceptors; by reafon whereof, and by the cuftom of merchants, the acceptors
became liable to 'pay the value of the bill to the
plaintiffs. He had looked in vain where the places
were to be found of this ufage and cuftom of merchants applying to fuch a cafe. What logician
could draw fuch a conclufion from fuch premifes?
Where was fuch a rule to be found? If no fuch
rule was to be found exprefsly laid down, was it to
be collected by inference? In his apprhenfion nothing could warrant fuch a conclufion.

He was ready to admit, that by the law of England, no man fhould be permitted to allege his own
crime; and in that fenfe he agreed, that no man
fhould take advantage of his own fraud, to fet it up
by way of defence; but ftill a plaintiff muft recover by his own ftrength; and the plaintiff on a
Bill of Exchange, like a plaintiff in every other cafe,
muft fhew a fufficient title. He muft prove his
cafe, and when that was done, it fhould not be permitted to the defendant to fet up his own fraud, to
infift that the payee was fictitious, and turn that
into a defence in anfwer to the plaintiff's cafe; but
here

here was the fundamental fallacy in the arguments used by the judges on the other side of the question, arising from not observing this proposition—That the plaintiffs must first prove their case and make out their title before the defendants were called upon to say any thing. But here the plaintiffs, in making out their own case, were driven to shew the facts, which the defendants, by way of defence, were attempting to shew against them. Where the plaintiffs could not make out a fair *bonâ fide* case, the defendants were not bound to say any thing.

HE considered the interests of commerce to be deeply concerned in the support of fair credit, and the discouragement of false.—The interests of commerce, and of gentlemen who dealt in discounting paper money, were not exactly the same. Trade might receive a deep wound from the failure of a number of capital houses, when the dealers in paper might receive twenty shillings in the pound, by proving their debts under twenty different commissions. While their Lordships were attending to the interests of the holders of bills circumstanced like the present, they ought not to forget the interests of the trade and commerce of the country. To support such instruments as this, was to encourage a spirit of loose adventure, a spirit of gaming in commerce, a spirit of fraud of every kind, the weight of which must necessarily cramp and depress every honest man, who traded on his own capital. No evil could arise by giving judgment against these bills; but if they were held to be recoverable

coverable in a court of law, there would always be found people who would avail themselves of the advantages to be derived from the negociation of such bills; this fictitious credit would go on, and where the mischief would end no man could tell.

Such were the reasons which induced his Lordship to think that the judgment of the Court of King's Bench ought to be reversed.

Mr. Justice Heath concurred with the Chief Baron, and argued in a similar manner.

Lord Kenyon observed, that if their Lordships could support this judgment, they would be glad to do it, and make it subservient to the honesty of the case.

In order to make out a title in a manner conformable to the words of the instrument, the indorsement of John White must be proved; this could not be done in this instance, because the special verdict had found, that no such person existed. From the nature of this bill, it could not be negociated in the terms in which it was drawn; but melancholy indeed must be the case of many persons, if there were positive rules of law that no instrument should operate at all, unless it operated in the very terms in which it was written. But deeds operated in a variety of ways, in order to effectuate the intentions of the parties. He was surprised at the observation that deeds admitted of a more lax construction than Bills of Exchange. This doctrine was new to him. In deeds that were intended to act on real property,

and

and where the affiftance of conveyancers was called in, he fhould have thought as much ftrictnefs at leaft ought to be obferved in the conftruction of inftruments of that fort, as in Bills of Exchange, which were drawn by men of plain common fenfe, who were engaged in trade, and who had no legal affiftance. He faw nothing that could prevent fuch a bill as this being negociated according to its legal operation.—There was the cafe of a Bill of Exchange which came extremely near to this, tried before Lord Mansfield in 1769, where his Lordfhip had held, that the holder was entitled to recover.

In anfwer to the obfervation, that it would be hard if fome remedy were not to be given to the party who had paid a valuable confideration for this bill, it had been faid that the plaintiffs ought to have brought their action *ex delicto* againft the acceptors. But it muft be remembered, this was a remedy not negociable in its nature; it could not be transferred, and died with the party who was guilty of the fraud. An action *ex contractu* did not die with the party entering into the contract.—His Lordfhip faw no reafon why the judgment of the King's Bench fhould not be affirmed.

The Lord Chancellor began with obferving, that this queftion did not turn on any general rule of fubftantial juftice, or on policy, but on the form of the action; and the queftion was, whether the plaintiffs' method of complaining, and the mode in which they fought redrefs, did or did not apply to their particular cafe.

In

In the whole courfe of the argument, no doubt had been entertained of the wifdom of the law, which had ordained fpecific remedies for fpecific cafes.

By the fpecial verdict, the plaintiffs were not found to have any cognizance of the fraud; the bill being drawn in the manner in which it was, it became important to fay whether there was no fraud. The reafon of making the bill payable to the name of John White, was in order to give it a greater degree of currency, and a more extenfive circulation. It was to give countenance to a thing which was unreal, and which, in his Lordfhip's ap-prehenfion, muft be deemed a fraud.

His Lordfhip, after remarking on the diftinction between bills payable to order and payable to bearer, proceeded to obferve that the fpecial ver-dict had ftated all the facts neceffary to be known, except one, which would have been very material, and that was, whether Gibfon and Johnfon, at the time they accepted this bill, knew that the defend-ants in error had paid the drawers value for it. In confequence of accepting this bill, the acceptors came under all the obligations to pay it which the nature of the inftrument required.

The thing which firft required explanation was this: what was the true conftruction of the law on this inftrument, with refpect to all the parties to the tranfaction? Under what obligations had they come to the public or to the individuals concerned in the bill? This was a very material article in the

inquiry.

inquiry. The learned judges had confined their
anſwers too cloſely to the ſpecial verdict, and had
not given him that ſatisfaction which he had ex-
pected on this part of the caſe.. It had indeed
been hinted, that if a forgery had been ſtated in
the ſpecial verdict, this might have made a difference; and it had been doubted, whether the acceptance would have been a felony, though the indorſement had been found to be a forgery with
reſpect to the drawers: as on the ſpecial verdict,
however, no forgery was ſtated, nothing of this
ſort could be implied: it was for the ſafety of mankind that the forms of law ſhould be obſerved, and
that nothing ſhould be aſſumed beyond what was
expreſsly found by the ſpecial verdict. Though the
evidence were ever ſo cogent, a court of law could
not draw the concluſion;—that was the province
of the jury.

THIS was indeed a melancholy caſe, with reſpect
to the parties. For, whatever became of this bill,
with reſpect to the very next that came before the
court, it muſt be decided, whether this was or was
not a forgery: whether the putting the name of
John White, or any other forged name, on a Bill of
Exchange, was not matter within the ſtatute. This
he could have wiſhed to have been ſtated. It muſt
therefore be found. It muſt be decided, whether
thoſe who call themſelves merchants ſhall be permitted to put fictitious names, or the names of any
other perſons on bills, and write thoſe names
themſelves.

IT

It was a queftion which deferved a folution, how far fuch an inftrument as this was or was not to be confidered as made for the purpofe of obtaining money under falfe pretences?

The criminality of this inftrument ought, in his Lordfhip's opinion, to prevent the holders of it from bringing an action on it. He was rather inclined to go on the fair and clear rules of law, let the lofs fall where it would, than to ftrain a rule of law to do fubftantial juftice in a particular cafe: for by the latter, more harm was done to the public than good to individuals.

The next queftion which arofe in this inquiry was, whether this was a bill payable to bearer in the terms of the the fifth count? And here his learned friend, who had immediately preceded him, had difappointed him. He thought it material to be determined, at what period this inftrument began to be a bill payable to bearer. Did it begin, in the language of the fixth count, after it came into the hands of the holders, and before they carried it to the acceptors?—Suppofe the holders of this bill had known that John White was a nominal perfon, at the time they took it,—he wifhed to know whether, in that cafe, it would have been a bill payable to bearer. He wifhed alfo to know, if this bill had been loft, and had got into the hands of a ftranger without any of thofe names upon it, whether that ftranger could have come to the acceptors and demanded payment; could he have recovered in

an

an action againft the acceptors, and have put the acceptance out of doors?

As a meafure of general policy, it was of extreme importance that tranfactions of this kind fhould be ftopped. Fictions on bills would be the conftant courfe, if their Lordfhips made fuch bills payable to bearer.

WITH regard to the hardfhips of the cafe, he obferved there muft be fome remedy. The law always found a proper remedy for every injury.—— The queftion was fairly reduced to this: was it ever according to the avowed policy of the law of England, that the contents of a Bill of Exchange fhould be proved by any thing but by the words of the bill? He conceived that no bill could have a fenfe introduced upon it, but what was agreeable to the words of the bill; and it was on account of its deviation from this rule that he diffented from the prefent judgment. If it were faid, that a Bill of Exchange was what it purported to be, the holder knew what he had to expect, and would not be afraid of advancing his money; but if it were held that a bill, which, on the face of it, appeared to be payable to order, was a bill payable to bearer, it was impoffible for the holder to know what would happen. The Court of King's Bench had given a judgment on this bill contrary, not only to all the notions which the holders had on the fubject, but contrary to every expectation which they could poffibly entertain when they took it—they had

taken

taken it as a bill payable to order, and it had turned
out to be a bill payable to bearer.

IT had been humoroufly faid, that it could not be
told what a will was, 'till it had gone through the
Houfe of Lords; but he had never heard this of a
bill of exchange.

HIS lordfhip next adverted to the *nifi prius* decifion of Lord Mansfield, in 1769.—He conceived
that cafe did not apply to the prefent; becaufe
Lord Mansfield had faid, he would not permit
parties to avail themfelves of their own fraud; and
held, that the inftrument fhould be confidered to
be what it purported to be on the face of it.   But
in the prefent cafe directly the contrary was attempted; it was wifhed to convert a bill which on
the face of it purported to be a bill payable to
order, into a bill payable to bearer.—He conceived
that more authority had been given to that cafe
than Lord Mansfield intended.

IT had been faid, that this judgment might be
fupported from analogy to deeds which regulated
the conveyances of real eftates.   In deeds, there
muft be certain words ufed, as *dedi*, *conceffi*, &c.
without which the conveyance would be void.
There muft be a fubject grantable; there muft be
a perfon capable of granting; and there muft be a
perfon capable of receiving.

IN like manner he conceived there muft be a
certain form of words ufed in bills payable to
order, and a different form in bills payable to
bearer.   It muft appear clearly on the face of the

R

bill,

bill, whether it be a bill payable to order, or a bill
payable to bearer.   On thefe grounds he differed in
opinion from thofe who thought the judgment could
be maintained on the fifth count.

IF he were to fupport the judgment on any count
it would be on the firft.   This was not a Bill of
Exchange, affignable according to the law and
cuftom of merchants, but it was an undertaking.
If the defendants in error had given money to the
drawers for this bill, and the acceptors had known
that they had done fo, and on that account had accepted the bill, he conceived this would have been
an undertaking to pay the debt of another : for in
that cafe the drawers would have been indebted to
the holders, and the acceptors would have been
apprized of that circumftance ; and the confideration would have been, that they, by interpofing
their credit, would have prevented the holders from
going back on the drawers: It would not have
been a *nudum pactum.*

BUT his Lordfhip conceived it would be impoffible the judgment could be fupported even on
the firft count, and he faw no ground on which it
was poffible to affirm the judgment.   Their lordfhips ought not to forget the numerous inconve-
niences that would attend the tranfactions of commercial men.   *Who* was to know that John White
was a mere fiction ? *When* was it to be known ?—
When the holders come againft the acceptors, they
refufe payment, and ftand an action ; and at laft
the holders are told that the inftrument which they
took

took as a bill payable to order, was a bill payable to bearer. Let it be fraud or not to make such an inftrument, it muft be an affignable bill. The acceptors fhould not be allowed to urge fraud in their own defence: they fhould be bound by the fraud: they fhould be tied down to their tranfaction, as if it had been honeft and *bonâ fide*. But the obfervation of the Chief Baron appeared unanfwerable, that until the plaintiffs had made out their title, the defendants could not be called upon to make a defence.

LORD Loughborough faid, that he continued of the fame opinion which he had originally delivered in the Common Pleas; that this inftrument ought to be confidered as a bill payable to bearer.

THE Lord Chancellor had very properly propofed to the confideration of the judges, a queftion preliminary to the difcuffion on the merits. This queftion was, whether by the matter found in the fpecial verdict, the acts done by the parties to this bill imported an utterance of it, knowing it to have been forged?

THE anfwer which had been received was, that from the matter found in the fpecial verdict, it was impoffible to fay any forgery had been committed refpecting the bill. One of the judges had hefitated whether the acceptance amounted to an utterance; but the general opinion was, that there was no forgery on the bill. The ground on which the judges delivered this opinion was inconteftable. The fpecial verdict did not ftate that the writing

of

of the name of John White on the bill was done with an intent to defraud any particular perfon.

On the fpecial verdict, the tranfaction was ftated thus—Livefey, Hargrave, and Co. made this paper in the form of a bill, and directed it to Gibfon and Johnfon, defiring them, three months after date, to pay to John White, or order, 721l. 5s. for value received. After that, and before the bill was prefented for acceptance, it got into the hands of Minet and Fector, for a valuable confideration. But a very material circumftance had taken place, by the drawers having indorfed it. The indorfement of the drawers was certainly unneceffary with refpect to the bill itfelf; but the jury feeing the indorfement of the drawers before the value of the bill was actually paid, thought it a demonftration that no deception had been practifed on the holders, but that it muft have occurred to Minet and Fector, that White was not in fact the payee of the bill; for that if he had, it muft have come from him, and not from the drawers; and that it was impoffible to account for its coming back again to the drawers, if it had come out of the hands of the payee, which it muft have done had he been a real perfon. This demonftrated that it was completely indifferent whether White exifted or not; whether he was worth a fixpence or not; whether he was to be found or not. Gibfon and Johnfon accepted it as the draft of Livefey, Hargrave, and Co. with their indorfement upon it, as the indorfement of a bill that had never been out of their cuftody.

cuftody. Finding it with the name of Livefey, Hargrave, and Co. indorfed upon it, as well as that of John White, they accepted it. On what ground, and under what circumftances did they accept it? Was it an acceptance to pay to the order of John White? They knew at the time the name of White was nothing. They knew it was a bill that had come immediately out of the hands of Livefey, Hargrave, and Co. and therefore they accepted it, to pay to the perfon who for value held it of the latter, which was to pay it to whoever fhould be the bearer.

The diftinction between bills payable to order, and bills payable to bearer was this, that the former muft be affigned by the real payee; they could never get back to the hands of the drawer but by being difhonoured. A bill payable to bearer was fuch a bill that any man who picked it up in the ftreets, might maintain an action on it. The ftate of the bill in queftion, when prefented for acceptance, negatived the idea that there was any fuch perfon as John White. The acceptors knew, that the words *John White*, or order, were merely colourable.

There was a convenience in trade for merchants to be able to raife money; and this was frequently done through the medium of Bills of Exchange. The bills were fent to market and negociated by means of the brokers. The broker put a name upon them, and did not difclofe his principal until he had found a perfon who would deal with him;

the

the principal was then difcovered, who then put his name on the bill, and from the moment the buyer got that indorfemeñt, he was perfectly indifferent.

THE acceptance was fubfequent to the indorfement by the drawers: the bill had ceafed to be payable to the order of John White, becaufe the acceptors, at the time they put their acceptance to it, took John White to be merely matter óf form ; and therefore his lordfhip was of opinion, that, in its proper and legal operation, and in the real ftate of the tranfaction between the parties, this was a bill which Gibfon and Johnfon undertook to pay to whoever fhould produce that bill to them with the indorfement of Livefey, Hargrave, and Co. and to whoever had paid a valuable confideration to the drawers.

THE Chief Baron had conceived the queftion to be, Whether the plaintiff had made out his title to recover on this bill, and that the defendant was not obliged to move one ftep in the caufe until the plaintiff had produced evidence of an affignment made by White, by fome circumftances that would amount to a proof againft the perfon who difputed that fact. They muft previoufly eftablifh the fact, that an affignment had been made of that bill by John White, before they could call for payment.

THIS objection had operated ftrongly on his mind ; but he thought he could anfwer it : it femed to him to proceed on a miftaken ftate of the queftion.

HE

He conceived that the plaintiffs had clearly and distinctly proved their title to the bill, by proving that they had paid value for it to the person from whom they received it.

A few observations would make this sufficiently clear. The defendants in error had proved they paid value for the bill to Livesey, Hargrave, and Co. Whether the name of White or order could be proved or not, an action might be brought against them as indorsors. For a long series of years, the courts had held, that in an action by an indorsee against an indorsor, it was only necessary to prove the indorsor's hand ; and it was on this ground that an indorsement made a new bill. In the present bill he could prove that the drawers wrote the name of White with the privity of the acceptors. It was in vain, therefore, to say that he had not made out his title; he had met the difficulty suggested ; and the only question was, whether he had made out such a title as would give him a right to recover.

He confessed, that when the justice of the case stared him fully in the face, he did not find himself pleased to be knocked down by a formal objection. He conceived that substantial justice was of much more importance than the beauties of special pleading.

This was an engagement, on the part of the plaintiffs in error, to pay to whoever should hold this bill under the indorsement of Livesey, Hargrave, and Co.—Was not this, in fact and in truth,

an

an undertaking to the bearer. It was not an engagement to pay exprefsly to Minet and Fector,
but to any perfon who could entitle himfelf under
an indorfement from Livefey, Hargrave, and Co.
The true effect of the bill, in every form in which
it could be put, was, that it was a bill payable to
bearer. This bill was never fent into the world as
a bill payable to order; for while it was in the
hands of the drawers it was not; and the moment
it was fent into the world, it was a bill payable to
bearer. It was no ftraining of the law, therefore,
to fay, that this bill, to all intents and purpofes,
was a bill payable to bearer.

It had been faid, that if this judgment were affirmed, it would be productive of numerous incon-
veniences. He durft not truft himfelf to look into
futurity, to fee what would be the confequence of
checking this, or the utility of fetting up a fictitious
payee. If this were really ufeful to merchants, and
was prohibited by the decifion in the prefent cafe,
their lordfhips would only tell them, inftead of a fictitious name, to fubftitute the name of the meaneft
cobler in the ftreet, or the loweft clerk in the houfe.

Their lordfhips knew that the parties had all
become bankrupts; fuppofe the prefent holders
could not recover in an action brought upon this
bill, what would be the ftate of thefe parties?—At
the time when the credit of thefe different houfes
was broken up, a vaft amount of their engagements
ftood on fuch bills, which had been given to tradefmen for goods fold and delivered. The confe-

quence

quence might be, that if fuch bills were held to be
a nullity, thefe gentlemen might finifh their bankruptcy; would have their certificates in their
pockets, and a large furplus to themfelves. It
would be a great reproach to juftice, and to the
laws of England, not to be able to overtake the
extravagance of defperate adventurers.

HE was, on thefe grounds, of opinion, that the
judgment of the Court of King's Bench ought to
be affirmed.

LORD BATHURST faid, that at firft he had felt
great weight in the objection of the Chief Baron,
refpecting the infufficiency of the plaintiffs' title,
but he was now fatisfied that this had always been
a bill payable to bearer.—But if the caufe had been
tried before him, he would have followed the ex-
ample of Lord Mansfield, and not have permitted
the defendants to infift on the proof of an affignment by John White, which they had always known
was impoffible. It was confiftent with juftice that
the holders fhould recover the amount of the bill
for which they had given a valuable confideration;
and Gibfon and Johnfon having accepted this bill,
they fhould not be now permitted to fay they would
not be bound.—His lordfhip therefore thought, that
the judgment ought to be affirmed.

THE Lord Chancellor then put the queftion, that
the judgment be reverfed, when, without a divifion,
it was affirmed.

SINCE this decifion the queftion has been again
agitated, in the cafe of Hunter, in the character of

indorfee,

indorfee, againſt Gibſon and Johnſon, in that of acceptors.

THE cauſe came before Lord Kenyon and a ſpecial Jury at Guildhall, at the ſittings after Michaelmas term, 1791, when the defendants demurred to the evidence offered on the part of the plaintiff.

THE bill was dated " Falmouth, 11th March, 1788, and purported to be drawn by Nathaniel Hingſton, payable to *William Fletcher or order*, and was addreſſed to Gibſon and Johnſon, Bankers, in London; the acceptance of the latter appeared on the face of it; and it was indorſed " William Fletcher," and " by procuration of Liveſey, Hargrave, and Co. A. Goodrich."

THE declaration contained 13 counts: The firſt of theſe ſtated, in the uſual form, the drawing of the bill by Hingſton in favour of William Fletcher, and its direction to Gibſon and Johnſon, ſuggeſting that Hingſton, at the time of drawing it, well knew that no ſuch perſon exiſted as William Fletcher, mentioned in the bill; it then ſtated, that on the ſaid bill a certain indorſement was made, purporting to be the indorſement of William Fletcher named in the bill, and to be ſubſcribed with his name, requiring the ſum of money mentioned in the bill to be paid to certain perſons uſing trade and commerce as copartners, in the copartnerſhip, name, and firm of Liveſey, Hargrave, and Company, *or their order*; that the bill was afterwards preſented to Gibſon and Johnſon for acceptance, who

who, according to the cuftom of merchants, accepted it, knowing that no fuch perfon exifted as
William Fletcher in the bill named, and that the
name of William Fletcher fo indorfed on the bill
was not the hand-writing of any perfon of that
name; and that the faid perfons ufing trade and
commerce in the name and firm of Livefey, Hargrave, and Company, afterwards, by a certain indorfement on the bill, fubfcribed with the hand
and name of one Abfalom Goodrich, by procuration of Livefey, Hargrave, and Company, according to the cuftom of merchants, appointed the
money, in the bill mentioned, to be paid to the faid
Robert Hunter, and delivered the bill fo indorfed,
as well with the name of the faid William Fletcher
as with the name of the faid Abfalom Goodrich to
the faid Robert Hunter, by reafon whereof, &c.

THE fecond count ftated, exactly in the common
form, the drawing and direction of the bill; the
delivery of it to William Fletcher as a real perfon;
the prefentment of it to Gibfon and Johnfon; its
acceptance by them; a fpecial indorfement by
William Fletcher to Livefey, Hargrave, and Company, or their order; and the indorfement to
Hunter, by their procuration by Abfalom Goodrich.

THE third count defcribed the bill as drawn by
Hingfton on Gibfon and Johnfon, payable to the
bearer.

THE fourth count, after ftating that the bill was
drawn by Hingfton on Gibfon and Johnfon, and
made

made payable to William Fletcher or order, and that it was prefented to Gibfon and Johnfon, and accepted by them, averred, that at the time when it was drawn, or at any time afterwards, there was not any fuch perfon as William Fletcher, the fuppofed payee, but that the fame name was merely fictitious, by reafon of which it alledged the fum of money mentioned in the bill became payable to the bearer; and it then averred, that the plaintiff, in due form of law, became the bearer and proprietor of it.

THE fifth count defcribed the bill as drawn on Gibfon and Johnfon by Livefey, Hargrave, and Company, " with the hand and name of the faid Abfalom Goodrich, by procuration of the faid Livefey, Hargrave, and Company, thereunto fub-fcribed," and made payable to Robert Hunter, the plaintiff, or order.*

THESE were all the counts framed on the bill itfelf.

THE fixth count, reciting " that the faid Nathaniel Hingfton was indebted to the plaintiff Robert Hunter for money had and received for the ufe of the plaintiff, and for money paid, laid out, and expended by the plaintiff for the ufe of the faid Nathaniel Hingfton; and that the laft-mentioned fum of money, at the time of making the promife

---

* This count was evidently framed on the principle that the indorfement by the procuration of Livefey, Hargrave, and Co. was as between them, the acceptors, and a fubfequent indorfee, to be confidered as a new bill.

and

and undertaking thereinafter mentioned, was
wholly due and owen and unpaid from the faid
Nathaniel Hingfton to the faid Robert Hunter,"
alleged, that the defendants, Gibfon and Johnfon,
in confideration of the premifes, and alfo in confideration that the plaintiff, at their fpecial inftance
and requeft, would forbear and give day of payment of the laft mentioned fum until the 14th day
of May, 1788,* and would not fue the faid N.
Hingfton for the recovery of that fum at any time
before default fhould be made by the defendants in
payment of it, according to their promife and
undertaking next thereinafter mentioned, undertook and promifed to the plaintiff to pay him that
fum on the 14th day of May, 1788: It then averred
that the plaintiff, confiding in this promife and
undertaking, forbore and gave day of payment till
the 14th of May, 1788, and did not fue or profe-
cute the faid N. Hingfton for the recovery of the
faid fum, or any part of it, at any time before the
defendants had made default in paying the faid fum,
according to their promife and undertaking; and
that the plaintiff had not at any time *fince* the
making of that promife and undertaking fued or
profecuted the faid N. Hingfton for the recovery
of that fum or any part of it, but had wholly for-
borne fo to do; *and that the faid laft mentioned fum
of money remained wholly due and unpaid, &c.*

---

* This was the day the bill became due.

THE feventh count differed from the fixth only in this, that it alleged the undertaking of the defendants to pay on the 14th of May to be conditional, " if the faid fum of money fhould then remain unpaid to the faid Robert Hunter;" and, inftead of averring " that the faid laft mentioned fum of money remained wholly due and unpaid," averred " that, on and after the faid 14th day of May, 1788, it had remained, and had been, and ftill remained, and was wholly due and unpaid, &c."

THE eighth count refembled the fixth, ftating Livefey, Hargrave, and Company as the original debtors to Hunter, inftead of Hingfton.

THE ninth differed from the eighth only as the feventh did from the fixth.

THE tenth was for money had and received; the eleventh for money paid; the twelfth for money lent and advanced; and the thirteenth on an account ftated—The plea was the general iffue.

The record proceeded in thefe words :—

" AND the jurors of the jury, whereof mention is within made, being called, likewife come, and being chofen, tried and fworn, to fay the truth of the premifes within contained, the faid Robert Hunter produced to the jury aforefaid a certain inftrument in writing, in the words and figures following, that is to fay—

£. 521. 7s.

Falmouth, March 11, 1788.

" Two months after date pay to Mr. William Fletcher, or order, five hundred twenty-one pounds feven fhillings, value received, with or without advice.

NATHANIEL HINGSTON.

To Meffrs. Gibfon and Johnfon,
    Bankers, London.   No. 2068.

G. *and* J.

AND whereupon are the following indorfements, " William Fletcher," " by procuration of Livefey, Hargrave, and Co." " A. Goodrich;" and the faid Robert Hunter, to prove and maintain the iffue within joined on his part, fhews in evidence to the jury aforefaid, by Robert Booth, a witnefs duly fworn in that behalf, that he, the faid Robert Booth, was a clerk to certain perfons ufing trade and commerce as copartners, in the copartnerfhip, name, and firm of Livefey, Hargrave, and Company, and that one Nathaniel Hingfton was, at the time of drawing the faid inftrument, a fhop-keeper, at Falmouth, in the county of Cornwall; that the name of Nathaniel Hingfton fubfcribed to the faid inftrument was the hand-writing of the faid Nathaniel Hingfton, and that he drew the fame as
agent

agent to the faid Livefey, Hargrave, and Company;
that Livefey, Hargrave, and Company ufed to
fend down to the faid Nathaniel Hingfton blank
bills of Exchange for him to fign as the drawer
thereof; that many fuch blank bills were fent down
together; that when they were returned to the
faid Livefey, Hargrave, and Company, they filled
up the blanks with the fum to be paid, and the
name of the perfon to whom the fame was to be
payable; that when the bills were fo drawn and
filled up, they were carried, indifcriminately with
other bills, to the houfe of Thomas Gibfon and
Jofeph Johnfon, the defendants, for their acceptance; that Livefey, Hargrave, and Company gave
Gibfon and Johnfon advice of the bills fo drawn
by the faid Nathaniel Hingfton; that fuch bills,
indifcriminately with the faid other bills, ufed to be
carried two or three times a-day from the houfe of
Livefey, Hargreave, and Company to the houfe of
Gibfon and Johnfon for acceptance, and were often
carried wet; that the acceptance of the bill produced was the acceptance of the defendants, Thomas Gibfon and Jofeph Johnfon; that the faid
Robert Booth upon thofe occafions ufed to fee the
defendant Johnfon; that Livefey, Hargrave, and
Company were generally indebted to the defendants,
Gibfon and Johnfon, on the balance of accounts,
for cafh advanced by the faid Gibfon and Johnfon
to the faid Livefey, Hargrave and Company; that
the defendants, Gibfon and Johnfon, were covered
for thefe acceptances by Bills of Exchange given

as

as a security for the same, but that the said bills so given as a security have not been paid; that no such person as William Fletcher in the said instrument and indorsement named, existed; and that the name William Fletcher, so indorsed on the said instrument, was not the handwriting of any person of the name of William Fletcher. And the said Robert Hunter further shews in evidence to the jury aforesaid, by one Stephen Barber, a witness duly sworn in that behalf, that he negociated the instrument now produced, with the plaintiff Robert Hunter; that he carried it from Livesey, Hargrave, and Company, to get it discounted for them; and that he told the said Robert Hunter from whom he came: that the said Robert Hunter gave him the value for the said instrument in money, and he took it back to be indorsed by Livesey, Hargrave, and Company; and that it was indorsed by Absalom Goodrich, by procuration of Livesey, Hargrave, and Company: that the said instrument had been accepted by Gibson and Johnson before it was carried to be discounted."

AFTER stating the demurrer to this evidence, and the joinder in demurrer, the record proceeded thus:—

" WHEREUPON it is told to the jurors aforesaid, that they shall inquire what damages the said Robert Hunter has sustained, as well by reason of the matter shewn in evidence as aforesaid, as for his costs and charges by him about his suit in this be-

S half

half expended, in cafe it fhall happen that judgment fhall be given upon the evidence aforefaid
for the faid Robert Hunter; and the jurors aforefaid, upon their oaths aforefaid, thereupon fay, that
if it fhall happen that judgment fhall be given for
the faid Robert Hunter upon the evidence aforefaid, then they affefs the damages of the faid Robert
Hunter, by him fuftained by reafon of the matter
fhewn in evidence as aforefaid, befides his cofts and
charges by him about his fuit in this behalf expended, to 521l. 7s. and for thofe cofts and charges
to 40s.—and thereupon the faid jurors, by the
affent of the faid parties, are difcharged from giving
any further verdict upon the premifes."———Then
followed the entry of judgment for the plaintiff.

In Hilary term, 1792, this demurrer to evidence
was fet down for argument before the Court of
King's Bench; but it being the underftanding of
both parties that a writ of error was to be brought,
the court gave judgment for the plaintiff, without
argument.

On this judgment a writ of error was brought,
returnable in Parliament, and the general errors
affigned.

The cafe having been fully argued at the bar
of the Houfe of Lords, the following queftions
were propofed to the judges :—

1. Whether, upon the ftate of the evidence
given for the plaintiff in this cafe, it was competent
to the defendants to infift upon the jury being difcharged

charged from giving a verdict, by demurring to the evidence and obliging the plaintiff to join in demurrer?

2. WHETHER, on this record, *any* judgment can be given?

3. IN cafe *no* judgment can be given, what ought to be the award?

To thefe queftions Lord Chief Juftice Eyre delivered the unanimous anfwer of the judges.

HIS Lordfhip, after explaining the nature of demurrers in general, and concluding his explanation by obferving, that before the queftion between the parties could be referred to the decifion of the judges "the *fact* muft be firft afcertained," proceeded to difcufs the firft queftion in the prefent cafe.

"ALL the books," he obferved, "agreed, that if a matter of *record*, or other matter in *writing*, were offered in evidence to maintain an iffue joined between the parties, the adverfe party might *infift* on the jury being difcharged from giving a verdict, by demurring to the evidence, and *compelling* the party offering the evidence to join in demurrer: that the books alfo agreed, that if *parol* evidence were offered and the adverfe party demurred, he who offered the evidence *might* join in demurrer if he *would*; but that, on the queftion whether the party offering *parol* evidence fhould be *compelled* to join in demurrer, the language of the books was very indiftinct. That the reafon affigned, why he fhould be *obliged* to join in demurrer, when the

evidence

evidence he offered was in *writing*, was this, " *that
there could not be any variance of matter in writing.*" *
That *parol* evidence was fometimes *certain*, and no
more admitted of any variance than matter in
writing; but it was alfo frequently loofe and indeterminate, frequently circumftantial.—That the
reafon for obliging the party offering evidence in
writing to join in demurrer, applied to the *firft*
fort of *parol* evidence, but did not apply to the
fecond, which might be urged with more or lefs
effect to a jury; leaft of all would it apply to evidence of circumftances' which was meant to operate
beyond the *proof* of the *exiftence of thofe circumftances,*
and to conduce to the proof of the exiftence of *other
facts*—yet, if there could be no demurrer in fuch
cafes, there would be no confiftency in the doctrine
of demurrers to evidence, by which the application
of the law to the fact on an iffue was meant to be
withdrawn from a jury, and transferred to the
judges.   If the party who demurred would *admit*
the *fact*, the *evidence* of which fact was loofe and
indeterminate; or in the cafe of *circumftantial*
evidence, if he would admit the *exiftence* of the
fact, which the *circumftances* offered in evidence
conduced to prove, there would then be no more
variance in this parol evidence than in a matter
in writing, and the reafons for *compelling* the party

* Middleton v. Baker, Cro. El. 753. S. C. 5 Co. 104.

who

who offered the evidence to join in demurrer would then apply, and the doctrine of demurrers to evidence would be uniform and confiftent."

AFTER fhewing, from an elaborate examination of the cafes * on the fubject, that this was the fair refult of the principles adopted in them, his Lordfhip faid, that the anfwer on which the judges had agreed to the firft queftion propofed to them was this, " That upon the ftate of the evidence given for the plaintiff in this cafe, it was *not* competent to the defendants to infift upon the jury being difcharged from giving a verdict, by demurring to the evidence, and obliging the plaintiff to join in demurrer, *without diftinctly admitting upon the record every fact and every conclufion which the evidence given for the plaintiff conduced to prove.*"

To the fecond queftion it was anfwered, that no judgment could be given ; that the examination of the witneffes had been conducted fo loofely, or the demurrer had been fo negligently framed, that there was no manner of certainty in the ftate of the facts upon which any judgment could be founded."

To the third queftion it was anfwered, " that a *venire facias de novo* ought to be awarded," which was accordingly done.†

* Baker's cafe before-mentioned, Wright v. Pindar. Al. 18. S. C. Stile 22. Worfley v. Filifker, 2 Rolle's Rep. 117.

† Gibfon and Johnfon v. Hunter, in error. 2 H. Blackftone 187—209.

THE

THE caufe came on to be tried a fecond time before Lord Kenyon, at Guildhall, at the fittings after Trinity term, 1793, when the defendants tendered a bill of exceptions to his Lordfhip's direction to the jury, the record of which, after ftating the bill with the indorfements, proceeded thus :—

" AND the faid plaintiff thereupon proved, and gave in evidence to the faid jury, that the name Nathaniel Hingfton, purporting to be fubfcribed to the faid paper writing fo produced to the faid jury, was of the proper hand writing of the faid Nathaniel Hingfton, and that the faid Nathaniel Hingfton fo fubfcribed the faid paper writing, as the drawer of the fame, and as the agent of the faid Livefey, Hargrave, and Company, and was accuftomed to draw bills of exchange for them, in his own name, as their agent, and that the faid Nathaniel Hingfton refided at Falmouth ; that no fuch perfon as William Fletcher the fuppofed payee ever exifted, and that the name *William Fletcher* was merely fictitious ; and that the faid paper writing, fo fubfcribed by the faid Nathaniel Hingfton, and before the fame was indorfed with the name of " A. Goodrich, by procuration of Livefey, Hargrave, and Co." and alfo before the letters and figures No. 2068, and the letters G. and J. were fubfcribed thereto, was fent by the faid Livefey, Hargrave, and Company, being the fame perfons mentioned and defcribed in the faid indorfement, by the name or firm of Livefey, Hargrave, and Co. to the faid defendants for acceptance, who accordingly

ingly accepted the same, by subscribing thereto the said letters and figures, No. 2068, and also the said letters G. and J. as the initials of their respective names. That the indorsement of the name *William Fletcher*, was made by a clerk of Livesey, Hargrave, and Company, whose name was not William Fletcher, and that the said bill was afterwards indorsed with the words, " by procuration of Livesey, Hargrave, and Co. A. Goodrich," by the said A. Goodrich, a clerk of the said Livesey, Hargrave, and Co. and paid and delivered by them to the said plaintiff for a valuable consideration then paid to them by the said plaintiff, who did not know that the payee named in the said paper writing was fictitious. And the said plaintiff, in further maintenance of the said issue so joined as aforesaid, on his part, and to shew that the said defendants, at the time of their said acceptance of the said paper writing, either knew that the said name *William Fletcher*, contained in the same paper writing, and indorsed thereon as aforesaid, was a fictitious name, or that the said defendants had given authority to the said Livesey, Hargrave, and Co. to draw the said paper writing, so produced to the jury, upon them the said defendants, by and in the name of the said Nathaniel Hingston their said agent, expressed therein to be made payable to the order of a person who did not in fact exist, and whose name was a fictitious name, by having given a general authority to the said Livesey, Hargrave, and Co. to draw Bills of Exchange upon them the said defendants, by and in the name of the said Nathaniel Hingston their said agent expreffed therein, to be made payable to the order of perfons who did not in fact exift, and whofe names were fictitious names, did further prove and give in evidence to the said jury, that the said Livefey, Hargrave, and Co. ufed to fend down to the faid Nathaniel Hingston, at Falmouth, printed forms of Bills of Exchange, upon paper duly ftamped for that purpofe, with blanks therein for the dates, the times of payment, the names of the payees, and the fums to be made payable therein, to be figned by him the faid Nathaniel Hingston, who ufed to return the fame figned by him the faid Nathaniel Hingston accordingly, to the faid Livefey, Hargrave, and Co. who then filled up the bills fo returned according to their convenience, with dates, the times they were made payable, the payees names, the greater part of which were fictitious, and the refidue real, and the fums for which they were to become payable, and that this was done as the exigencies of the houfe of Livefey, Hargrave, and Co. required. That when the bills were thus filled up, they were taken to the defendants for acceptance ; fome of the faid bills, when fo taken for acceptance, being unindorfed, and others of fuch bills, at the time they were fo taken for acceptance, having the names of the fuppofed payees in fuch bills indorfed in various hand-writings. That this happened in a great variety of inftances, and to the amount of 20,000l. That the faid bill or paper writing produced in evidence, although

dated

dated at Falmouth, was not in fact filled up with
the date, the time of payment, the name of the
payee, or the fum of money therein mentioned, at
Falmouth, but in London. That bills fo drawn
by the faid Nathaniel Hingfton, and dated from
the fame place, were frequently carried at feveral
different times on the fame day, by the faid Livefey, Hargrave, and Co. to the defendants for acceptance, and accepted by them accordingly. That
it requires three days to tranfmit a bill from Falmouth to London by the poft. That in feveral inftances, fuch bills drawn by the faid Nathaniel
Hingfton, as from Falmouth, have been prefented
by the faid Livefey, Hargrave, and Co. on the fecond day after the date of them, to the defendants
for acceptance, and that they have accepted them
without objection. That in many inftances, bills
fo drawn by the faid Nathaniel Hingfton, were prefented by the faid Livefey, Hargrave, and Co. to
the defendants for acceptance on the days on which,
by the courfe of the poft, the fame bills would have
arrived, if fent on the refpective days of their refpective dates, but before the hours of the poft's
arrival on thofe days, and that they were accepted
by the defendants without objection. That in
fome inftances, fuch bills were carried for acceptance after the arrival of the poft from Falmouth, and other bills of the like kind at different
times afterwards on the fame day. That in many
inftances, fuch bills were carried for acceptance on
the

the day on which they were filled up by the faid
Livefey, Hargrave,. and Co. the inftant they were
filled up, and whilft the ink with which they were
fo filled up has been wet. That the houfe of the
faid Livefey, Hargrave, and Co. where the faid
bills were fo filled up, was not three minutes walk
from the defendants' houfe. That this was the general courfe of dealing between the faid Livefey,
Hargrave, and Co. and the defendants. That the
ink has been apparently fo wet at many times when
the bills were fo delivered for acceptance, that the
perfon who delivered them was careful in carrying
them that they might not be fmeared. That at
the time of carrying them in this manner, it was
apparent that the fignature of Nathaniel Hingfton
was dry, and an old writing, and that what had
been written to fill up the bills was frefh and wet.
That the witneffes, by whofe teftimony the plaintiff
gave the faid evidence of the feveral inftances of
the manner of prefenting and accepting the faid
bills, had no particular memory to diftinguifh the
bill or paper writing produced in evidence from
the reft of the bills prefented, and accepted by the
defendants : that the date of the faid bill or paper
produced in evidence, the name of the payee, and
the fum therein expreffed to be made payable, were
filled up by a clerk in the houfe of Livefey, Hargrave, and Co. in London, and that was a general
courfe before defcribed with refpeĉt to the other
bills that were carried to the defendants wet for acceptance.

ceptance. That the defendants paid bills under thefe circumftances to a large amount, and for a confiderable length of time."

THE record then ftated the objection by the defendants' counfel to the admiffibility of this evidence; the direction of the judge to the jury that it was proper evidence to maintain the iffue on the third count, which confidered the bill as payable to the bearer: the verdict of the jury according to that direction; the tender of a bill of exceptions to his Lordfhip; and his Lordfhip's putting his feal to the latter.

IN Michaelmas term, 1793, the Court of King's Bench gave judgment for the plaintiff, on which the defendants brought a writ of error in Parliament, and affigned the common errors.

AFTER argument at the bar of the Houfe of Lords, the following queftion was propofed to the judges :—

" WHETHER the circumftances mentioned in the bill of exceptions was fufficiently relative to the propofitions therein alfo mentioned, viz. that the defendants in the action knew the name Fletcher was fictitious, or that the defendants had given authority to Livefey and Company to draw bills upon them the faid defendants, payable to fictitious payees, fo that they ought to have been received, and left to the jury as evidence thereof?"

ON this queftion there was a divifion among the judges, who, in Eafter term, 1794, delivered their refpective opinions *feriatim*; but the majority of them,

them, together with the Lord Chancellor and Lord Kenyon, having declared that they thought the evidence ought to have been received and left to the jury, the judgment was affirmed.*

It may be obferved, that the *only* queftion made in this cafe, was, whether the evidence ftated was fufficient for the jury to conclude that the defendants knew that in the particular inftance of this bill, the payee was fictitious? *or* that they had given a *general* authority to Livefey and Co. to draw fuch bills upon them? If either of thefe conclufions could be drawn from the evidence, it feems to have been admitted without difpute, that the evidence was fufficient to maintain the action on the bill, as a bill *payable to the bearer.*—It follows from hence, That,

In all cafes, where the holder of fuch a bill declares againft the acceptor, as on a bill *payable to the bearer*, it is fufficient to maintain the action, that he fhould prove ; 1. That the payee was fictitious, and, 2. That the defendant knew this at the time when he accepted the bill :—or, 1. That the payee was fictitious, and, 2. That the defendant had given a *general* authority to the drawer, &c. to draw bills upon him in the name of fictitious payees.

In an action by an indorfee againft an indorfor, it is not neceffary to prove either the hand of the

1 Ld. Raym. 174. Str. 444. 2 Bur. 675.

* Gibfon v. Hunter, in error. 2 H. Blackftone 288—298.

drawer

drawer or of the acceptor, or of any indorſor before him againſt whom the action is brought; for by his indorſement, he virtually undertakes to every ſubſequent holder, that the names of the drawer, acceptor, and previous indorſors, are really in the hand-writing of thoſe to whom they reſpectively purport to belong.

THE ſame diligence alſo, with reſpect to the drawee, and the ſame notice to the defendant as indorſee, muſt be proved in this action, as in that againſt the drawer, every indorſor being, with re-ſpect to ſubſequent indorſees or holders, a new drawer. But proof of a demand from the drawer, and notice of non-payment by him, is not ne-ceſſary.

WHERE the action is by an indorſor who has paid the money, proof muſt be given of the pay-ment. ^{1 Ld. Raym. 743.}

IN an action by the drawer againſt the acceptor, it is neceſſary to prove the hand-writing of the latter; demand of payment from him, and refuſal; the return of the bill, and payment by the plaintiff; but it does not appear neceſſary to prove, that the acceptor had in his hands effects of the drawer; his acceptance is preſumption that he had, and if he had not, the proof muſt lie upon himſelf. ^{Vid. Lou-viere v. Laubray. 10 Mod. 36, 37. Symonds v. Parminſter. 1 Wilſ. 185.}

IN an action on the caſe by the acceptor againſt the drawer, the plaintiff muſt prove the hand-writing of the defendant, and payment of the money by himſelf, or ſomething equivalent to that, ſuch as his being in priſon in execution. ^{Vid. 3. Wilſ. 18.}

IT

IT does not seem clear, whether, in the case of a simple acceptance, the acceptor in this action must not be put to the proof that he had no effects of the drawer in his hands, either at the time of the acceptance, or at the payment of the bill; but the presumption of law, being that he had effects, it would therefore seem that the proof of the contrary lies on him.

IN the case however of an acceptance or payment under protest, there can be no doubt, but the protest is sufficient presumptive evidence of no effects at the time when the protest was made; if therefore it was made on payment, it is certainly presumptive evidence of no effects, and it lies on the drawer to shew the contrary: but if the protest was only at the time of acceptance, it is natural to presume that at the time of payment the acceptor had effects, and the proof that he had not must lie on him.

12 Mod.
345.
Gilb. L. E.
118.

IN actions against the drawer or indorsor, the protest is sufficient evidence that the bill is not paid; and the mere production of the protest is sufficient; it is not necessary to prove either the writing of the notary, or to give any account how the plaintiff had the protest; for that would be destructive to public commerce, and throw too great a difficulty on transactions of this kind: and beyond seas, it is said, that it is sufficient to shew the court the protest without producing the bill itself,

G. L. E.
119.

but here in general the bill itself must be shewn, as well as the protest, because the whole declaration

must

muft be proved, which cannot be without giving the bill in evidence.

BUT in an action againft the drawer of a bill which was loft, it was held by Holt, C. J. that proof of the defendant's having owned that he had made the bill was fufficient. Hart v. King. 12 Mod. 309.

WITH refpect to a Promiffory Note, the fame rules, of what is neceffary to be proved, apply, as in a Bill of Exchange; the maker being in the place of the acceptor; the payee, after indorfement, in that of the drawer; and the indorfors and indorfees the fame in each.

IN general direct proof is required of the fignature of thofe parties whofe indorfement muft be proved: But with refpect to the party himfelf againft whom the action is brought, proof of other circumftances may be fufficient to fupply the place of actual proof of his fignature; particularly, confeffion. Thus, where the defendant was fued as indorfor of a note, and it was proved, that a perfon to whom application had been made to difcount it, fent it to the defendant, who looked on it, and faid it was his hand, and that the note, which had fome months to run, would be paid when due; the Chief Juftice would not permit the defendant to fhew forgery, by fimilitude of hands, becaufe that would tend to deftroy all negociation of Bills and Notes. But he feemed inclined to have admitted actual proof of forgery, if the defendant could have given it, but this he was unable to do, and the plaintiff had a verdict. Ld. Hardwicke. Cooper v. Le Blanc. 2 Str. 1051.

So,

Dale v.
Lubbock.
1 Barnard.
B. R. 198.

So, where a letter was produced under the defendant's hand, in which he wrote to a friend that he had received a Bill of Exchange from the drawer on the acceptor, bearing date fuch a day, and payable to him or order fix months after date, and in all thefe circumftances the bill agreed with the letter, though no fum was mentioned in the letter, this was thought fufficient evidence that the defendant had had the bill in queftion in his poffeffion ; and to fhew that he had indorfed it over, it was proved that he had faid he had come to town to haften the trial of a caufe brought against him on an indorfement he had made on a Bill of Exchange, and that in fact he had brought down this very caufe by provifo.

Barnes,
3d ed.
oct. 436.
Hemmings
v. Robinfon.

But where, in an action againft any one party, proof of the fignature of another is neceffary to fupport the action againft the defendant, that proof muft be direct; confeffion of the party whofe fignature it purports to be, will not be fufficient evidence. Thus in an action againft the drawer or acceptor of a bill, or maker of a note, a confeffion of an indorfor that he indorfed the bill or note, will not be proper proof of the indorfement.

Whitcomb
v. Whiting.
Doug. 652.

But where an action was brought againft one, on a joint and feveral Promiffory Note, figned by him and others, proof of payment by one of the others, of intereft and part of the principal within fix years before the action brought, will be fufficient to bind the defendant, and take the cafe out of the ftatute as to him.

Where

WHERE a bill is accepted, or a bill or note is drawn or indorfed by one of two or more partners, on the partnerfhip account, proof of the fignature of the partner accepting, drawing, or indorfing, is fufficient to bind all the reft.

Pinkney v·
Hall.
1 Salk. 126.
1 Ld. Raym.
175. vid.
Carvick v.
Vickery.
Doug. 653.
Gil. L. E.
117.

WHERE a fervant has a general authority, to draw, accept, or indorfe bills or notes, proof of his fignature is fufficient againft the mafter; but his authority muft be proved.

SUBSEQUENT affent, it would feem, is evidence of authority.

Comb. 450.

A GENERAL cuftom of the fervant's fignature, and payment by the mafter, is fufficient proof of a general authority; and a general authority will continue to bind the mafter till its determination be generally known. Therefore if a fervant, having authority, draw a Bill of Exchange in fo fhort a time after he is difmiffed, that the world cannot take notice of his being out of fervice; or if he were a long time out of fervice, but that kept fo fecret, that the world could not take notice of the bill in thofe cafes will bind the mafter.

12 Mod.
346.

WHERE notice is to be given by the poft, it would feem that proof of putting the letter into the poft is fufficient, that being in general all that is in the plaintiff's power to prove, though this in one place is denied.

1 Barnard.
B. R. 198.

WHERE the defendant fuffers judgment by default, and the plaintiff executes a writ of inquiry; it is fufficient for the latter to *produce* the note or bill, without any proof of the defendant's hand:

T   This

This was determined so long ago as the 14th Geo. II. in a case in the King's Bench, where the plaintiff having offered *collateral* evidence to prove the defendant's hand, the court not only held that this was sufficient, but said, that the note being set out in the declaration, was admitted by the default, and that the only use of producing it was, to see whether any money was indorsed on it as paid.

NOTWITHSTANDING this, about four years afterwards the court of Common Pleas gave a different decision, holding not only that the note ought to have been produced, but both the note and indorsement proved.

AND they gave the same decision in a case which occurred soon after.

LONG subsequent to this, the same court is, in one book, reported to have given a similar opinion on the authority of the two last cases.

IT appeared that the declaration contained two counts, one on a note of hand, and another for money expended; the defendant pleaded a set-off; the plaintiff replied, and denied the set-off, and for want of a rejoinder, signed judgment: The note was produced on the execution of the writ of inquiry, but not proved; and the defendant offered to confess damages on being allowed a month's time to pay the debt and costs; this was not granted, but the jury found the value of the note.

THIS case coming before the court, Lord Chief Justice De Grey is reported to have expressed himself thus: Damages must either be proved or admitted,

mitted. The prefent cafe does neither; for the
fet-off confeffes only general damages on both
counts. The note therefore ought to have been
proved. But the confeffion of the defendant's attorney makes this cafe particular in its circumftances, and on that ground only I am for difcharging the rule for fetting afide the inquiry.
The reft of the court agreed.

BUT in another report of the fame cafe, the
opinion of the court is reprefented in very different terms; it is faid they were of opinion the
jury had done right; the plea of fet-off amounted
to an acknowledgment of a debt, and the clerk to
the defendant's attorney had offered, in the hearing
of the jury, to confefs damages. And *Gould* added,
on a judgment by default in an action on a Promiffory Note, or a Bill of Exchange, the fum due
on it is admitted, and needs not to be proved on
the execution of a writ of inquiry.

BUT this point is clearly decided by a late cafe
in the King's Bench. It was an action againft the
acceptor; he fuffered judgment by default, the
plaintiff *produced* a bill in the fame terms as that
ftated in the declaration, but it did not appear to
have been accepted; and no other evidence was
produced. It having been objected that the bill
produced did not correfpond with that mentioned
in the declaration, the court obferved that it might
have been accepted, though not in writing; and
that, by fuffering judgment to go by default, the
defendant had admitted the caufe of action to the

T 2   amount

3 Wilf. 155.

3 Term
Rep.
P. 29. G. 3.
Green v.
Hearne.

amount of the bill, becaufe that was fet out on the record, and the only reafon for producing it to the jury on executing the writ of inquiry, was to fee whether or not any part of it had been paid.

Morris v.
Lyne.
B. R. H.
26 G. 3.
Bayley's
App. No. 7.

AND in a cafe before this, it had been held that it was not even neceffary to *produce* the note or bill; for that if the defendant had paid part of it, he might have pleaded that, but he had let judgment go for the whole.

Ruled
anon.
B. R. H.
26 G 3.
Bailey 67.
Rafhleigh v.
Salmon.
C. B. T. 29
G. 3. Bl.
Term Rep.
252.

AND now, on fuch judgment, a writ of inquiry is not neceffary, for the court on application by the plaintiff will, if no good reafon fhewn to the contrary, refer it to the proper officer to afcertain the damages and cofts, and calculate the intereft.

BESIDE the different fubjects of defence which may be collected from the general principles laid down in the preceding chapters, the moft ufual are thofe which arife either from the total want of confideration, or from the illegality of the confideration for which the bill or note was given.

THE want of confideration, it is evident, will be a fufficient defence to an action by one party againft another, from whom he has immediately received the inftrument; for according to the general principles of law, no contract can be fupported without a confideration, and accordingly it frequently occurs, that the defendant refts his cafe on the circumftance of the bill or note having been given merely for accommodation.

BUT where the plaintiff has in fact given a confideration to the perfon from whom he immediately

mediately received the inftrument, any preceding party being fued on it, cannot protect himfelf, by faying that he himfelf had no value of the party to whom he gave it; for by making himfelf a party to the inftrument, he contributed to its currency, and that circumftance was, perhaps, one reafon that prevailed on the plaintiff to part with his money: And that in this refpect there is no difference, whether the perfon who actually gave a good confideration, knew that the inftrument was actually given without one or not, appears evident from the cafes which have been cited on a former occafion.

Vid. Pillans v. Van Miernp. 3 Bur. 1663. Ruffell v. Langftaffe. Doug. 514.

WHERE a confideration is illegal, that, as between the parties to the tranfaction, is a fufficient reafon to preclude the plaintiff from recovering, and it is immaterial, whether the illegal confideration be, by the plaintiff himfelf, made the foundation of his fuit, or fet up by way of anfwer by the defendant; and therefore the defendant may fhew that the note or bill on which he is fued, was given by him to the plaintiff for an illegal confideration.

Guichard v. Roberts. 1 Bl. Rep. 445. Vid. Biggs v. Lawrence. 3 Term Rep. 454.

WHERE the original tranfaction however is not morally bad, its illegality arifing only from its being prohibited by a pofitive ftatute, every thing done in confequence of the prohibited act, will not, of *courfe*, be confidered as void: Thus where two partners enter into illegal contracts with third perfons, and on a lofs falling on the partnerfhip, one of the partners takes upon himfelf to pay the whole lofs, he cannot recover againft the other his proportion of it. But if the other give him an exprefs

authority,

authority, or do any act which amounts to an exprefs authority, or even to a fubfequent affent to pay his proportion of the lofs; this will be binding on him.

Vid. St. 7 G. 2. c. 8.

THUS, where one of two partners, concerned in a ftock-jobbing tranfaction, paid the fum of 3000l. the amount of the lofs they had fuftained, and the other gave him a bond conditioned for the payment of half that fum, it was held that the obligee fhould recover on this bond, becaufe it was a debt of honour which the obligor was in confcience bound to pay, and this bond was not within the ftatute, though one from the lofers to the winners would have been fo.

Faikney v. Reynous. 4 Bur. 2069. 1 Bl. Rep. 638.

Petrie. v. Hannay. 3 Term Rep. 418.

THE fame principle prevailed, and the authority of this cafe was recognized in another which oc-curred very lately. *Keeble* and *Hannay*, with two other perfons, had engaged together in illegal fpeculations in the ftocks, and having incurred confiderable loffes, on the 8th of January, 1774, came to a fettlement with *Portis* their broker, who had paid all the differences. On that occafion Keeble repaid to *Portis* the whole fum advanced by him, except 811l. which was part of Hannay's fhare of the lofs, and for which Keeble drew a bill on Hannay in favour of Portis, which Hannay ac-cepted. This bill not being paid by Hannay when due, Portis brought an action on it againft the exe-cutors of Keeble, and recovered the amount, no defence being fet up on account of the illegality of the tranfaction. Keeble's executors afterwards

brought

brought an action againft Hannay, to reimburfe themfelves the fum recovered againft them by Portis, the declaration being for money paid by the plaintiffs to the defendant's ufe, on which they obtained a verdict, and the matter being agitated in court on a rule to fet afide the verdict, that rule was difcharged. *Kenyon, C. J. tamen dubitante.*

WHEN the legality of a tranfaction is impeached, on account of its being in contravention of a pofitive law of this country, there is a material diftinction between the cafe, where both plaintiff and defendant refide in this country, and that where the plaintiff refides abroad. In the latter cafe, though the plaintiff knew that the defendant intended to tranfgrefs the laws of this country, yet if the contract be complete, before thefe laws can attach, he fhall recover on that contract. Thus, where the plaintiff who refided in Dunkirk, together with his partner, who was a native of that place, fold and delivered a quantity of tea, for the price of which the action was brought, to the order of the defendant, knowing it was intended to be fmuggled by him into England; but had no concern in the fmuggling fcheme itfelf, having fold the tea to the defendant in the common and ordinary courfe of trade, with an intention of being paid in ready money, or in bills drawn perfonally on him in this country; here it was held that the intereft of the vendor being totally at an end, and his contract complete by the delivery of the goods at Dunkirk, the plaintiff had been guilty of no vio-

Holman v. Johnfon. Cowp. 341.

T 4

lation

lation of the laws of this country, of which he was not bound to take notice, and therefore he had a right to recover. If indeed the plaintiff had engaged in the rifk of fmuggling the goods into England, he would then have been privy to the guilt of the defendant, and would not have been affifted by the laws of that country, whofe laws he had contributed to elude.

Biggs v. Lawrence. 3 Term Rep. 454.
BUT where the plaintiffs or fome of them refide in a place fubject to the crown of Great Britain, and thofe of them fo refiding affift in the execution of the fmuggling fcheme, the others, though in fact unacquainted with the tranfaction, fhall be confidered as affected by the knowledge of their partners, and fhall not be affifted by the courts in this country.

Vid. Powell on Contracts Vol. I. 152 to 234.
WHAT is or is not a good confideration it is not intended here to inquire, any farther than, as it is neceffary to point out a material diftinction which the legiflature has thought proper to eftablifh, with refpect to the effect which the illegality fhall have, in general, and in fome particular cafes.

Vid. Doug. 636. (614)
IN general no advantage can be taken of the illegality of the confideration, but as between the perfons immediately concerned in the tranfaction ; any fubfequent holder of the bill or note, by a fair confideration, cannot be affected by it.

BUT there are cafes, in which it has been determined, that by the conftruction of certain ftatutes, the innocent indorfee fhall not recover againft the acceptor of the bill, or drawer of the note.

By

By ſt. 9 Ann. c. 14. ſ. 1. " All notes, bills,
" &c. where the whole or any part of the con-
" ſideration, ſhall be for any money or other va-
" luable thing whatſoever, won by gaming or
" playing at cards, dice, tables, tennis, bowls, or
" *other* game or games whatſoever, or by betting on
" the ſides or hands of ſuch as do game at any of the
" games aforeſaid, or for re-imburſing or re-paying
" any money knowingly lent or advanced for ſuch
" gaming or betting, or lent and advanced at the
" time or place of ſuch play, to any perſon or per-
" ſons ſo gaming or betting as aforeſaid, or that
" ſhall, during ſuch play, ſo play or bet, ſhall be
" utterly *void, fruſtrate, and of no effeƐ, to all intents*
" *and purpoſes whatſoever.*"

AFTER this ſtatute, there occurred a caſe in which
it appeared, that the defendant had given to one
Church, certain Promiſſory Notes for money knowingly advanced by him to game with at dice; that
Church indorſed them to the plaintiff for a valuable
conſideration, who had no notice that any part of
the money for which the notes were given had been
lent for the purpoſe of gaming. After two arguments, the court were of opinion, that the true
conſtruƐion of the words, " ſhall be utterly void,
&c." was, that no recovery could be had againſt
the defendant on the note, even in the hands of an
innocent indorſee.

By ſt. 12 Ann. ſt. 2. c. 16. ſ. 1. " All bonds,
" contraƐs, and *aſſurances* whatſoever, made for
" pay-

Bowyer *v.*
Bampton.
Str. 1155.

" payment of any principal, or money to be lent,
" or covenanted to be performed upon or for any
" ufury, whereupon or whereby there fhall be re-
" ferved or taken above the rate of five pounds in
" the hundred, fhall be utterly *void*."

Lowe v.
Waller.
Doug. 736. On this ftatute, and on the authority of the cafe
on the ftatute of gaming, it has been determined
that no action can be maintained by an innocent
indorfee, againft the acceptor of a bill given on an
ufurious confideration : The court were of opinion
that the words of the ftatute were too ftrong not to
extend to this cafe, the word *affurances* being a
general term, comprehending all kinds of *fecurities*,
notes and bills as well as bonds, and that the former cafe ftood directly in the way.

By ft. 5 G. 2. c. 30. f. 11. " Every bond, bill,
" note, contract or agreement, or other fecurity
" whatfoever, made or given by any bankrupt, or
" by any other perfon, unto or to the ufe of or in
" truft for any creditor or creditors, or for the
" fecurity of the payment of any debt or fum of
" money due from fuch bankrupt at the time of his
" becoming bankrupt, or any part thereof, be-
" tween the time of his becoming bankrupt, and
" fuch bankrupt's difcharge, as *a confideration*, or
" to the intent to perfuade him, her, or them, to
" confent to or fign any fuch allowance or certifi-
" cate, fhall be wholly *void*, and of no effect ; and
" the monies thereby fecured or agreed to be paid,
" fhall not be recovered or recoverable ; and the
" party

" party fued on fuch bond, bill, note, contract, or
" agreement, fhall and may plead the general iffue,
" and give this act and the fpecial matter in evi-
" dence."

THERE can be no doubt, from a comparifon of
the words of this ftatute with thofe of the two preceding ones, that the fame determination would be
given againft an innocent indorfee in this cafe as in
the two former: But in none of the cafes is he al- Str. 1155.
together without remedy, for he may fue the indorfor on his indorfement, becaufe as between them
it is a new bill, and no inquiry can be made into
the original confideration.

IT has been obferved, that except in the particular cafes above-mentioned, the defence arifing
from the illegality of the confideration, cannot be
fet up againft any other plaintiff than the perfon
who was privy to the original tranfaction: But this
rule muft be confined to the ordinary cafe of a bill
or note, indorfed before it was due; for it has been   D. per Buller
repeatedly ruled at Guildhall, that wherever it ap-   J. at Laun-
pears that a bill or note has been indorfed over,   Affizes 1788
fome time after it is due, which is out of the ufual
courfe of trade, that circumftance alone throws
fuch a fufpicion on it, that the indorfee muft take it
on the credit of the indorfor, and muft ftand in the
fituation of the perfon to whom it was payable.

THEREFORE in an action by the indorfee of a Pro-   Banks v.
miffory Note payable on demand, againft the maker;   Colwell, at
                                                      Launcefton
the defendant was admitted to give evidence that   fizes, 1788,
the note had been indorfed to the plaintiff a year   ler J. cited
                                              and   3 Term
                                                     Rep. 81.

and a half afterwards; and to impeach the confideration by fhewing that it had originally been given for fmuggled goods, and that payments had been made upon it at feveral times. And though no privity was brought home to the plaintiff, Mr. Juftice Buller nonfuited the plaintiff.

BUT the generality of this rule was doubted by Lord Kenyon, though the other three judges adopted it in its extent. It is however generally agreed that it fhall prevail, wherever it appears on the face of the note or bill, that it has been difhonoured, or if knowledge can be brought home to the indorfee that it had been fo.

Brown v. Davis. 3 Term Rep. 80.

THEREFORE in an action by the indorfee of a Promiffory Note againft the maker, where the note appeared to have been noted for non-payment, and indorfed after it became due, the defendant fhall be admitted to fhew that the note was paid as between him and the original payee, from whom the plaintiff received it.

INDEX.

A

CCEPTANCE,
 What, 68.
 How made, 69.
 What fhall amount to, 80—87.
 Verbal or written, 69—72.
 Collateral, or by writing on the bill, 72—74.
 When it may be made, 72.
 By whom, 73, 153—156.
 To whom, 73.
 Abfolute, 74.
  Cannot be revoked, 156.
 Conditional, 75—80.
  May be difcharged, and how, 161—165.
 General, 74.
 Partial, 74, 75.
 How ftated in pleading, 190.
 Muft be proved, and how, 205, 271—273.
 On account of a third perfon, 153.
 Supra Proteft, 153—156.
 How ftated in pleading, 190.

ACCEPTOR,
 His undertaking, 156.
 How difcharged, 156—165.

ACTION,
 What, may be brought on a bill or note, 175—177.

BANK OF ENGLAND, 27, 32.

BANK NOTES, 40.

BANKERS' CHECKS, &c. 41—46.

BILLS OF EXCHANGE,
 Definition of, 3.
 Their origin, 2.
 Their nature, 2, 3, et infra.
 Their different forms, 13—16.

BILLS

BILLS OF EXCHANGE,
> Their different kinds.
> > Foreign and inland, 11, 12.
> > > Their difference at common law, 142, 143.
> > Payable to order or bearer, 35—38.
> Refemblance they bear to Promiffory Notes, 35.
> When payable.
> > At fight, 4.
> > After fight, 4.
> > After date, 4.
> Parties to them,
> > Who may be, 28—33.
> Transfer of them,
> > By delivery, 88.
> > By indorfement, 89, et infra.
> Their privileges, 46, et infra.
> Requifites to render them good, 49—67.
> How ftated in pleading, 177—190.

CHARGES,
> On the difhonour of a bill, 140, 141.

CONSIDERATION,
> What a good one, 280.
> Want of, 276.
> By whom taken advantage of, 277.
> Illegal, 276, 277.
> > Where it renders the bill or note void in the hands of an innocent indorfee, 280—283.
> > Where only as between the parties to the tranfaction, 277—280.

CORPORATION,
> When it may be party to a bill or note, 32.

DATE,
> Where abfolutely neceffary, 66, 67.
> How fupplied when wanting, 7.
> Not neceffary to be exprefsly ftated in pleading, 187.

DEFENCE,
> What a good one, 276—284.

DEMAND,
> When it muft be made, 41—46, 117—129.
> When neceffary to be ftated in pleading, 192.

DELIVERY,

INDEX.

DELIVERY,
> Date calculated from it, 7.
> Stated in pleading, 190.

EVIDENCE,
> What neceffary on a bill or note, 202—284.

FORGERY,
> Of an indorfement, confequence of, 104.
> Of acceptance, 203, 204.
> Of drawer's fignature, 203, 204.

GRACE, days of,
> What, 9.
> When allowed on Bills of Exchange, 9.
> When not, 10.
> Whether to be allowed on Promiffory Notes, 121—125.

INDORSEMENT,
> Its effect, 112.
> When neceffary, 88.
> In full, or in blank, 88—96.
> Where it may be made at any time after iffuing the bill or note, 89.
> May be made on a blank note or bill, 89, 90.
> When it muft be made before time of payment, 66.
> When attefted and how, 67.
> Need not contain the words " to order," 96—100.
> May be reftrictive, 100—102.
> By whom it may be made, 106, 107.
> When the bill is to the ufe of another than the payee, 108.
> Muft not be of part only, 109.
> When neceffary to be ftated in pleading, and how, 191.
> When neceffary to be proved, 206—208.
> Fictitious, 208—268.

INDORSOR,
> His undertaking, 112.
> How difcharged, 112—120, 165, 166.

INFANT,
> Cannot be fued on a bill or note, 28, 102.
> May fue, 30.
> Indorfement by him, its effects, 102.

INTEREST,
> When payable on a bill or note, 140.

INTEREST,

INDEX.

INTEREST,
> By whom, 140.
> To what time calculated, 140, 142.
> When allowed on a bankruptcy, 201.

LOSS of a BILL or NOTE,
> What muft be done thereon, 173, 174.
> Legal confequences of, 102, 103, 173, 174.

MARRIED WOMAN,
> Where fhe may be a party to a bill or note, 30, 31.

NEGOTIABILITY,
> Whether abfolutely neceffary to conftitute a bill or note, 63, 64.
> By what words conftituted, 63.
> May be reftrained by indorfement, 100—102.
> How ftated in pleading, 192.

NOTES, PROMISSORY,
> Origin of them, 18.
> Definition, 18.
> Their forms, 20.
> Payable to order or bearer, 19, 35.
> Who may make them, 28—34.
> Refemblance they bear to Bills of Exchange, 34, 35.
> Requifites to make them good, 50—65.
> How ftated in pleading, 181, 186, 187.

NOTICE
> Of non-acceptance, 118, 119, 125.
> Of non-payment, 125.
> By whom to be given, 126.
> To whom, 119.
> Within what time to be given, 126, 127—129.
> When not neceffary, 129—136.
> Difference in the form of it, in foreign and inland bills, 136—139.
> How ftated in pleading, 192—194.

PARTIES
> To a bill or note, who may be, 28—34.

PARTNERSHIP,
> Acceptance by one partner binds the reft, 31.
> Indorfement, 106.
> How ftated in pleading, 189.

PAYMENT,

PAYMENT.

 Diſtinction anciently taken between a bill given in payment of a precedent debt, and for a debt newly cotnracted, 171, 172.

PLEA,

 To an action on a bill or note, 200.

 Pleadings on a bill or note, 175—200.

PRESENTMENT,

 For acceptance, when neceſſary, 118, 119.

  At what time to be made, 125.

  When neceſſary to be ſtated in pleading, 190.

  How ſtated, 190.

 For payment,

  At what time to be made, 120, 125.

  Within what time, 120, 121.

  When it muſt be ſtated in pleading, 192.

  How ſtated, 194.

PROCURATION,

 What, and how it operates, 33.

PROTEST,

 What, 136.

 Noting and Notary, 136, 137.

 Within what time to be made, 137.

 For non-acceptance, 136.

  How ſtated in pleading, 193, 195.

 For non-payment, 138.

  How ſtated in pleading, 193, 195.

 For better ſecurity, 139.

 Effect of, 140.

 Where original bill loſt, may be made on copy, 139, 140.

 On inland bills, 143—148.

 Acceptance, ſupra, what, 152, 153.

  By whom it may be made, 152.

  How made, 153.

 Payment, ſupra, 154, 155.

  How ſtated in pleading, 196.

REMEDY on a BILL or NOTE.

 By Action, 175—177.

 By whom, 175—178.

 Againſt whom, 175—178, 199.

 In caſe of bankruptcy, 200—202.

U   SATISFACTION,

SATISFACTION,

What shall be, 112, et infra.

Holder can have but one, 198, 199.

SERVANT

May accept, &c. for his master, 33.

When his acceptance shall bind himself, 86, 87.

Whether necessary to be stated in pleading, 189.

SET.

Bills in sets, 12.

Their form, 14.

How stated in pleading, 190.

SIGNATURE

Of the drawer, whether necessary to be stated, 188, 189.

Of the acceptor, needs not be expressly stated, 190.

By two jointly or severally, how stated, 186.

By partners, how stated, 189.

By a servant, 33, 86, 87.

How stated in pleading, 189.

When necessary to be proved, 203—206, 268—270.

How proved, 268—270, 273.

STAMPS.

Where bills and notes must be stamped, 21, 22.

Where not, 27.

Penalty, &c. 24.

STYLE,

Old and new, 7.

TIME,

How calculated on a bill or note, 6, 7, 8.

TRANSFER of BILLS and NOTES,

How effected, 88, et infra.

By whom made, 102—108.

UNDERTAKING

Of the drawer of a bill, 109, 110.

Of the acceptor of a bill, or maker of a note, 156, et infra.

Of the indorsor, 111, 112.

Of the holder, 117, et infra, 125.

USANCE,

What, 4.

Its length, 4, 5.

Must be stated in pleading, 188.

WAIVER

WAIVER

    Of acceptance, what will amount to, 156, 157, 160.
    Of remedy againſt indorſor, 165.
    ——————— drawer, 165, et infra.

WITNESS

    To a bill or note, when neceſſary, 65—67.
    To an indorſement, 67.

FINIS.

THIS DAY IS PUBLISHED,

In Two Volumes Octavo, Price Sixteen Shillings Bound,

A TREATISE

ON THE

LAW OF CORPORATIONS.

BY STEWART KYD,

OF THE MIDDLE TEMPLE, ESQ. BARRISTER AT LAW.

LONDON: Printed for J. BUTTERWORTH, Fleet-Street.

Of whom may be had, by the same Author,

A TREATISE ON THE LAW OF ARBITRATION,

PRICE 5s. BOARDS.